INTERNATIONALIZING SOCIAL WORK EDUCATION
Insights from leading figures across the globe

Gurid Aga Askeland and Malcolm Payne

First published in Great Britain in 2017 by

Policy Press
University of Bristol
1-9 Old Park Hill
Bristol
BS2 8BB
UK
t: +44 (0)117 954 5940
pp-info@bristol.ac.uk
www.policypress.co.uk

North America office:
Policy Press
c/o The University of Chicago Press
1427 East 60th Street
Chicago, IL 60637, USA
t: +1 773 702 7700
f: +1 773-702-9756
sales@press.uchicago.edu
www.press.uchicago.edu

British Library Cataloguing in Publication Data
A catalogue record for this book is available from the British Library

Library of Congress Cataloging-in-Publication Data
A catalog record for this book has been requested

ISBN 978-1-4473-2870-4 hardcover
ISBN 978-1-4473-3527-6 ePub
ISBN 978-1-4473-3528-3 Mobi
ISBN 978-1-4473-2872-8 ePdf

Cover design by Policy Press
Front cover image: istock
Printed and bound in Great Britain by CPI Group (UK) Ltd,
Croydon, CR0 4YY
Policy Press uses environmentally responsible print partners

Contents

List of tables

List of abbreviations

AASSW	American Association of Schools of Social Work (1919-52) – precursor to CSWE
AIETS	Association Internationale des Ecoles de Travail Social, Association International de Escuelas de Trabajo Social (French and Spanish names of IASSW)
APASWE	Asian Pacific Association for Social Work Education (regional association of IASSW)
ASWEA	Association of Social Work Education in Africa (precursor of ASSWA)
ATSMAC	Mexican Social Workers' Association
BA	Bachelor of Arts (first degree title, sometimes for social work degrees)
BSc	Bachelor of Science (first degree title, sometimes for social work degrees)
BSW	Bachelor of Social Work (title for qualifying degree in social work, commonly used in the US, also in some other countries)
CBE	Commander of the Order of the British Empire (UK honour)
CCETSW	Central Council for Education and Training in Social Work (former UK governmental development and regulatory body for social work education, 1970–2001)
CDP	Community Development Project (UK government-financed local projects, 1970–8)
CESEM	Municipal Study Centre (Mexican local organization)
CFA CID	Canada's Foreign Aid Canadian International Development platform
CONFITEA	International Conference on Adult Education
COS	Charity Organization Society (nineteenth–twentieth century UK and US charitable organizations)
CSA	Central Union for Social Work (Swedish professional body)
CSWE	Council on Social Work Education (1952 to date) – successor to AASSW and NASSA
CV	Curriculum vitae (document setting out career achievements; résumé, in US English)

DSW	Doctor of Social Work (title of a professional doctorate commonly used in the US and some other countries)
EASSW	European Association of Schools of Social Work (regional association of IASSW)
EEsrASSW	Eastern European sub-regional Association of Schools of Social Work
EEC	European Economic Community (1957-93) – precursor to EU
ESRC	Economic and Social Research Council (UK state research funding body)
EU	European Union – regional economic and political association of European states
FAO	Food and Agriculture Organization (UN agency aimed at defeating hunger)
HIV/AIDS	Human Immunodeficiency Virus/Acquired Immunodeficiency Syndrome
HMSO	Her Majesty's Stationery Office (UK government publisher in the twentieth century)
IASSW	International Association of Schools of Social Work
ICSD	International Consortium for Social Development
ICSW	International Council on Social Welfare
IFSW	International Federation of Social Workers
IJSW	International Journal of Social Welfare
ILO	International Labour Organization
INDOSOW	International Doctorate in Social Work (joint project of five universities, led by the University of Ljubljana)
INGO	International non-governmental organization
IPPF	International Planned Parenthood Federation
JASW	Jamaican Association of Social Workers
KAKI	Katherine A Kendall Institute (of CSWE)
LSE	London School of Economics (part of the University of London)
MDG	Millennium Development Goals (of the UN)
MSc	Master of Science (higher degree title)
MSW	Master of Social Work (title for qualifying masters degree in social work commonly used in the US, also in some other countries)
NACASSW	North American & Caribbean Association of Schools of Social Work (regional association of IASSW)
NASSA	National Association of Schools of Social Administration (US, 1942-52) – precursor to CSWE

NASW	National Association of Social Workers (US)
NCSW	National Conference on Social Work (US) – annual professional conference
NCSSW	Nordic Committee of Schools of Social Work (sub-regional association of IASSW; part of the European region)
NGO	Non-governmental organization
PGU	Urban Management Programme (Latin American UN programme)
PhD	Doctor of Philosophy (initial research doctorate)
SARS	Severe acute respiratory syndrome
SIDA	Swedish International Development Agency
SME	Sindicáto Mexicano de Electricitas (Mexican Electricians' Syndicate)
SSA	School for Social Services Administration (University of Chicago)
SSR	Akademikerförbundet SSR (Union for social science professionals, Sweden)
UNAM	National Autonomous University of Mexico
UNESCO	United Nations Educational, Scientific and Cultural Organization
UNFPA	United Nations Fund for Population Activities
UNICEF	United Nations Children's Emergency Fund
UK	United Kingdom of Great Britain and Northern Ireland
UNCRC	UN Convention on the Rights of the Child
UN(O)	United Nations (Organization)
US(A)	United States (of America)
USAID	United States Agency for International Development
WHO	World Health Organization
YMCA	Young Men's Christian Association

Acknowledgements

This book is a result of decisions by the board of the International Association of Schools of Social Work (IASSW). It builds on an original proposal by Gurid Aga Askeland, when she was a vice president of the Association, developed in association with Brian Littlechild, the publications officer of the Association at the time. We are grateful to Brian and to Julia Watkins (CSWE) for their hard work on the early stages of the project and to members of the board for their guidance and support. We also want to acknowledge the efforts of the interviewers of the Katherine Kendall awardees:

Pia Aronsson, University Lecturer, School of Law, Psychology and Social Work, Örebro University, Sweden.

Gurid Aga Askeland, Professor Emerita, VID Specialized University, Campus Diakonhjemmet, Oslo, Norway.

Andrea Bediako, Coordinator of International Programs, Katherine A. Kendall Institute for International Social Work Education and Council on Social Work Education (CSWE), Washington DC, US.

Darja Zaviršek, Professor, Faculty of Social Work, University of Ljubljana, Slovenia.

Lynne Healy, Board of Trustees Distinguished Professor Emerita, University of Connecticut, School of Social Work, West Hartford, US.

Brian Littlechild, Professor of Social Work, Research Lead, Department of Nursing and Social Work, University of Hertfordshire, UK.

Vimla Nadkarni, retired professor, Tata Institute of Social Sciences, Mumbai, India; Past President, IASSW.

Helle Strauss, Senior Lecturer, Metropolitan University College, School of Social Work and Administration, Copenhagen, Denmark.

Bertha Mary Rodríguez Villa, Faculty Member, ENTS–
Universidad Nacional Autónoma de México, Mexico City,
Mexico.

Chapters 6 and 7 are reproduced from the internet journal *Social Work and Society*; details are given on the first page of each chapter. We have added some explanatory footnotes and a list of selected publications by the subjects of the biographies reprinted in those chapters.

Every effort has been made to trace all the copyright-holders, but if any have been inadvertently overlooked, the publishers will be pleased to make the necessary arrangements at the first opportunity.

Gurid Aga Askeland, Oslo, Norway
Malcolm Payne, Sutton, UK

A note on terminology

In literature about international issues, people argue about how to refer to the economic and social development of particular countries. Should we say that a country is developed or developing, which hides an assumption that development is a desirable outcome to social change? Should we say that a country is a Western country, meaning an economically developed country whose culture originates from European and North American models? Some writers refer to the Global North and Global South, implying that most countries in the northern hemisphere are economically developed and most countries in the southern hemisphere are not. But some countries in the southern hemisphere, such as Australia, are Northern and Western in their social and economic development and culture. Some countries do not fit into any such category. Examples might be Indonesia, experiencing rapid economic and social change and development alongside substantial poverty and inequality, or Eastern European 'transition' economies, which have been moving from being part of the Soviet sphere of influence to participation in European economic markets.

Ways of understanding and talking about the development of countries have changed over the period covered by this book, so different interviewees in Part 2 refer to these issues in different ways. In Part 1, we have chosen to refer to the Global North as a collective term denoting rich and economically developed nations and the Global South referring to poorer nations with less developed economies.

Gurid Aga Askeland and Malcolm Payne

Preface

The book's aim

Our aim in this book is to document the history of an important period after World War II, in which international social work education become firmly established across the globe, building on its initial base mainly in Europe and the US. We look at this process through the eyes of distinguished social work educators, who have been selected because they received the Katherine Kendall Award from the International Association of Schools of Social Work (IASSW). These people promoted social work education by developing programmes, offering consultation to local people or through exchanges with colleagues.

Social work is an international profession and there have always been international exchanges. In this book, we examine the awardees' contributions and achievements in the social, historical and political context in which they did their work. This preface introduces the Kendall Award and how the book came about. We clarify the interview process and how we analyzed the material, then outline the book's structure.

The award

The Katherine A. Kendall Distinguished Service Award, established in 1992, is the only international accolade for promoting social work education internationally. The announcement described it as follows:

> It is entirely appropriate that the IASSW Board has decided to establish the Katherine A. Kendall Award for service in international social work education. This award does not honor Katherine. It is she who honors us by her association with the IASSW. This award, to be given no more frequently than once every two years, is to identify someone whose service to international social work education makes her or him worthy to be considered a colleague of Katherine Kendall. One is hard-pressed to think of a higher honor.

The criteria established by the board in 1992 have not changed, and are as follows:

- educational activities to promote equality and social justice in all societies;
- research and production of professional literature of interest and value to social work educators everywhere;
- curriculum development that advances social work education worldwide;
- innovative educational approaches leading to improvement of the quality of social services and usable in different countries as models in teaching social work practice;
- application for social work education, nationally and regionally, of successful practice strategies from the fields of social welfare and social development;
- worldwide interpretation of professional education for social work as essential for preparation of well-qualified social work personnel.

The Katherine Kendall nomination committee solicits nominations through the IASSW website home page, from regional and national associations of schools of social work and from individual members. It then proposes a candidate for the award to the board, which makes the appointment. A diploma is presented to the awardee at IASSW's biennial international conferences. Until 2004, when it was done in a video presentation, Katherine Kendall herself introduced the recipients to the conference audience, and presented the diploma. The award ceremony now includes a lecture by the awardee and a board dinner.

How this book came about

In 2007, the board decided to publish interviews with the awardees. Since they were recognized pioneers in social work education, it was considered important to make their experiences accessible for future generations of social workers, as part of our professional heritage. An interview guide was accepted by the board, and interviewers identified who were mainly present or former board members. The interviews were recorded and transcribed.

Following a debate about how the interviews should be used, two projects were carried forward. A publication by the Council on Social Work Education (CSWE) in the US was launched in 2014 to honour Katherine Kendall and American awardees (Foxwell, 2014a). The current writers then agreed to prepare a book to present the interviews about all the awardees fully, within a framework of contextualizing information for readers unfamiliar with IASSW and international social work education. In Part 1, we also seek to draw some preliminary views and conclusions on the contents of the interviews.

Presenting and editing the interviews

Each of the awardees is represented in named chapters in Part 2, in most cases through a version of the interviews, edited by the authors of this book. The interviews took place between 2004 and 2016. Three awardees were not available for interview. Herman Stein and Robin Huws Jones died before the board decided on carrying out interviews. They are represented by articles written by Katherine Kendall and reprinted from the internet journal *Social Work & Society*, with the journal's permission. We have not edited these two chapters, except by adding some footnotes for information. Harriet Jakobsson, although aware of the planned publication, was too ill to be interviewed. A colleague agreed to write a chapter based on an interview she had carried out earlier and some other information about her. This chapter is slightly edited to make it conform as far as possible with the other chapters.

The content of the interviews differs for various reasons. The topics of the interview guide are used as subtitles in the chapters. These differ slightly depending on whether the interviewee was retired or in the middle of their career. We have tried to align the content of the interviews along the interview guide's main flow of questioning, so that each chapter is roughly comparable. The interviewers were colleagues who were acquainted with the interviewees and their achievements. This made the interviews richer since they knew of topics on which they wanted the interviewees to elaborate. Some questions in the guide were emphasized or omitted, and some other topics are covered under additional subheadings where the interviewer or interviewee moved the discussion in particular directions.

Preparing spoken interviews for reproduction in text form raises questions of veracity. The aim of publishing the interviews is not to permit textual analysis, but rather to present ideas and experiences from the interviewees in a readable form. We also needed to edit the texts to a British English publication style. The awardees' personal emphases and mode of expression are, however, important in our view. In the editing, we have ironed out spoken infelicities, and corrected obvious linguistic errors but without removing all signs of the awardee's personality and vernacular. We hope that the authentic person speaks, even in the edited texts.

All but one of the interviews was in English, though sometimes one or both participants were not native English speakers. Some interviews might therefore be affected by language use, and we have checked meaning with the interviewees where we were unsure. The interviewees have gone through drafts of their chapters to update and correct them and suggest deletions for brevity and clarity. One interview in Spanish was translated into English, and both the awardee and the interviewer have had the same opportunity.

In editing the transcripts, we shortened longer texts. To do this, each of us separately proposed deletions or rephrasing of the interview texts without losing the meaning of the material. We also identified and amalgamated in one place repetitions and related issues stimulated by different questions. We then looked at the other's suggestions, discussed our reasoning and came to a final conclusion.

Where people or events mentioned in the conversation might not be familiar to readers, we have added a note at the end of the chapter. The original names of organisations and publications appear in the text with translations in brackets.

As an introduction to each chapter, we created brief biographies of the awardees and at the end included a bibliography of five titles selected by the awardees themselves from their work. For two of the three awardees who were not interviewed, we selected titles from bibliographic searches; we have been unable to find publications representing Harriet Jakobsson's work.

Reviewing the interviews

The interview chapters contain what, in research methodology, might be described as 'elite interviews'. An elite interview is not necessarily of '... someone of high social, economic, or political standing; the term indicates a person who is chosen by name or position for a particular reason, rather than randomly or anonymously' (Hochschild, 2009: np). In this case, the reason for selection is that they have received the Katherine Kendall Award, for their successful participation in social work education internationally. Kezar's (2003: p 397) analysis points to an elite interview following a schedule or guide that reflects the interviewer's analysis of the situation, to meet the objectives in carrying out the study. In this case, as we have seen, decisions by the IASSW board and the chosen interviewers influenced the subjects covered in the interviews. The outcome of the interview, however, reflects the interviewee's definition of the situations in which they have been involved. They had free rein to interpret the open questions in the interview schedules. In this way, the interviewees are not just responding to the guided questions, but had latitude to raise their own concerns and ideas.

To provide the analysis of the interviews in Chapter 2, we each separately read the interviews and listed themes raised within them. We then met to agree a single list of topics. As part of our discussion, we noted points to be made about each issue, then divided the drafting of the sections of the analysis between us. Having made our contributions, we met to debate and resolve areas of disagreement. In this way, we jointly contributed to the review. While we recognize that the way in which the interviews were set up influenced what the interviewees said, our review focuses on their themes and concerns. Where possible, we included comparable material from the three chapters about awardees who could not be interviewed.

We are conscious that we are writing about an international topic, but jointly can only read a few European languages. In creating the introductory chapters, our access to untranslated professional literature and research published in languages other than English is inevitably limited. Large areas and important issues might therefore unintentionally be excluded. What we are describing in this book may therefore be lopsided due to our language limitations.

Outline of the book

The book is divided into two parts, after this preface. Part 1, *International social work education: past and future*, consists of three chapters. Chapter 1 seeks to identify some important factors and trends that over time have influenced social work and its education around the world, as well as providing information about IASSW, the organization that makes the award. This provides a basis for our review of the interviews in Chapter 2, summarizing and comparing the awardees' experiences and views. The Tables in Chapter 1 provide reference points for some of the changes and trends in international social work education. Considering the interviews offers an opportunity to explore professional educators' personal experiences of social work education around the world, and some of the realities of its development. Rich and diverse though these experiences are, information drawn from just a few people in leadership positions cannot fully represent the totality of experiences of international social work education, but these accounts also provide a reference point for evaluating others' experiences. Chapter 3 picks up and extends awardees' views on the future of IASSW and contains some discussion of future perspectives on international social work education and the Award.

Part 2, *International social work education: notable figures,* consists of 14 chapters. Chapter 4 discusses Katherine Kendall's achievements in social work education around the world for 60 years to outline the milieu in which the ideas underlying the award have developed.

Chapters 5 to 17 portray the awardees, each in their own chapter, and their contributions to establishing and securing international social work education during the last half of the twentieth century and the first decades of the twenty-first. These biographies and interviews show something of the lives, professional experiences and achievements of leaders in international social work education during this period.

PART 1

International social work education: past and future

ONE

The changing contexts for international social work education

Aims

Social work and social work education are partly created by general historical changes and movements. Ideas and values also change. Some of the movements leading to change have been international, with influence exerted across national borders. The way in which international social work and its education have crossed borders to achieve influence and development is complex and controversial, because 'travelling knowledge' (Harris, Borodkina, Brodtkorb, Evans, Kessl et al, 2015: p 481) changes the context for the indigenous knowledge that forms local practice and how local social workers are educated to do their jobs. In the concluding section of this chapter, we look at this issue, drawing upon some of the contextual historical information reviewed here to examine debates about the nature of international social work and its education.

To make a critical evaluation of the contribution made to international social work education by the awardees, we need to understand the links and relationships that they worked within and what the circumstances of history faced them with, so that we can begin to understand how their ideas and efforts interacted with their historical, political and social context. The aim of this chapter is not to provide a complete and complex history of the social professions, but to help readers understand the currents and trends in social work and the social issues that it faced during the period in which the awardees were working. The focus of this book on international social work and its education requires looking at broad international trends, not local or national changes that may be more familiar to many readers.

The changing nature of international social work and its education

In this section, we identify three broad historical phases into which these developments may be divided.

Early pioneers in the first decades of the twentieth century were mainly concerned to develop international support for social work and its education. They therefore founded structures for exchange and development by building international organizations, including IASSW, for cooperation and influence.

This foundation phase was followed by the period covered by this book, in which the main concern was to establish and secure social work as a widespread, even universal, profession. This eventually came to be supported by a global understanding of its potential and by acknowledged acceptance of structures for its professional education in most countries. Most of the awardees interviewed in Part 2 were active in this establishment phase of the development of international social work.

From the interviews, we draw out in Chapters 2 and 3 a shift in focus for the awardees and for international social work and its education towards developing a role for social work in addressing issues of global importance. Issues-based international social work is emerging as an important objective for international organizations and thinking in social work, and engaged the awardees whose contribution was in the later twentieth and early twenty-first centuries.

Table 1.1 offers a timeline which places Katherine Kendall, after whom the award is named, and the awardees in their historical context. Katherine Kendall was born early in the twentieth century, and most of the awardees in the period 1930–60, just before and after World War II. Their careers covered the final third of the twentieth century and the beginning of the twenty-first century. Thus, the social trends of the last half of the twentieth century form the historical context of their contribution to social work education. In the following sections, therefore, we look briefly at the foundation phase, and particularly the origin of the organization that was to become IASSW. They deal in more detail with the development of social work education and IASSW in the establishment phase from the 1950s onwards and then review the later shift to issues-based international social work.

Table 1.1: Timelines of the careers of Katherine Kendall and the Kendall awardees in the context of the development of social work education

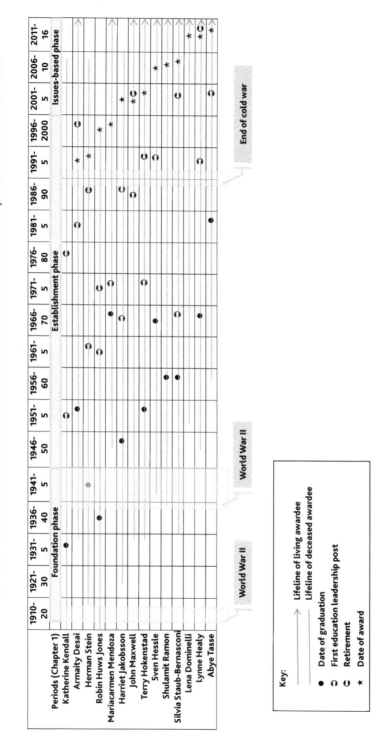

The foundation phase

All societies have some form of social welfare. Studies of the history of social welfare can identify indigenous responses to social need, often based around families and local communities, and cultural and religious traditions. Examples from around the world include Indian and Japanese Buddhist, Hindu and Confucian traditions (Akimoto and Majumdar, 1968; Goodman, 1998; Takahashi, 1997). Islamic traditions in the Middle East and Africa are also important (Ashencaen Crabtree et al, 2008). So, too, are a range of African traditions (Kreitzer, 2009; Graham, 2002; Ragab, 2016). These traditions are neglected in the social work literature, in favour of a European tradition influencing Western culture in the Global North dating from the ancient Greeks and Romans and medieval Christianity (Payne, 2005).

Present-day social work is usually considered to have emerged from the social changes brought about by industrialization and consequent urbanization in European countries and the US beginning in the mid-nineteenth century (Payne, 2005). By the beginning of the twentieth century, it looked as though societies in the Global North were going to develop active social provision and this was seen as an important area of social progress.

Social work education emerged from discourses about services and methods in Europe and the US and as the concept 'social work' became the organizing idea of these developments in the period 1900-30. Table 1.2 collects information about when the first social work schools were set up in different countries. This tells us something about the dispersion of social work education from its beginnings in the early twentieth century to virtually universal coverage by the early twenty-first century. Both major and some minor European countries, Canada and the US had schools of social work before the World War I; by the end of the World War II, all European countries had some form of social work education.

Table 1.2: Dispersion of social work education

Country	Innovation	Date	Source
Netherlands	Institute for Training in Social Work, Amsterdam	1899	World Guide (see Sources); Kendall (2000)
United States	New York School of Philanthropy	1904	World Guide
United Kingdom	Liverpool School of Social Science	1904	Walton and Elliott (1995)
France	Practical School of Social Formation (1907) (Roman Catholic); Practical School of Social Service (1913) (Protestant)	1907	Rater-Garcette (1996); Jovelin (2010)
Germany	Women's School for Social Work (Berlin-Schöneberg)	1908	World Guide; Kendall (2000); Otte and Olsson (2007)
Switzerland	Schule für Soziale Arbeit, Zurich (1908); Ecole d'Etudes Sociales (1918)	1908	World Guide
Austria	'Combined welfare courses', Vienna	1912	Zierer (2010)
Austria (Bulgaria)		1912	Vladinska (1994)
Canada	Department of Social Service, University of Toronto (1914) (Anglophone); University of Montreal (1942) (Francophone)	1914	Watts et al (1995); Jennison and Lundy (2011)
Belgium	Central School of Social Service	1920	World Guide
Norway	Norwegian Women's National Social School	1920	World Guide; Sundt Rasmussen (1991)
Czechoslovakia	Higher School of Social Care, Prague	1921	Stoškova and Chytil (1998)
Italy	Social Service School, San Gregorio in Celio, Rome	1921	Martino (1960)
Sweden	Socialinstitutet in Stockholm	1921	World Guide
China	Department of Sociology, University of Yanjing	1922	Chow (1997)
South Africa	University of Cape Town	1924	Ntusi (1997)
Chile	Escuela de Trabajo Social Elvira Matte de Cruchaga, private Catholic foundation affiliated with the Catholic University of Chile in Santiago	1925	World Guide; Kendall (2000)
Finland	School of Social Sciences in Helsinki, moved to Tampere in 1960, becoming the University of Tampere	1925	World Guide
Poland	College of Socio-Educational Work, Independent Polish University, Warsaw	1925	Les (1997)
Japan	Central Social Work Association	1928	Maeda (1995)

Country	Innovation	Date	Source
Argentina	Argentine Social Museum proposal to create a school of social service	1930	Queiro-Tajalli (1995)
Spain	School of Welfare for Women, Barcelona	1932	Sabater (2001)
Australia	Melbourne University	1933	World Guide
Ireland	Department of Social Science, University College Dublin	1934	Kearney (1999)
Mexico	Centre for Technical Studies	1933	Aguilar (1995)
Egypt	Higher Institute of Social Work, Alexandria (Francophone); Cairo School of Social Work (Anglophone)	1935	Abo-el-Nasr (1997); Ragab (1995)
Estonia	Tallinn Institute for Social Work and Household Economics, Estonian Women's League	1935	Tulva (1997)
Portugal	Instituto Superior de Serviço Social (Lisbon)	1935	World Guide
India	Sir Dorabji Tata Graduate School of Social Work	1936	World Guide
Denmark	Den Sociale Højskole, Copenhagen	1937	World Guide; Hermansen (1991)
Uruguay	School of Social Work of Uruguay	1937	World Guide
Costa Rica	Foundation by local agencies, 1944; part of the University of Costa Rica	1942	World Guide
Brazil	School of Social Service, Catholic Brazilian Young Women of Natal (northern Brazil)	1945	World Guide
Colombia	Antioqueña Normal School for Girls	1945	World Guide
Ghana	School of Social Welfare, Department of Social Service	1946	Blavo and Apt (1997); Kreitzer (2012)
Panama	School of Social Work, University of Panama	1947	Aguilar (1995)
South Korea	Department of Social Work EWHA Women's University	1947	Furuto (2014)
Greece	IAKE (formerly XEN) School of Social Work	1948	World Guide
Guatemala		1949	Aguilar (1995)
Hong Kong	University of Hong Kong	1950	Furuto (2014)
New Zealand	School of Social Science in Victoria University College of Wellington	1950	World Guide
Philippines	School of Social Work affiliate school of the Philippines Women's University	1950	World Guide
Taiwan	Provincial Junior College of Administration	1950	Furuto (2014)

8

Country	Innovation	Date	Source
Singapore	Department of Social Work, National University of Singapore	1952	World Guide; Hodge, 1980
Uganda	National Training Institute of Social Development, Entebbe	1952	World Guide
Yugoslavia (Serbia)	Social policy, University of Zagreb	1952	Guzzetta (1995)
El Salvador		1953	Aguilar (1995)
Pakistan	Department of Social Work, University of Punjab	1954	World Guide
Sri Lanka	Institute of Social Work	1954	World Guide
Thailand	Faculty of Social Administration Thammasat University	1954	World Guide; Furuto (2014)
Peru	Educational Program for Social Work, Pontifical Catholic University of Peru	1956	World Guide
Honduras		1957	Aguilar (1995)
Indonesia	Social work training course, Ministry of Social Affairs	1957	World Guide; Furuto (2014)
Yugoslavia (Slovenia)	Two-year course	1957	Guzzetta (1995)
Pakistan (Bangladesh)	University of Dhaka Institute of Social Welfare and Research	1958	World Guide
Israel	Paul Baerwald School of Social Work, Hebrew University of Jerusalem	1958	Cohen and Guttmann (1998); Kendall (1986)
Iran	Tehran School of Social Work	1958	Farman Farmaian (1992)
Venezuela	Central University	1958	World Guide
Jamaica	Department of Sociology, University of the West Indies Mona	1961	World Guide
Nicaragua	School of Social Work	1961	Aguilar (1995)
Turkey	Hacettepe University (social services academy)	1961	World Guide
Zambia	Oppenheimer College of Social Service	1961	World Guide
Kenya	Kenya School of Social Work	1962	World Guide
Zimbabwe	Harare School of Social Work (Jesuits)	1964	World Guide
Iraq	University of Baghdad	1968	Ragab (1995)
Guyana	Department of Sociology, University of Guyana	1970	World Guide
Papua New Guinea	Department of Anthropology and Sociology, University of Papua New Guinea	1972	World Guide
Libya	University of Tripoli	1972	Ragab (1995)
Saudi Arabia	University of Riyadh	1974	Ragab (1995)
Tanzania	National Social Work Training Institute of Ministry of Labour and Social Welfare	1974	World Guide

Country	Innovation	Date	Source
Kuwait	University of Kuwait	1975	World Guide
Malaysia	Universiti Sains Malaysia	1975	World Guide; Furuto (2014)
Nigeria	University of Nigeria Nsukka	1976	Okafor (2004)
Micronesia	University of Guam	1980	Furuto (2014)
Yugoslavia (Bosnia)	Faculty of Political Science, Sarajevo	1980	Guzzetta (1995)
Iceland	Samfunnsvetenskapliga fakulteten, Islands University	1981	Jónsdóttir (1991)
Yugoslavia (Macedonia)	Institute for Social Work and Social Policy, University of Skopje	1987	Guzzetta (1995)
Cambodia	Royal University of Phnom Penh	1990	Furuto (2014)
Russia	Moscow Academy of Pedagogical Sciences	1991	Guzzetta (1995)
Slovak Republic	Comenius University, Bratislava	1991	Guzzetta (1995)
American Samoa		2008	Furuto (2014)

Sources: Our source for each foundation date is listed in the column on the right. The starting point was IASSW's World Guide to Social Work Education (Rao, 1984), 'World Guide' in the source column. This was created through a questionnaire to IASSW members, so it reflects responses from the countries questioned, although the research did not intend to identify first foundations, so its listing is not definitive.

Note on method: We have tried to identify the first admissions to the first full-time course of one academic year or more, or part-time equivalents, leading to an educational award considered at the time to be a vocational qualification in social work. In search of accuracy, we compared start dates given by different sources, and tried to understand why the differences arose. Common reasons for variations are that some sources were concerned only with full-time, degree-awarding and/or post-graduate courses. Also, some sources give dates of school opening, while others note dates of first graduations. Another issue is that some sources focus on adoption by a university or national regulation, not crediting earlier developments by private or charitable bodies. We preferred evidence in documents produced by people native to the country concerned.

In Austria, Pakistan and Yugoslavia, first foundations in constituent countries that are now independent are listed separately under the name of the country of original foundation, with the new country in brackets after it.

There are, however, weaknesses in looking at first foundations. First, early developments were small–scale and tentative, and did not lead to more extensive education. For example, in Norway, early social courses for women in 1920 remained isolated incidences but were identified as a development of social work education by Salomon's (1936) international survey (Salomon, 1937). They did not fully bear fruit until developments in public services led to the foundation of a governmental school of social work alongside a local government college in Oslo in the 1950s. Second, knowing the timing of first developments does not tell us about the diversity of provision. For example, in the US, developments in urban private universities connected with large, charitably funded urban agencies (such as settlements and charity organization societies) differed in role and philosophy both from schools in state universities covering rural areas and also from schools serving black populations in Southern states, such as New Orleans and Atlanta (Green, 1999; Ross, 1978: pp 422-51). Third, the timing of developments does not tell us why they happened. For example, early development of social work education in Chile came about through the influence of the Roman Catholic Church and the fortuitous involvement of important medical supporters of social intervention. Fourth, when developments took place does not identify what different intellectual and practice traditions were engaged. For example, in an early international survey, Macadam (1925: pp 188-9) observed a difference between US developments, with a focus on social treatment, and European moves to emphasize environmental and economic issues as an important area of social work. Salomon (1937) argued that government regulation and training programmes in Belgium, France and the Netherlands were important reasons why social work and its education became strongly established in these countries in the first decades of the twentieth century.

An important marker of attempts, during the foundation phase, to create cooperation and mutual influence across borders was the first international social work conference, held in Paris for two weeks in 1928. It was the initial attempt at collective international action among social workers and their educators. Participants numbered 2,481 educators, students, volunteers and administrators, representing 42 countries (Kniephoff-Knebel and Seibel, 2008); a parallel wider public sector conference attracted even larger numbers. One of the conference sections was on social work training. This was led by Alice Salomon, a German pioneer, and René Sand, a Belgian medical doctor and promoter of social work and its education in Europe and in Latin America. Salomon and Sand had travelled to the US to gain support from educators there in 1919.

The conference asked Salomon to develop the ground for an organization in the field of education. Approaches were made to 111 training schools identified at that time. Forty-six schools from 10 countries agreed to join an association (Kendall, 1978). The founding meeting of the International Committee of Schools of Social Work (ICSSW) took place in Berlin in 1929, with representation only from European schools and the International Labour Office (ILO) (Wieler, 1989; Healy, 2008).

The purpose of ICSSW, defined by the founding meeting, was:

> ... to bring about an exchange of opinion and experience between schools of social work and to deal with all problems of international co-operation of these schools, such as the exchange of teachers and students, the organization of a centre of documentation and information, the formation of international social study courses and the participation in the preparation of international congresses for social work. (International Committee of Schools of Social Work, 1929, cited by Healy, 2008: p 115)

Salomon was elected the first president, recognizing the international standing arising from her role in the German and international women's movements and in the foundation of the important pioneer school in Berlin. At the time, she had been a leading member of the International Council of Women, and had many American friends. In an exceptional career, Salomon published 28 books and about 250 articles. Kendall (1978: pp 10-15) regarded her and her ideas as among the important foundations of international social work.

In the 1930s, ICSSW organized biennial seminars or summer schools in Europe, mainly involving presentations of successful service development in the host countries rather than education (Kendall, 1998: p 10). The membership and board were mostly Europeans, although there were links with the US, with the eminent Chicago professor, Sophonisba Breckinridge, being a member of the 'secretariat' (in effect, an organizing committee) from 1931. By the later 1930s, Salomon, who had Jewish origins, had been driven from Germany by the Nazi government and took refuge in the US (Salomon, 2004). The 1940 conference was cancelled on the outbreak of World War II. During the war, members were only rarely able to keep in touch, and the ICSSW records were lost in bombing.

The establishment phase

Economic and social development from the 1940s to the 1970s

After World War II, twentieth century history threw up circumstances propitious for the development of social work and its education. Physical and social reconstruction after World War II led to a long period of economic growth, ending in the 1970s. During this expansionist time, Katherine Kendall and the early awardees, Armaity Desai, Robin Huws Jones and Herman Stein, were active, and it formed the background to the early careers of most of the other awardees.

Many Western European countries pursued social democratic policies by developing state welfare, with the state taking responsibility for meeting a wide range of social needs from taxation, including the provision of education, health, housing and social security. Increasingly, social responsibility in such regimes provided ideal soil for social work. Social work and its education became more strongly institutionalized in many countries where it was already strong, because social expectations in the new welfare states, and consequently governments, supported the development of appropriately trained workforces for the social services. This was extended by international work through aid organizations, of which awardee Harriet Jakobsson's activities in several countries are an example, transferring expertise and building support for social provision in the Global South.

Much of this social reconstruction was helped by substantial financial aid from the US in its areas of political interest, particularly Europe, Latin America and the Pacific Rim. UN agencies also gave important support, pursuing a policy of promoting social work education as a way of stimulating social and economic development during the 1950s and '60s. This policy derived in no small measure from the early work of Katherine Kendall and her report in social work education internationally and successor reports (United Nations, 1950). Social work education was revived after the discontinuity caused by fascist regimes and war in the 1930s and '40s. For example, in 1950 Doshisha University in Kyoto started the first masters in social work in Japan, and this became the model for later schools as they developed. In 1988, the Japanese government introduced new regulatory legislation for the registration of social workers.

ICSSW held its first post-war meeting in 1946. Sand was elected president and, in 1947, an initial post-war conference took place in Scheveningen, Netherlands, on 'urgent social problems in the war-stricken areas of Europe'. Sand tried to build a link from Europe to the North American schools, addressing an embarrassingly small international session at the US National Conference of Social Work in 1948: only six representatives of the US schools attended. The Committee was nevertheless revitalized and renamed IASSW at the first full international congress in Paris in 1950. Since then, conferences have focused on social work education and research. When conferences are held jointly with the other international social work organizations, social work practice is also included. In 1952, the first IASSW meeting on social work education outside Europe was held in Madras, India, at the same time as the Sixth International Conference of Social Work. After that, interest in a worldwide organization seemed to take off

(Kendall, 1998: p 6). In 1956, IASSW had 350 school members in 46 countries. In comparison, there were 389 institutional school members from 53 countries in 2014. In the late 1950s and '60s, new procedures broke the European and North American dominance and schools from Australasia, Asia, Africa and Latin America became members. The board also became more international, with members being elected from across the world (Kendall, 1978: p 18).

Balancing its communication and networking role, since the early 1950s IASSW has sought to promote policy objectives relevant to the social work profession and its education (Kendall, 1978: p 14). The UN accredited IASSW in 1947 with consultative status as an NGO. The International Federation of Social Workers (IFSW – representing social workers' associations) achieved this status in 1959 and the International Council on Social Welfare (ICSW – representing social welfare agencies) in 1972. All three have, therefore, for many decades had formal consultative status with UNESCO and other UN and related agencies and committees. The main involvement has been with the Economic and Social Council (ECOSOC), one of the six principal organs in the UN, whose focus on economic, social and humanitarian problems effecting social welfare and human rights is particularly relevant to the three organizations' interests. This involvement is reflected in the careers of awardees including Terry Hokenstad and Lynne Healy. IASSW and its sister organizations' consultation teams are represented at ECOSOC's annual four-week session.

The post-war period of opportunity for social work in Europe was not universal. Central and Eastern European countries, and the huge land area of China, fell within a communist sphere of influence. Communist regimes assumed that social ills came from social class divisions and exploitation inherent in capitalist economies; China was an example (Chan and Chow, 1992). This view led to the end of official support for social work in Soviet Asia, Eastern and Central Europe, Ethiopia and other communist spheres of influence. In these countries, there was a 'period of silence in social work' (Bagdonas, 2001: 45). Welfare provision through work-based units and social provision of employment, housing and income by the state was thought to make the interpersonal help of social work methods irrelevant. Here, there was an ideology of universal social provision through state management of the economy and industry. Such regimes denied the value of social work as a service, in favour of broad social provision, incorporating social assistance in education, housing and work-based provision. Existing social work institutions in communist countries were dismantled or frozen in a very restricted form. A 'cold war' developed between countries in the Global North ('First World') and Soviet communist ('Second World') spheres of influence. It was called a 'cold' war because armed conflict was displaced in favour of ideological conflict around what were seen as opposing economic and social systems. Social provision, including social work, continued to be seen by states from the Global North in this context as a bulwark against revolutionary social disruption. It was therefore promoted across Western European states and in 'Third World' countries, particularly in Africa, Asia and Latin America that were politically non-aligned in the cold war partly as an instrument of that ideological conflict.

Growing movements for independence affected many European colonies. Eventually, after the conclusion of World War II in 1945, independence was achieved – sometimes with conflict and difficulty – for many former British, French and other European colonies in Africa and Asia and for former colonial protectorates in the Middle East, such as Egypt, Israel/Palestine, Iran and Iraq. Some financing and planning was contributed to help them develop some welfare provision, although in most cases, particularly in Africa, this was minimal and reflected European assumptions about what was appropriate.

Kreitzer (2012), in the broadest analysis available of developments in African social work education, shows how the colonialist lack of awareness of indigenous values and culture and the continuing interest in maintaining a legacy of influence, led to an emphasis on models of university education deriving from the Global North. These valued knowledge and methods of academic discourse expected in the Global North and delayed the adoption of indigenous alternatives. Local authoritarian leaders also adopted these techniques to control the pace and direction of development in support of their own political objectives. When it came to social work education, practical education in local colleges favoured charitable or missionary welfare activities and devalued local cultural and religious values. Also, as African universities gained independence from Western academic sponsors, knowledge derived from understanding of indigenous family and community supports was devalued in favour of psychological knowledge based on academic discourses accepted in the Global North. A similar pattern emerged in Asia, where early university social work departments in former colonies employed British academic and professional leadership in the 1950s and '60s, for example Jean Robertson in Singapore and Hong Kong and Peter Hodge in Hong Kong (Robertson, 1980; Hodge, 1980). Belgian, British and French colonies in Africa and Asia took up colonial 'social development' to create collective social action in local communities to meet local social needs (Sinha and

Kao, 1988; Yimam, 1990; Singh, 1999; Kreitzer, 2012). This colonial experience led to conceptual development which influenced ideas about community work in Europe and the USA.

An important counterbalance to these colonial influences was the growth of regional organizations of social work educators, which sought to reestablish the importance of indigenous values and social traditions. These associations also shifted the emphasis of social work education towards social development rather than individual social practice.

During this period of growth, a psychoanalytic and individualistic model derived from US casework continued to have a strong influence on social work thinking, and the generic model of education connected with it continued the priorities of the influential US model of social work education. CSWE's founding curriculum policy in 1952, for example, was:

> ... directed toward the creation of an integrated, unified, two-year programme of class and field instruction and research as the educational base for the profession of social work. The objectives ... were those of a generic curriculum designed to produce social workers with a common foundation of knowledge and values ... . (Kendall, 1978: p 93)

This kind of thinking set international assumptions about what would be the best standard of professional education for social workers.

The psychoanalytic casework model continued to have influence for two main reasons. First, many of the new welfare states of the Global North were organized to value, for example in their social security arrangements, a family pattern of the male breadwinner with a domestic role for women and a subservient role for women and children. Psychoanalytic ideas about maternal roles influenced family casework, which supported this social pattern in these welfare societies. It therefore became part of social work's mission to create successful family life on this pattern. It also claimed to deal with problems with deprived and neglected children, in school attendance, in the disciplining of young offenders and – new cultural creations of this period – 'teenagers' and 'juvenile delinquents'. Iacovetta (1998: p 316) argues that the social reconstruction after World War II and during the cold war period were times of 'heightened domesticity', when the family was idealized after the end of the period of relative independence for women and young people in wartime. Working-class parenting was disdained and disciplining children to achieve success in education was valued.

The second reason for the worldwide impact of psychodynamic family casework was the political and professional policies of the US state. The US sought to use social interventions in post-war social reconstruction and to promote democratic liberal economic values in the cold war. The US was also the world's economic powerhouse at this time. Its publishing industry served a large population, and it was economic to produce books and journals even in a small academic specialty such as social work; these could then have worldwide circulation. Finance was available to allow travel by American administrators and academics to other countries, and to enable scholars and professionals from other countries to visit and learn from the US. The ambition to have a universally applicable method overcame doubts about its validity in different cultures mainly because social workers hoped to promote successful professionalization. A leading French social work educator commented in 1963:

> The trend to provide a professional education which is sufficiently generic to prepare the student to work in any of the areas of activity of social work should be encouraged ... A world-wide approach in social work gives us a better basis for work in the developing countries ... From the point of view of professional social work, we cannot recommend too strongly this worldwide approach ... and to interpret social work so that it is better understood as a profession both nationally and internationally. (Ginet, 1963: p 26)

The dominance of psychodynamic family casework as the primary social work method was challenged increasingly strongly from several sources from the 1960s onwards This was an important issue for awardee Armaity Desai. There are many examples in India (Yelaja, 1970; Nagpaul, 1972). Shawky, a UN regional consultant on social work education identified some of the tensions in Africa:

> Most of the trained social workers are still clinging to the western-oriented type of service which calls for therapeutic individual attention for special groups in need of assistance, such as juvenile delinquents, orphans, the elderly, the destitute and the physically handicapped ... In the meantime, many African social workers seem to see the need to link social welfare programmes with the priority

needs of African peoples, and thus are more interested in preventive and developmental programmes like community development and youth service schemes. (Shawky, 1972: pp 5-6)

There was thus a growing sense of the failure of the pre-eminent mode of social work to meet the emerging needs of people in the Global South. Significant social movements arose in many parts of the world concerned with the civil rights of oppressed population groups, confronting racial discrimination in the US, apartheid policies promoting racial segregation in South Africa and other historical injustices affecting particularly African and Asian nations and populations. There was also renewed concern that economic growth had failed to eradicate poverty in Europe and the US and that development policy was not achieving social progress in wide swathes of the developing 'Third World'. At the same time, a 'second wave' of feminist activism reflected continuing inequalities for women in work and in public services and discriminatory attitudes towards women throughout society.

All these social movements led to an increase in concern about cultural assumptions, inequality and social justice in political discourse. In Latin America, liberation theology (Gutiérrez, 1988) built on a radical view of the aims and role of Christianity to proclaim that a politics of salvation through community organization could address poverty and other important social problems. The radical Brazilian educationalist, Freire (1972), proposed a method of informal education relying on 'conscientization' (consciousness-raising) through group discussion of social issues. This had a worldwide impact.

Many Western countries, too, experienced a flowering of community action, informal education, youth work and citizen participation in urban planning, picking up the social reform tradition of social work more strongly. This led to a period of service development and financing of special projects concerned with urban development and confronting the causes of poverty, for example in the American 'war on poverty' and 'great society' programmes (Katz, 1996: pp 259-99). Other projects such as the influential 'mobilization for youth' in New York (Helfgot, 1981) and European projects such as the UK urban and community development programmes (Loney, 1983) also influenced political and social thinking. This led in turn to a growth in interest and practice development in community interventions within social work, and in areas such as informal education, youth work and citizen participation in urban planning. Lena Dominelli's early community work experiences, described in her interview in Part 2, took place in these programmes.

An influential development was 'reconceptualization' in Latin America, a 'widespread and extremely diverse movement seeking structural and political changes …' (Saracostti, Reininger and Parada, 2012: pp 470-1), with the aim of creating a social work capable of responding to local problems and needs. Based on 'conscientization', it was redirected towards social work. These developments became widely known across the world. The influence in Latin America of such approaches to social work is identifiable in the work of the 1998 awardee, Mariacarmen Mendoza.

As IASSW developed during this period, international networking was at its heart and laid a foundation for other activities. Conferences and seminars gave a unique opportunity to meet like-minded colleagues, exchange ideas, and be informed about developments and trends. Five regional associations were established and some sub-regional associations developed later. Promoting international exchange led to a journal where opinions, experiences and research could be published. *International Social Work* was founded in 1957 in cooperation between IASSW and ICSW, with IFSW joining as co-sponsor in 1959. The journal was made possible by a grant from the National Cash Register Corporation. It was said to be an experiment (Healy, 2008), but celebrates its 60th anniversary in 2017.

Group and community methods gained renewed international prominence at an IASSW congress in the Netherlands in 1972. Contributions on social pedagogical and community methods of practice from the Netherlands and France and on conscientization from Latin America were connected to curriculum development in India (Desai, 1972) and the US (Pernell, 1972).

A product of this period of expansion and community endeavour was the most important development project ever undertaken by IASSW, the family planning project (1971-78; Kendall, 1977). IASSW has always offered consultation to countries and universities that are developing social work programmes, and the interview chapters in Part 2 show awardees contributing to this. The family planning project used this consultation model to draw social work education into international movements for policy and practice change.

Encouraging family planning was an important policy objective in the Global South during the period after World War II. The aims varied. One was to reduce poverty by reducing the number of mouths that a poor family had to feed. An important healthcare aim was to reduce the stress and ill health to mothers of repeated childbearing. These clinical objectives were the most important in the early stages of family planning policy in India, until the mid-1960s, and social workers with a medical background were therefore the most important contributors (Pathak, 1974). At this point, though, policy changed to a community education approach, designed to change cultural assumptions to favour a norm for small families, and to reduce the number of street children (Farman Farmaien, 1992). The aim was to facilitate national economic growth, by shifting families and communities from mere subsistence towards economic development.

Initiated in Asia and the Middle East, the IASSW project extended to Africa, Latin America and the Caribbean. Two important aims for social work emerged from the outset. The first was, perhaps unrealistically, to shift national programmes away from quantitative targets and towards human and cultural development. Second, social work education offered very little to prepare practitioners for work in this field, and it was hoped to rectify this. Important forerunners were a national programme in India, starting in 1951 (Pathak, 1974) and the Tehran School of Social Work, which integrated family planning into its students' work in the 1960s (Farman Farmaien, 1992). Sattereh Farman Farmaien, its director, was an influential IASSW vice president from 1972.

Most of the work took place in 31 schools of social work, in 13 developing countries, with some additional work in seven other countries. Population and family planning were added to the curriculum, and reference and teaching materials were developed and published (Oettinger and Stansbury, 1972). In Asia, more than 7,000 students were reached. The project was successful in three regions: Africa (where the project started later and was consequently less well developed), Asia and the English-speaking Caribbean. Attempts to make progress in Latin America were largely unsuccessful, due to opposition from the Roman Catholic churches, with their religious objection to contraception.

Retrenchment and reaction from the 1970s

The period of growth for social programmes internationally and for social work came to an end when conflicts in the Middle East led to a significant rise in the price of oil in 1976, threatening global economic development. This in turn led to a reassertion of neo-liberal ideology, based on a concern that tax incomes could no longer support generous government social provision. Doubts were also raised about expectations that economic development would eventually lead to a level of social development similar to that of the Global North in Africa, Asia and Latin America. This generated a political environment that questioned social interventions. It also sought to restrain their growth through 'new public management', emphasizing economic and managerial constraints on expansion (Pollitt, 1993).

Social work therefore became more constrained, less concerned with achieving personal fulfilment and well-being for its clients and more an instrument of governments' political priorities. Public choice theories of economic and social policy were dominant, assuming that the role of public social intervention is a product of rational economic management, rather than to respond to social concern (Jordan, 2000, 2008, 2014). Earlier social policy gains were also increasingly constrained by the demands of a globalized economic system; this promoted deregulation of restrictions on the free operation of markets worldwide, which favoured the economic interests of developed economies. Neo-liberal values also devalue collective social provision, such as social services. Such policies tend to exclude poor and minority social groups from access to good service provision, and devalue public sector social professions.

Sociological critique of the potential self-interest of 'producer interests' in professions led to questions about social work's efforts to achieve professional status. Globalized market economies favoured the industrialization and routinization of social professions, splitting broad professional roles into tasks that could be performed by less broadly trained employees. In many countries of the Global North, 'tough love' policies were enforced, focusing on providing financial incentives and restrictive social interventions to manage service user behaviour. Service user participation in the control of services also limited professional discretion. All these trends shifted the role of social workers in public sector social services in developed economies towards surveillance and behaviour management roles.

Neo-liberal policies also affected universities. For example, Brauns and Kramer (1991) noted tendencies in European universities, which are also typical of processes elsewhere, towards increasing:

- 'academization': shifts from training organized by agencies or governments towards education in higher education institutions, with further moves towards university provision, and consequently greater concerns for university priorities, such as research production;
- Europeanization: shifts towards aligning the organization of training according to regional norms, assisted in Europe by the later Bologna

Agreement among European Union nations to harmonize university qualifications (Martínes-Román, 2007);

- secularization and an increasingly 'generic' approach, that increased the influence of universities over the design of curricula and objectives for social work education, rather than that of founding agencies and institutions, such as churches and aid charities.

Such moves reduced opportunities for creative social work in public services and for social work to empower people to fulfil their personal potential and enhance social solidarity. In the US, a different social trend in the development of social work became apparent. The continuing focus on individual methods of practice, the demand for private counselling and psychotherapy, and the continuing focus on social work as a mental health profession allowed many social workers to make a living through private practice. This also followed the political impetus towards privatization of services from collective public control. Specht and Courtney (1994), in a trenchant and controversial polemic, attacked the US social work profession for abandoning its mission to help people in poverty and seek social change for the betterment of the whole population. Thus, a substantial section of the US profession retained its focus on individualized psychotherapeutic practice. One of the most striking responses was in Billups' (2002) series of interviews with 'international social work notables', including Katherine Kendall and some existing, or to become, Kendall awardees. In his book, Billups contests individualized practice in the US social work profession by demonstrating the achievement of broader social purposes, social development and political activism in social work internationally.

Disillusionment with social work education based on models from the Global North during the 1980s spread across African, Asian and Middle Eastern countries. This led to trends towards social development and incorporating indigenous knowledge and values into social work. A variety of factors were identified (Cox 1995; Ragab, 1995: Kreitzer, 2012, Butterfield and Tasse, 2013):

- rejection of the policy of economic growth at any price;
- giving importance to cultural and religious diversity;
- assertion of Islamic, Hindu, Buddhist and other important ideological or cultural positions as important bases of social work education;
- displacing values deriving from the Global North with local values and philosophies;
- emphasizing development and modernization as a focus for practice;

- identifying the reality that most areas of need are mass social problems, so de-emphasizing individualized responses to needs;
- concern that the main social problems that dominate the country are not tackled by what the social work schools offer. Curricula in the Global North primarily prepare workers to work with individuals in urban areas, neglecting both more collective practice and people in rural areas and their problems.

One of the drivers for the success of neo-liberal political policies was the collapse of the Soviet political and economic regimes, ending the cold war. Also, changes in economic policy in China, Eastern and Central Europe, which were already industrialized, took on faster-paced economic development and altered social policies. This enabled another important extension of social work internationally, in which awardees such as Sven Hessle, Terry Hokenstad, Shulamit Ramon and Silvia Staub-Bernasconi were involved. Another factor was the final Soviet collapse and the shift in management of the Chinese Communist Party towards a more open capitalist economy. These political regimes became more open to social interventions and social work during the 1990s, enabling another phase of international extension of social work education. In many countries in Africa and the Middle East, developments were influenced from neighbouring countries and regional UN development agencies. Asia and Latin America saw significant economic growth in a succession of countries following Japanese development in the 1960s. Countries such as Brazil, China, Korea, Indonesia, Malaysia and Mexico faced the same process of urbanization and social disruption that led to the emergence of social work in Europe in the later nineteenth century, but at a very accelerated rate. Furuto (2014) notes that countries in East Asia often sought university development of social work education as an instrument to develop welfare services.

The period of retrenchment had its effects on IASSW. The family planning project, which had funded Katherine Kendall's full-time secretary-general's post, came to an end in 1978. When she retired that year, the secretariat was moved, with a grant from the Austrian government, from New York to Vienna, close to another UN office. Two secretaries-general followed her, Marguerite Mathieu and Vera Mehta, until the Vienna office closed in 1992. An internal conflict arose in IASSW in the 1970s about whether to allow South African schools to continue membership during the period in which the South African government maintained a policy of apartheid. The early stages of debate about this issue is described in Part 2, in Kendall's biographies of Robin Huws Jones, who was in the chair at the time the issue first arose, and of Herman Stein, who succeeded him. Aside from internal conflicts on this issue, UNICEF threatened to withdraw consultative status from IASSW because of its South African members. Stein negotiated a compromise, retaining the consultancy status by subjecting the South African membership to continuing review. In late 1980s and 1990s, the Nordic schools of social work suspended their membership over this issue. IASSW went through a serious financial crisis, due to the consequent loss of membership fees. The Austrian government's grant aid towards maintaining IASSW's office in Vienna also ended, and IASSW could no longer afford to have a paid secretary-general. From then on, the administration has been maintained by a paid assistant situated in the home country of the president. Once again, IASSW became a voluntarily run organization as the president, secretary and treasurer are all elected positions.

Extending IASSW's cooperation role

Networking opportunities have been at the centre of IASSW's value to its members from the outset. New international social work priorities have led IASSW to seek ways to extend these opportunities on a more equal basis to the whole membership through developing policies around how it organizes its conference and minimizes the impact of language and other differences across its regions. In this way, it aims to model in its organization the equalities and social change agenda it promotes in its issues-based work. From the first conferences outside Europe and North America in Asia (Madras, 1952) and in Africa (Nairobi, 1974), present policy today is to rotate biannual conferences between the different continents. This is because it facilitates attendance from surrounding countries and over time spreads opportunities for international contact. Even so, most congresses are in the Global North, where they are more easily financed. Probably for the same reason, representatives from the Global North often predominate. The regional associations of IASSW organize biennial conferences, either with IFSW and ICSW or separately alternating with the global conferences.

In 2003, IASSW launched a fund for international projects in social work education, aiming to find more ways to stimulate exchange and cooperation. The idea is to get members to work together, learning across borders. Criteria for grants require a minimum of three members representing at least two countries and different cultures in social work education to participate. This initiative has borne fruit in networks studying social work in areas of political and social conflict, referred to in the interview with Shulamit Ramon, and in work on gender and on health inequalities, which connects with extensive work from the World Health Organization on this issue.

IASSW has also been concerned that educational institutions around the world should be able to find others to collaborate with. In the tradition of Salomon's world survey in 1936, IASSW published *The world guide to social work education* in 1973 and 1984 (Rao, 1984). It contained accounts of social work education programmes around the world, describing similarities and differences in social work education in member countries (Healy, 2008). A World Census initiated in 1996 (Garber, 2000) – and significantly referring to social development education, the Global South priority, alongside social work – has been updated several times since, and presented in reports, conference papers and articles (Barretta-Herman et al, 2016).

Another important development, reflecting the internationalizing of its work, has been the implementation of a language policy, which enables better participation in networking opportunities. IASSW's official languages were for many years English, French and Spanish, which were all used in correspondence and documents among the founders (Healy and Thomas, 2007). The Japanese schools, the largest membership group, raised the question of language use in the early 2000s. The IASSW board focused on the important role that language plays in enabling member schools to benefit from IASSW's work and participate fully in its activities. Recruiting and serving members globally meant that the board needed to address the language issue more seriously, and a permanent language committee was appointed.

Responding to these issues, in 2005 the board passed IASSW's language principles and policy, adopting four official languages: English, French, Spanish and Japanese. Most member schools were considered to have access to one of these languages, although the growing number of Chinese schools is a renewed challenge to this policy. Nevertheless, English is the dominant language due to lack of financial resources for translation. An additional principle is that at conferences translation into one or two regional languages should be provided to include participants from nearby countries, who might rarely have access to international conferences. As IFSW and ICSW do not have the same language policy as IASSW, this latter principle has been difficult to put into practice at joint conferences.

Shifting to the issues-based phase: IASSW's advocacy work

The Soviet collapse removed the spectre for capitalist countries of their potential replacement by an alternative communist economic system. Awareness rose of the adverse impacts of globalized economic growth on climate and the environment, poverty and social development generally. Programmes to achieve the UN Millennium Development Goals (MDGs) for reducing problems associated with poverty and making progress with education, equality and health aims by 2015 were replaced by successor sustainable development policies. Social concern with equalities for oppressed social groups and for women also became important objectives for international social development.

Changes in social work education in the Global South and in Europe after the end of the cold war also renewed interest in international issues within social work education generally and in IASSW from the beginning of the twenty-first century. The twentieth-century focus on achieving a wide spread of social work education internationally had largely been achieved. International links in social work education have increasingly focused on knowledge transfer and offering students opportunities for exchange. One example is the extensive cooperative networks promoted by finance from the European Union for contacts between Western European universities and the former Soviet countries (Seibel, 2003). Links have also developed elsewhere, such as the Caribbean-USA connections described in Part 2 by Lynn Healy and John Maxwell.

Attempts to promote shared action on social issues that have importance for countries in both the Global South and North also gained interest, renewing the long-standing involvement in international policymaking associated with UN and other international agencies. IASSW's mission statement on promoting cooperation and exchange today is much the same as it was in 1929. The present version does, however, contain a commitment to policymaking and advocacy and to promoting human rights and social justice as a platform in the late twentieth century to renew a more active policy agenda (IASSW, 2016b). IASSW and its regional associations work to support oppressed members, social workers and its educators around the world. From the late twentieth century onwards, IASSW has sought to engage its members more actively in policy influence and policymaking, and members' benefits have developed through a website and international and regional magazines. Today, activities are divided into five themes with 22 committees (IASSW, 2016a), indicating an enormous voluntary contribution from members. A broader range of interests therefore began to influence IASSW. One sign of this was a shift in leadership towards the Global South. Until 2004, all the presidents had come either from Europe or the US. Since then, there have been three consecutive presidents from Africa and Asia; Abye Tasse's interview in Part 2 shows this is a significant development in recognition for members in those continents.

The UN continues to offer an important arena for action for IASSW. With its 193 member states, it is a tool for promoting advocacy and lobbying for change around the world in areas of importance in social work and its education. While national governments negotiate UN policy and actions, NGOs like IASSW can significantly influence those decisions. Joint action often enables IASSW to increase its influence. Cooperation with IFSW and ICSW in the international social welfare arena has continued intermittently since the 1928 Paris conference. From 2010, joint conferences have become a permanent arrangement.

Since 1992, IASSW and IFSW have had consultative status with UNICEF to add to their UN connections. The IASSW and IFSW consultation team has representatives in committees on the family, ageing, children's rights, mental health, disability, women, indigenous people, and human rights. The organizations have representatives not only at the UN's main delegation in New York, but also in Geneva, Vienna and Addis Ababa. Awardees interviewed in Part 2, including Terry Hokenstad and Lynne Healy, have been involved with the UN policy and advocacy work.

Since 2010, the three organizations have joined forces with the UN in developing and pursuing the *Global agenda on social work and social development* (IASSW, ICSW and IFSW, 2012), again placing in the foreground a commitment to collective social development.

The organizations have committed themselves:

> ... to work together, with people who use services and with others who share our objectives and aspirations, to create a more socially-just and fair world that we will be proud to leave to future generations. (IASSW, ICSW and IFSW, 2012: p 1)

In 2012, the intended focus for the following years was on:

- promoting social and economic equalities;
- promoting the dignity and worth of peoples;

- working toward environmental sustainability;
- strengthening recognition of the importance of human relationships (IASSW, ICSW and IFSW, 2012:1).

Conclusion: debate on international social work education

This chapter has shown that, during the early twentieth century, social work developed in Europe and North America, soon followed by professional education. For most of the period covered by this book, the latter half of the twentieth century, the focus of international social work education has been on establishing new education programmes in areas other than the educators' home countries. Consequently, both the profession and its education have spread worldwide, to become virtually universal. Education in social work, as with all professions, is concerned with imparting knowledge, understanding and relevant skills and values in a process of socializing new entrants to a profession. Doing this internationally has raised – and continues to raise – questions about relevance and applicability as we cross borders. The nature of social work, its theories, practices, organizational position and professional activities vary in different countries, and this reality has become clearer. While the structures and ideas developed in the Global North have been influential, they have also been contested. Social structures and cultures in countries adopting or interpreting social work developed indigenous ideas of practice and education to meet their own social needs and sought to resist, or at least adapt, ideas about social work developed in the Global North. Eventually, there have been attempts to incorporate alternative conceptions and objectives into a broader global social work.

IASSW has been a channel of some of these processes of influence and contestation, and we can see many of these debates in the experience of the awardees as they participated in this century of dispersion. The culmination of the foundation and establishment phases of social work is exemplified and represented by the creation by IASSW and IFSW of a 'Global definition of social work' (IASSW/IFSW, 2014), 'Ethics in social work: statement of principles' (IFSW/IASSW, 2004) and 'Global standards for the education and training of the social work profession' (Sewpaul and Jones, 2004). These are claimed to be valid for members of both associations, and propose a universal basis for social work and its education. Gray and Fook (2005: p 628) define 'universal social work' as 'a form of social work that transcends national boundaries and which gives social work a global face such that there are commonalities in theory and practice across widely divergent contexts'. Despite this claim for acknowledgement of a universal social work, the two associations nevertheless have recently accepted the need for adjustments to be made in these international benchmarks to reflect national diversities.

While the 'Global definition of social work' offers guidelines for all social work thinking and practice, the experience of the diffusion of international social work and its education revealed alternative meanings of the 'international' in social work and its education. Several authors have discussed the concept since it was first used in 1943 by George Warren (Xu, 2006; Akimoto, 2008; Payne and Askeland, 2008; Hugman, 2010; Huegler, Lyons and Pawar, 2012; Healy, 2012; Cox and Pawar, 2013). Many refer to Healy's (2008: p 10) description of international social work as 'international professional practice and the capacity for action by the social work profession and its members'. Elaborating this, she identified four dimensions of international work: 'internationally related domestic practice and advocacy, professional exchange, international practice, and international policy development and advocacy'.

None of these is concerned with establishing social work or its education: this is taken for granted. Instead, she is identifying new forms of international interaction. These include social workers practising with particular cases in their home country, with migrants or refugees or working across national borders, and social workers leaving their familiar contexts to work in foreign countries. The former is growing due to globalization and increasing migration of people, related at least in part to natural and human-made catastrophes. Opportunities for practice abroad are decreasing in developmental aid organizations, which increasingly prefer to employ local personnel. On the other hand, worldwide mobility and exchanges of social workers as part of their education are growing with the pressures and opportunities offered by globalizing economies and technical development. So, the opportunities for, and form of, international practice are changing within the established structure of international social work and education. Healy's fourth dimension, however, draws attention to the developing issues-based focus of IASSW's concerns in the twenty-first century.

Writers such as Ife (2001) and Dominelli (2010) have identified the tenets of issues-based international social work when they ask us to think globally and act locally, having a dual perspective whether working in our home country or internationally. If we take up this focus on global challenges, Estes (2010) argued that social work education lacks a body of knowledge and skills for influencing national and international social situations. This makes it difficult to find sustainable solutions to recurrent issues. Consequently, international interchange and collaboration within the social work profession and education continues to be needed. Thus, more recent awardees have participated in a different form of international social work education.

Akimoto (2008) distinguished international social work from internationalization in social work. He does not consider Healy's first three dimensions to be international social work. His definition is: 'International social work is social work which deals with problems caused between nations or across national boundaries or efforts beyond national boundaries to solve those problems' (Akimoto, 2008: p 1). He claims that: 'International social work is irreconcilable with egocentrism, ethnocentrism, and xenophobia', and has to be performed as if we have a map without national borders, with 'world citizens'. He seeks an equality of people and services, regardless of where they live. He asks how international social work can advance social work as a discipline in a globalized world. The Global Agenda of the international social work organizations (IASSW, ICSW and IFSW, 2012) is a manifestation and symbol of a shift towards an issues-based international social work; this shift was made possible for recent awardees by the success of the establishment phase of international social work in which the early awardees made their mark.

Diversity in how international social work is conceived may be identified in the work of the awardees and their views expressed in the interviews and biographies in Part 2. In the next chapter, we have sought to tease out these diversities and the discourses about the 'international' and about social work found in their work and experiences.

TWO

The awardees' contribution reviewed

Introduction

To enable readers to identify and explore issues about international social work education that arise from the interviews presented in Part 2, this chapter highlights and summarizes the achievements, experiences and concerns of the recipients of the Katherine Kendall Award. Building on this, we discuss how they promoted and contributed to international social work education.

In this chapter, we ask a range of questions. Who are the awardees? The interviews indicate variations between them in many aspects of their careers. What are their characteristics? Where did they come from, where did they travel in their international work, what did they do and how did they do it? In what ways have the awardees promoted social work education internationally? Are the differences related to the historical, social and political context to which they belonged?

The awardees and their work

Between 1992 and 2016, thirteen social work educators have received the distinction of the Katherine Kendall Award. Table 2.1 provides some basic information, listing them by forename and surname in alphabetical order. Of the 13 awardees, seven (53.8%) are women and six are men, even though social work is a predominantly female profession in most parts of the world. Three are from the US, two from the UK, one from Israel living in the UK, two from Sweden and one each from Switzerland, India, Mexico, Jamaica and Comoros. In percentages, 46% came from the UK or US, 69.2% came from a country in the European continent plus the US. A high proportion, 62%, lived in the largest 25 countries by population and the same proportion, 62%, came from a country where English is an official language.

Table 2.1: The awardees: some basic information

Awardee	Sex	Country	Pop'n rank	Official languages	IASSW office held
Armaity Desai	f	IN	2	Hindi 30%, English, + many local languages	Vice President
Lena Dominelli	f	GB	22	English + 2 local languages	President
Lynne Healy	f	US	3	English 82%, Spanish 11%	Vice President, Secretary
Robin Huws Jones	m	GB	22	English + 2 local languages	President
Sven Hessle	m	SE	89	Swedish + 2 minority languages	
Terry Hokenstad	m	US	3	English 82%, Spanish 11%	Secretary, Treasurer
John Maxwell	m	JM	140	English, Jamaican Creole	Vice President
Harriet Jakobsson	f	SE	89	Swedish + 2 minority languages	Vice President
Shulamit Ramon	f	GB	22	English + 2 local languages	
Maria del Carmen Mendoza Rangel (Mariacarmen Mendoza)	f	MX	11	Spanish + several local languages	
Silvia Staub-Bernasconi	f	CH	97	German 64%, French 20%, Italian 7%	
Herman Stein	m	US	3	English 82%, Spanish 11%	President
Abye Tasse	m	KM	163	Arabic, French + Shikomoro	President

Sources: ISO 2-letter country code: One Nation, 2016; Population rank: Worldometers, 2016; Official or recognized languages: Infoplease, 2016.

The Kendall Award is the only international opportunity for formal recognition for social work educators. Only one of the awardees, Mariacarmen Mendoza, reports recognition in the public media. Some have been honoured by their colleagues and home university, but not all. This lack of public recognition might be because the award is not well known, and the awardees do not promote it themselves.

Consequently, it does not raise the visibility of IASSW or social work education.

Upon receiving the award, interviewees were all well established in their career, as you would expect for an award that honours career achievements. Several were retired or close to retirement at the time, but continued to be actively involved in international work. The award seems so far to be a reward for involvement in IASSW; only four have not been members of the IASSW board. Four are former presidents, another five have had positions as vice presidents, treasurer or secretaries. Apart from the four non-board members, all the awardees knew Katherine Kendall well. Obviously, this personal link to the award will decline in the future.

All except two awardees (Huws Jones, Hessle) were social workers by education. The extent of awardees' experience in social work practice varies. All of them worked as social workers in the field before they moved into academic work, some before they became qualified social workers (Dominelli, Maxwell). Four shifted back and forth between practice and academic posts during their career (Stein, Jakobsson, Mendoza and Hessle). The earlier awardees gave greater importance to working in the field, while later awardees experienced a growing pressure to do research and publish, and had less time to continue with practice. Healy points out that, in recent years, social work educators have had less opportunity to continue to do social work, even on a voluntary basis. If educators are forced to favour non-practice engagements in their work, what influence might that have on the nature and quality of the education in a practical profession such as social work? Despite this trend, several awardees highlighted the importance of combining theory and practice in social work education.

About two-thirds of the awardees did not originally plan to become social workers, some using the words 'accidental' or 'hijacked'. Moving on to become an academic was also an unexpected journey for several. Just over half were offered their first academic role without applying for it, to their surprise, as they had never thought of it themselves. As one said: '… that was the way at the time to hire people.' There is a change with the later awardees, who were more likely to apply for their positions and go through appointment procedures. The latest, Abye Tasse, had a different career path, occupying various posts in France. After experience there, he was asked to re-establish social work education in his home country, Ethiopia. As a French citizen, he became involved in the French government secondment programme to other countries. A condition of this employment was to move on to different African countries, where he has also introduced social work education.

We noted in Chapter 1 that, during the twentieth century, most international social work education activity involved the dispersion of social work education from countries where it was well established, mainly in the Global North, to countries in the Global South, where it was less established. Changes in the Soviet and Chinese regimes, leading to economic and social transitions towards capitalism, created a new market for exchanges and transfer of social work education. This then led to the latest wave of international dispersion of social work education from the Global North to countries where it was less well founded.

We therefore sought to identify what kinds of links the awardees made in the context of these movements in international social work education. About two-thirds of the interviewees lived, studied or spent a sabbatical in countries other than their home country. Only two of the earliest awardees from the Global North continued working over a period of years in the countries where they engaged in developing social work education (Stein, Jakobsson). Other awardees were more like visitors: staying for shorter or longer periods. Two from the Global South (Desai, Tasse) gained much of their social work education and some educational and practice experience in the Global North, before pursuing their main involvement in educational development in Asian and African countries. The trend towards briefer visits raises the issues of the depth and quality of collaboration and the sustainability of links in international social work.

How did the awardees go about promoting social work education internationally? Their activities in foreign arenas included working as a social worker in the field (Jakobsson), offering consultation, running workshops and seminars to develop educational programmes, sometimes in close cooperation or looser partnership with local colleagues. Sometimes this extended to developing and publishing new ideas and approaches. Social work educational models and understanding about, and views of, social work might be transferred to the Global South when visitors from the Global North participate in developing new programmes.

The interviews show, then, that awardees stayed in foreign arenas for various lengths of time. Consequently, their activities differed and the opportunity to gain contextual knowledge and achieve a high level of cooperation varied. As a result, the sustainability of their achievements as they withdrew at the end of an international contact also varied:

longer or persistent involvement generally created wider ranges of activity and more intensive and long-lasting cooperation.

Kreitzer (2012) makes the point that expectations about scholarship and research in the Global North may demand that ideas are based on existing social and political science conceptualizations, rather than responding to insights from and relevance in the Global South. This is an ongoing critique (Osei-Hwedi, 1993; Gray et al, 2008, 2013; Osei-Hwedi and Rankopo, 2008; Mwansa, 2010; Butterfield and Tasse, 2013; Ragab, 2016). An increase in shorter visits within international social work education might focus on consultancy from internationally accepted intellectual positions, and fail to take into account the need to adjust or reject these when confronted with alternative conceptualizations from the Global South. Neither do shorter contacts facilitate incorporation of ideas from the South into those of the North. An example of how this may happen is the experience of one of the awardees from the Global South, Armaity Desai, whose wish to use her competence in social group work in the US was rejected. Mariacarmen Mendoza, on the other hand, was well received when called upon to share her competence from a disaster area.

What social issues were of concern to the awardees? We examined the interviews to identify social policy issues, client groups or social problems. Ignoring passing comments, we selected what they gave specific attention to in their careers. The outcomes of these analyses of the interviews are set out in Table 2.2. We would not want to read too much into this analysis: most social work educators, including the awardees, would be interested in a range of issues. It would be wrong to suggest that any awardee is ignorant of or uninterested in a topic because they did not happen to mention it in a brief interview. We must also see this in the light of the period in which they were actively involved in social work education. Examining Table 2.2, the notable absence is work with people with intellectual disabilities.

Table 2.2: Social interests of awardees

Social interest	Armaity Desai	Herman D. Stein	Robin Huws Jones	Mariacarmen Mendoza	Harriet Jakobsson	John Maxwell	Terry Hokenstad	Sven Hessle	Shulamit Ramon	Silvia Staub-Bernasconi	Lena Dominelli	Lynne Healy	Abye Tasse
Adult education				x									
Ageing							x						
Children	x	x		x		x		x				x	
Civic affairs				x									
Class										x	x		
Conflict				x					x		x	x	
Community/macro practice	x	x	x	x		x	x				x		
Disasters	x			x	x						x		
Drugs								x					
Environment/climate	x			x				x			x		
Gender	x			x		x				x	x	x	
Globalization							x				x		
Human/civil rights		x								x	x	x	
Indigenous populations											x		
Indigenous/local literature	x			x		x					x		
Inequality											x	x	
Integrated practice	x												
Macro practice						x	x						
Mental health		x						x	x				
Migration/refugees					x		x	x		x			x
New technology								x					
Peace								x					
Poverty				x				x		x	x		
Power/empowerment										x	x		
Racism		x								x	x	x	
School social work	x											x	
Social development	x			x				x					
Social justice		x						x		x	x		
User participation									x		x		
Youth work						x	x	x		x			

The nature of international engagements

How do social work educators become engaged internationally? In particular, how did the awardees reach recognition for their contribution in the international field? We saw in Chapter 1 that there was a continuing debate about the meaning of 'international' in social work and its education. Most social work practice is undertaken within national boundaries and within national, regional or local legal and administrative systems. Most social work education therefore focuses on national social concerns. International research and commentary is, therefore, a minor interest for most social work educators, practitioners and students. The awardees are unusual in being involved with international matters, as much as for their achievement and contribution.

How and why did the awardees begin to take up international concerns? The most common career sequence was to have pre- and post-qualifying social work practice experience, then to move into social work education; international interests emerged later. In some cases, professional development was an important motive, though this was a gain many awardees recognized in hindsight.

Armaity Desai was marked out early in her career for leadership in the social work field; she took up professional development opportunities in the US to pursue this. Harriet Jakobsson moved from practice experience in her own country into social work education, and started to attend international conferences, later using her practice experience in countries in the Global South. Others, like John Maxwell and Mariacarmen Mendoza, looked outwards as part of the process of developing social work education in their country or university. Herman Stein had international experience in military service in World War II, and renewed these interests in his social work education career. Lynne Healy, after learning about international social work in student practice education, developed international interests alongside the decision to work towards a role in social work education. Robin Huws Jones, not a social worker, became involved in education for British colonial administrators before taking up a role in social work education. Terry Hokenstad extended his concerns for ageing and services for older people at home into international learning and service development. Sven Hessle's strong motivation to help emerged when he was asked to become involved with local colleagues building social work education in post-war former Yugoslavia. Silvia Staub-Bernasconi worked with refugees in her own country.

Some awardees had a different path, because their life experience was international. Shulamit Ramon's Israeli background and Russian connections reinforced an international vision in her social work career. Lena Dominelli came to education and community work in the UK from her Canadian homeland and Italian family roots, and with knowledge and understanding of Islam and Arabic. Abye Tasse was a refugee from Ethiopia in France, received his social work education and practice experience there, then returned to establish social work education in African countries.

Lena Dominelli identifies herself as an internationalist. In doing so, she aligns herself with a principled political position that advocates action to increase political or economic cooperation among nations and peoples. This conception of the role of social workers as 'world citizens' connects with Akimoto's (2008) view, discussed in Chapter 1, that international social work should focus on global issues. Taking such a political view is likely to be a motivator towards involvement in international work, but the extent to which it alters the conception or practice of social work or international social work education is unclear.

How did their international leadership roles develop? Many were led or encouraged by colleagues. Several benefited from reassurance and help from Katherine Kendall herself. Others, such as Silvia Staub-Bernasconi, Shulamit Ramon and Lena Dominelli, went through a great deal of struggle in achieving their successes, both nationally and internationally. Sven Hessle and Lynne Healy find little interest in international issues among colleagues. Lynne Healy was discouraged by her supervisor early on in her career, and suggests that US social work educators are uninterested in international issues and feel that it is just 'nice to have a world view'. Healy's career, and the work of Silvia Staub-Bernasconi, Terry Hokenstad, Lena Dominelli and Abye Tasse reflect a twenty-first century approach that more than 'a world view' is required: they focus on issues such as promoting human rights or social justice.

Developing education in the awardees' careers

All awardees have developed educational programmes, either in their home country or abroad. A difference between earlier and later awardees is that, for the former, the emphasis was on courses leading to BSW and MSW qualifications; for the latter, it was more often on doctoral or other advanced study or research programmes. None of the interviewees discussed their view of social work, or teaching and learning approaches. It is therefore unclear what models of social work and its education they promoted. This lack of comment may be because it was not directly raised by the questions, however, it was not so central to their thinking that they raised it themselves.

Nevertheless, some indications of their views emerged. Many emphasize that an important facet of social work is to achieve social change. Several awardees are clear that professional social work intersects with political and social action. Their commitment to this view is expressed by their engagement in policy making and in social and political action. Their emphasis varies between those who are more action oriented (Huws Jones, Dominelli) to those who are more reform oriented, working for and influencing policy changes at the national (Desai, Mendoza, Hokenstad) or international levels, the latter through professional associations or the UN (Healy, Hokenstad, Tasse). The approach taken has depended on the political climate of the time. An example is Terry Hokenstad's discussion of being involved in social action and civil rights demonstrations in the 1970s and later being involved with the government and UN in promoting reform.

Because policy advocacy is integral to social work for the awardees, their representation of social work brings social solidarity objectives into the broad international policy agenda, which otherwise favours economic and other macro issues. Their activities highlight this as an important characteristic of social work. In selecting awardees with this particular orientation, IASSW is perhaps expressing a collective view about what should be valued in international social work and its contribution to a wider international discourse.

In most countries in the Global North, social work is oriented towards individual services. In the period after World War II, an emphasis in the US on casework, clinical work and mental health led to these focuses being transferred to international social work. A critique of such transfers developed in countries in the Global South partly because that focus on individuals does not emphasize action on poverty and other roots of social problems that affected these countries. For example, the Association of Social Work Education in Africa (ASWEA) discussed in a succession of meetings between 1971 and 1986 whether social work ideas from the Global North were culturally relevant in an African historical, social, economic and spiritual context (Association of Social Work Education in Africa, 1982a, 4: p 481). As part of this, ASWEA Information Centre collected 52 case studies of social development in Africa from local educators in seven countries, some in English and some translated to and from French (Association of Social Work Education in Africa, 1973, 1974). Nevertheless, most African social work curricula did not use these resources because of the privileged status of Anglo-American social science research and scholarship (Kreitzer, 2012). Armaity Desai describes similar initiatives to publish local studies by students and university staff. Lack of opportunities for publishing local study material is also a concern for other awardees from the Global South (Maxwell, Mendoza, Tasse). Terry Hokenstad, nevertheless, suggests that the US role in international social work education continues to be sought, although he also argues that it is important for Americans to learn from other countries.

Opposition to such knowledge transfers also grew in Europe, where social work had a strong role in public social services. In the later decades of the twentieth century, a radical critique of psychotherapeutic social work became widespread. A striking characteristic in several of the interviews is the lack of interest in individual clinical practice, even among those who are Americans themselves or have studied in the US. Clinical models of social work were considered inappropriate for their countries' needs or for the new programmes that awardees in the Global South were working on.

The awardees' orientation towards activism, advocacy and social change is in line with that critique. Earlier attempts at knowledge transfer were thought inappropriate. While several of the interviews reveal awardees' activist approach, the material does not show the extent to which this is visible in the educational programmes they were involved in developing. Awardees value and recognize social work's holistic approach, including both social action and helping individuals. All practised – and some researched and published about – individual, group and family work, but this is not highlighted as the core of their interests in the interviews. Perhaps professional interests in direct practice are displaced by broader concerns as their status and role broadens in late career. Nevertheless, Armaity Desai emphasizes the importance of social worker educators in leadership positions using all their social work skills and approaches, whatever arena of education, administration and leadership they are working in. In her view, interpersonal skills are highly valued and successful in policy work.

The strong role of mental health social work in the US is not replicated in many other parts of the world. Lynne Healy expresses her concern that the main body of work and licensing in the US is in mental health social work. It may be that – while the American emphasis on counselling and psychotherapy and its openings for private practice is distant from the main forms of social work elsewhere – a better recognition of the needs of mentally ill people is lacking in many other countries. This has not been clear policy focus of international social work education. The one awardee strongly committed to mental health social work (Ramon) is concerned that this important social issue does not generate interest and support.

There has been a growing awareness in the twenty-first century that climate and environmental changes will increasingly concern social work in the future, for example through work with refugees from climate and terrorism (Ife, 2001). Robin Huws Jones took up climate as an issue at an early period, while Mariacarmen Mendoza maintains environment as a priority, living in a region exposed to natural catastrophes. Lena Dominelli has recently picked up a focus on green social work. She has worked on developing crisis intervention in collaboration with local social work educators for people suffering from natural disasters. Political conflict is a related and important area of concern for Shulamit Ramon.

All the awardees discuss the necessity of contextualizing social work education to fit local problems, resources and areas, although from different perspectives. Some (Hokenstad, Ramon, Dominelli, Healy) focused on promoting education internationally around the social issues they are concerned with, socially constructed by the needs and culture of particular countries. The interviews offer no overview of the degree to which this is reflected in educational programmes.

A deconstruction of claimed universal elements of social work and its education are inevitably part of this process. Research and scholarship deriving from the Global North demand that students adjust knowledge that is claimed as universal to their local environment, rather than making use of local research and scholarship (Askeland and Payne 2001), which is a concern for Abye Tasse. Recently developed ideas about how knowledge travels between different cultures will increasingly influence future developments (Harris et al, 2015), but has not yet had a strong impact in social work education (Payne and Askeland, 2008). Ugiagbe (2015) and Kreitzer (2012), among many writers, argue that Western imperialism and colonial administration of higher education destroyed much indigenous knowledge. There have been attempts to retrieve and develop indigenous understanding, and this has become an important movement in social work, engaging the interest of the awardees. Lena Dominelli, however, is the only awardee who discusses spirituality as an aspect of holistic social work. Achieving a connection with local peoples' spiritual identities enables them to identify with and avoids alienation from educational programmes (Akimoto, 2013; Ragab, 2016).

We might draw from these experiences the importance of developing regional rather than international exchanges that make better connections with concerns of particular populations. Such initiatives might better contribute to developing mutual understanding in international social work than seeing broad international conferences as the main locations for exchange of ideas.

Another distinction between the Global North and the needs of the Global South is the universal acceptance that most social work education, research and literature focuses too much on urban environments, while almost half of the earth's population lives in rural areas. Nevertheless, Williams (2016) maintains that the development of social work today is left behind by growing urban challenges. In his interview, John Maxwell suggests that international social work organizations ought to organize conferences from the perspective of developing countries and rural areas. This is not a new idea: ASWEA and IASSW initiated this in Africa as early as 1982 (Association of Social Work Education in Africa, 1982b).

Academization and practice (field) education

'Practice education' is the current UK term for practice experience provided as part of a social work course in social work agencies under the supervision of social work practitioners. 'Field education' is the US equivalent. The term in use in different countries has varied over the past century. Since this book is published in the UK, we use the current UK convention, unless an interview or other quotation uses a different one.

UK and US social work education is historically connected to universities, while social work education on the European mainland was often offered in separate schools alongside other professional education. In the African, Asian and Latin American regions, most social work courses were established with university connections. Where new programmes are expanding, for example in China, Eastern Europe and Russia, they are integrated in universities. Over the last few decades, European social work has gradually been integrated into the university system, and this has led to concern about academization, a process of focusing on academic learning rather than practice (Brauns and Kramer, 1991). Education systems have become more consistent across Europe, due to the Bologna Agreement (see Chapter 1). This also aligns social work education with higher education programmes rather than with the requirements of practitioners in the field. The result of these trends is that social work education is exposed to the same expectations for research and publishing as traditional universities. This is problematic for the nature of social work and its education in connections with practice.

Being connected to universities gives status to the profession, but may raise difficulties because of differences between social work and other university disciplines. In a professional area of education, academization might threaten the quality of the practice elements of social work studies. Sven Hessle, for example, expresses concern about the standardization of university education, brought about by such developments as the Bologna process, may lead to reductions in practice teaching. The tension between the academic and practice in social work education is not new. Macadam's (1925: pp 23-4) early survey of the field argues that social studies were not new in early twentieth-century universities, but that social work linked theoretical studies with the practical and concrete, continuously related to real issues in social life and to the difficulty in dealing with its complexities. To link social science teaching and practice courses is of importance for Mariacarmen Mendoza, who refers to it as 'collective teaching'.

Earlier awardees, who were primarily from the Global South, were concerned to develop practice teaching in social work education and its supervision, and to raise its status to the same level as the theoretical courses (Desai, Jakobsson, Maxwell, Mendoza). From India, Armaity Desai describes how using field action projects raised public awareness of social issues of concern and contributed to social changes. This approach, with students and educators cooperating, is still in use. Similar issues about combining theory and practice experiences from fieldwork in classroom teaching was an issue in ASWEA conference papers in the 1970s, with a strong focus on supervision. Supervision was seen to be directed towards practice tasks and personal competence as '... a way of orienting and guiding them in their functions ... to gain confidence both in their work and in themselves' and to facilitate the '... development of human resources' (Imru, 1972: 1-8).

Publication

Demand for publication of scholarship and research is one of the marks of academization and an increasing demand on social work education.

Most of the awardees have published several books or edited works as well as articles in academic and other journals. There is a slight tendency for the later ones to have published more than earlier awardees. Those who have published less had their career at a time when publication was not as essential adjunct to academic seniority as it is now (Huws Jones, Jakobsson, Maxwell). Some awardees made important contributions to government and official reports (Desai, Huws Jones, Stein), which are not well represented by these listings.

The nomination process of the award is something of a counterbalance since it primarily values education, de-emphasizing empirical research and publications as decisive criteria. Nevertheless, we asked each awardee to identify no more than five publications which would represent their work. Three awardees (Stein, Huws Jones, Jakobsson) were not able to do this, so we have selected five publications based on Internet and British Library Catalogue searches, and publications known to us. Unfortunately, we have been unable to find any publications recorded for Harriet Jakobsson. In Table 2.3, we have listed the broad subject areas covered by the titles of publications identified in this way. Publications that link multiple topics are categorized for every relevant topic. This does not indicate the weight of the work, however, since we have not attempted to assess the length or quality of publications. It may be that our specification of only five publications for the select bibliography in their respective chapters does not allow for a full representation of the awardees' breadth of publication.

The subjects covered by awardees' publications reflect matters discussed in their interviews. Among the awardees, only Lynne Healy and Terry Hokenstad have published work developing the conceptual and theoretical basis for international social work education. Lena Dominelli and Abye Tasse point out that we have far to go in this arena. Nevertheless, a high proportion of awardees have published on international and educational issues. On the other hand, there are few publications on learning methods and social work practice. This may reflect the reality that people selected for an international social work education award will have fewer direct practice and teaching and learning interests, focusing instead on broader international and educational issues. Five awardees have published on theoretical development in human rights (Dominelli, Healy, Hokenstad, Staub-Bernasconi, Tasse).

All but one awardee, Mariacarmen Mendoza from Mexico, were competent in and published substantially in English. Mendoza's work has been translated into other Latin American languages. Major works by Silvia Staub-Bernasconi, Mariacarmen Mendoza and Abye Tasse have not been translated. This means that, as we said about IASSW's language policy in Chapter 1, such work does not have the opportunity it deserves to contribute to the academic debate conducted primarily in English that dominates international academic reputation.

Some awardees (Desai, Mendoza, Maxwell, Tasse) commented that many social work educators in their countries find little time to carry out research and publish. Resources for research and publishing are not equally distributed around the world. Thus, distinguished work

Table 2.3: Analysis of awardees' selected publications

Subject of publications	Armaity Desai	Herman D. Stein	Robin Huws Jones	Mariacarmen Mendoza	Harriet Jakobsson	John Maxwell	Terry Hokenstad	Sven Hessle	Shulamit Ramon	Silvia Staub-Bernasconi	Lena Dominelli	Lynne Healy	Abye Tasse
Adult education				2									
Ageing							x						
Behaviour		x											
Children and families								2					x
Community practice				x									
Conflict/crisis/disasters	x	x							3				x
Doctors			x										
Environment and sustainability								x			x		
International social work						x	2	x		x		x	
Gender	x			x							2		
Groupwork										x			
Higher education	2							x					
Human rights/social justice							x			2		3	x
Indigenous peoples				x									
Mental health									x				
Migration								x					x
Organizations		x				x							
Practice education						x							
School social work	x												
Social action										x			x
Social development								x					x
Social services		x	x			x			x				
Social theory/ social work theory		x		x						3	x		
Social welfare history						x							
Social work education	x	x	x			2	x	x		x		x	
Social work practice				2									
Social work values	x			x								2	
Student assessment						x							

Note: A cross marks coverage of a subject in the relevant column, and a number if there is more than one publication on that topic in that author's selected publications.

from some parts of the world remains unknown to the international professional society, an issue raised by Abye Tasse. Lynne Healy comments on the pressure to publish in journals assessed as having a high international impact factor. While this may generate a higher level of academic discourse in the subject, it may become an inappropriate priority in professional subjects in particular localities. Whether to publish in a world language or in local ones has not only to do with the presumed audience but also with the reward system in employing educational institutions. Healy is also concerned about colleagues belonging to small language groups, who are forced to publish in a world language, even if it would be more relevant for the material to be communicated in the authors' and practitioners' own languages.

Both research subject and language for publication in the international arena may fail to acknowledge achievements in research and in educational contact with agencies and practice education that contributes to good social work education. It might also exclude important areas in the Global South with few spokespersons able to meet the interests of the global academic community. It also contributes to a standardization and a hegemony of the Global North in deciding on the nature of social work, and disempowers alternative cultural and political discourses about international social work and its education. Kreitzer (2012: p 146) points out, as another barrier to equal international discourse, that if articles about African social work are published in high-cost English or French journals, they become harder for Africans to have access to.

Curriculum development

Curriculum content and learning methods are elements of the 'Global Standards for Social Work Education' promoted by IFSW and IASSW (Sewpaul and Jones, 2004). Curriculum development was an important focus for the awardees whose career was primarily in the twentieth century, particularly those from the Global South. They saw curriculum development as a way of responding to social needs and promoting and defining the role of social work in their country. Armaity Desai used conferences between social work schools as a vehicle for a curriculum shift towards social development. John Maxwell saw establishing the validity of the social work curriculum as a way of incorporating social work securely in his university. Mariacarmen Mendoza also worked on curriculum development to establish the role of community social practice and adult education, particularly for women.

Awardees in countries in the Global North working in a later period, focused on doctoral education to establish stronger academic and professional credibility. Both Silvia Staub-Bernasconi and Shulamit Ramon were involved in cross-European courses developed with EU finance, the INDOSOW doctoral education project. Terry Hokenstad and Sven Hessle were engaged in former Eastern European countries and China at all levels of education. Abye Tasse instituted MSW, then BSW and thereafter PhD programmes at the Addis Ababa University over six years. His idea was to use social workers with Masters degrees to teach BSW students, while continuing their PhD studies. He went on to initiate social work education in different African countries.

Community work and policy advocacy

Table 2.2 shows a striking concentration of focus on the connected topics of community development, social development and macro work. Nine of the twentieth-century awardees express interest in these areas of social work method, perhaps reflecting the importance of it in countries with developing economies.

Armaity Desai describes how IASSW's family planning project broadened Asian participants' focus on social development. Herman Stein led a university and city response to an urban civil rights crisis in the US, and worked for years in community development in Tanzania. Community education and development was central to Mariacarmen Mendoza's work. Robin Huws Jones brought together local educators, government and industry in the Swansea valley project against pollution and led a significant community work practice development in London. John Maxwell had wide involvement in community organizations in the Caribbean. Terry Hokenstad noted that community organization in the US shifted its focus from community-based social services in the 1960s towards grassroots social action later. Silvia Staub-Bernasconi worked with a street gang in Switzerland and had experience of urban community work with black women in the US, and Lynne Healy had early experience in a community information service. Lena Dominelli's involvement with social work continued her community work as an activist.

These practice experiences also affected awardees' conceptualization of social work. For awardees in the Global North (Dominelli, Hokenstad, Jakobsson), this issue is about incorporating community practice into social work curricula. Awardees working in the Global South, such as Armaity Desai and Mariacarmen Mendoza, regarded community and social development as an essential aspect of practice and the social work curriculum in the social context of their countries.

Social work and gender

Inequalities affecting women are clearly matters of continuing struggle in social work, as they are in academia. Historically, male academics have been in majority, however, that is not the case for the awardees. Nevertheless, gender has been an issue in several of the interviews, both as a personal experience and as a general concern. Table 2.2 confirms that gender was important to many of the awardees, particularly in the careers of Silvia Staub-Bernasconi, Shulamit Ramon, Lena Dominelli and Lynne Healy. The female awardees were concerned about academics' positions in universities and involved in fostering women's positions. A strong element of the female awardees' work has been related to feminist concerns in society, such as family planning, social development and poverty. The male awardees did not mention gender issues. Nevertheless, one man commented on a related subject. John Maxwell refers to the shortage of males in most areas of practice, and the challenge it creates that there are so few male role models among social workers. In doing so, he is accepting the status quo that women's professions do not have high status. Social work is a female profession in many countries in the Global North, but that is not necessarily the case all over the world. In some countries, where education is not equally distributed between the sexes, male students are in the majority.

During the second wave of feminism in the 1960s and '70s, several of the female awardees were engaged in women's movements, linked to other rights movements at the time. The IASSW family planning project took place during this period. Although it had a broader focus, it also was significantly concerned with women's rights and liberation.

Many women, including some of the awardees (Dominelli, Healy, Staub-Bernasconi) published on feminist social work. At the Beijing Conference on Women in 1995, the IASSW consultation team at the UN was involved in the voluntary sector (Dominelli, 1998: p 5). A Women's Interest Group achieved a permanent seat on the IASSW board from 1996 and has influenced IASSW policy.

ASWEA (Association of Social Work Education in Africa, 1982c; Selassie, 1989) was not only concerned about the role of women and their exclusion from economic and social participation but also encouraged men to take greater interest and involvement in women's participation in development in Africa. Feminism in the 1970s proclaimed 'sisterhood' and solidarity between women around the world. A more complex analysis of women's situations across the world has been important to many social workers, and this is reflected in writing by Lena Dominelli, among others. It is influenced by the context – by class, religion, culture and ethnicity. It often puts women in conflict about whose side to be on, and women from the Global South have criticized women in the Global North for not acknowledging their emancipatory successes. Women and children have always been at the heart of social work from the birth of the profession until today.

Funding

How did the awardees finance their work? It is an important question: with finance comes influence and power, and without funding development activities become more difficult.

Most of the awardees are from the US and Europe. Travelling for them has become easier and less costly with globalization and its technical advances. Globalization, however, has been driven by Western people, who benefit most from it (Stiglitz, 2002: p 9). The infrastructure for travel is not the same everywhere, and people do not have the same resources for travelling around the world to promote the profession, an issue raised by Abye Tasse.

The UN has been a source of international development aid. Several awardees (Desai, Stein, Huws Jones, Jakobsson, Hokenstad, Staub-Bernasconi) mentioned involvement with the UN and its agencies as a repeated element of their work. UN finance for international involvement in social work education was important to earlier awardees. Silvia Staub-Bernasconi received a UN Fellowship to finance her extended period of education in the US. She was significantly influenced in her thinking about human rights by involvement with the UN. The UN also contributed to travel for people from the Global South. Sven Hessle's work in the former Yugoslavia and Herman Stein's engagement in Tanzania were financed by UNICEF.

Several countries contributed to international projects through their development budgets or national foundations. Examples are Katherine Kendall's work in Paraguay and in the IASSW family planning project. Other financing came through international foundations, such as the Open Society Foundation. There is a growing demand for international exchanges at universities in the Global North. This is, however, often a one-sided exchange: universities in the South do not have the same resources for it, and the expenditure involved in going from a developing country to a developed one is much higher than the cost of travel from a rich to a poor country. Thus, knowledge travels on a one-way highway from rich countries in the Global North to the Global South.

Chapter 1 showed that funding from the US in the context of the cold war and from the UN was significant in the periods in which international work in social work education was substantially concerned with extending the reach of social work and its education across the world. The result was that US models of social work and its education became influential in countries, without contextualization. The method was often for the social work educators to be paid for consultation in advisory or supportive projects. Armaity Desai describes how, early in her career, American finance sent social work educators from the US to promote social work education in India, with funding used to develop local interests and priorities to support the foundation of an Indian Association of Schools of Social Work and Indian curriculum development work. Robin Huws Jones received Ford Foundation funding for his work with students from across the British colonies in the 1950s; which contributed eventually to ideas and practice in social development. Finance from foreign foundations in the Global North may also be important to countries in the Global South; for example, Mariacarmen Mendoza's work was facilitated by a German foundation. The later phase of extending social work and its education into communist or former Soviet regimes received funding from the European Union. Both Terry Hokenstad's and Shulamit Ramon's work in Eastern Europe is an example of international work financed from these sources.

Many awardees mention and acknowledge the importance of external finance in sustaining their work. An important skill for senior academics is building, maintaining and administering relationships with organizations providing funding: an example is Robin Huws Jones's skill in managing the group of funders of the IASSW family planning project and in negotiating the arrangements for the IASSW office to move from the US to Vienna. Leadership skills of this administrative and management kind seem to have been significant in the educators selected for the Kendall Award.

Much of the international work described by the awardees, however, was self-funded or funded by research or personal development grants from their university, often for attendance at IASSW's international conferences and other similar events. Even major speakers do not receive fees for speaking, but universities, at least in the Global North, often contribute to staff costs in taking up opportunities to present papers. Most of those attending international conferences, however, incur expenditure from their personal or family income; Silvia Staub-Bernasconi mentions this as a constraint on her career. Consequently, conference attenders from rich countries with a larger disposable personal income or greater support from their universities can more easily afford to cover expenses than participants from poorer countries; Abye Tasse draws attention to this. The advantage comes in two ways: they are more able to get their work noticed internationally, and they gain esteem in their own country because they present at international conferences.

For internal regional exchanges, there seems to have been fewer financial sources. However, ASWEA (Association of Social Work Education in Africa, 1982a, p 481) received financial support from the Frederic Ebert Foundation, West Germany, until 1981. When this ended, it became difficult to keep up both the activity and the secretariat in Addis Ababa. For the last few years, the EU has extended its portfolio to a two-way mobility grant for students and staff with educational institutions outside Europe.

Work with the UN

Two awardees (Hokenstad, Healy) discuss their considerable policy advocacy work with the UN and its agencies on behalf of IASSW in association with other international social work organizations.

Several awardees mention the UN Children's Charter as a statement of principle that is particularly relevant to social work. Social workers were engaged with children's and family rights before this became a UN priority for human rights thinking after World War II. More recently, these ideas have become coopted to become more central to more generalized human rights discourses. This has been one of the achievements of feminist analysis. The importance of children's and family rights in the general discourse creates space for women to become important players in national and international cooperation. Policy advocacy on these issues also helps social work to become an important player in human rights discourses, and brings social advocacy as a professional activity into the national and international arena.

Herman Stein's engagement with UNICEF in Africa lasted many years, covering a wide range of projects. One of the disadvantages of UN involvement, however, is illustrated by his effort to overcome bureaucratic requirements that development work in Africa should be funnelled through UN agencies. Eventually regional seminars resulted, and this was seen as permitting stronger African leadership. Such indigenous developments often needed to be fought for. A disadvantage of UN involvement in the Middle East, according to Ragab (1995), is that UN support for social work education tend to encourage relatively short and low-level training in response to immediate service needs identified by governments, rather than a longer-term focus on the development of professional education. Ragab's point suggests that the UN was only one path for influence on the development of policy and social work education.

Conclusion

In the next Chapter, we draw together some conclusions about what has been achieved in international social work education so far, looking at the evidence of the interviews. It goes on to consider the interviewees' reflections about what the future might hold for international social work education, for IASSW and for the Katherine Kendall Award.

THREE

Issues for the future of international social work education

Introduction

This chapter seeks to raise issues about the awardees, the award and how it functions, and future changes in international social work education and in IASSW. After an expansive period for international social work education, will growth and exchange continue along the same tracks or adjust to a changing world? If social work education must respond to *local* cultural, historical and social contexts, how can it at the same time be promoted *across* regions?

The awardees, in their interviews, represent more than a generation of social work educators and their achievements in spreading social work education around the world. They have accepted leadership in many different contexts, in their own countries, in their regions and in international organizations. In this way, they contributed to the secure establishment of social work education, took up a wide range of social work issues and developed perspectives on important international issues. Some have an extensive record of publications, often of innovative ideas. We ask here: what were the nature of the international developments that they sought to promote and how might this change in the future?

We draw from this experience that successful international careers in social work education require individuals to respond both to the needs of their own community and to international concerns. Educators require a strong concept of social work, administrative and leadership skills, and good social and networking skills. Not least, they need to be committed to social change and prepared to struggle. The international social work educator must be willing to undertake hard and time-consuming work, sometimes spending their own resources; they must be strong-willed, resilient and self-confident.

IASSW and the Katherine Kendall Award

Through launching an award and selecting awardees, IASSW expresses its values and concerns. What do the Katherine Kendall Award and the selection of its awardees say about the kind of people and achievements that IASSW values?

We are not considering here whether the awardees fulfil the formal criteria set out in the preface. These criteria are wide, and awardees are not expected to meet all of them. Rather the question is: on the evidence from the first 13 awards, selected over a quarter of century, what expectations do IASSW and its members have of their leaders? The IASSW board considered that the awardees should be honoured and appreciated for their accomplishments and '... worthy to be considered a colleague of Katherine Kendall'. Most of the awardees so far have known Katherine Kendall personally, and expressed a sense of honour and feeling valued at being selected for an award in her name. This might not be the case for future awardees, not having met her in person.

How does the award contribute to fulfilling IASSW's objectives of promoting, developing and supporting social work education internationally? In many countries, social workers and their educators, as well as awardees, do not see their profession as highly regarded. Early in the twenty-first century, Katherine Kendall claimed:

> I fear we have entered a period when we are not highly valued. It is very important that we continue to value ourselves, what we know and what we do, and try to overcome the obstacles in our way. Of course, the current climate is not in our favor. (Billups, 2002:162)

An award for educators might contribute to raising the status of social work. By continuing to make the award, we value our profession, as Katherine Kendall suggested we should. But the interviews indicate that the award is not well known and awardees get little public recognition, so it seems not to have raised the profession's valuation. Turning this round is a challenge for IASSW. Making an award is potentially an attractive story for the media. Part of the answer is for IASSW to be more assertive in marketing and publicizing the award in the local, national, regional and specialist press relevant to each awardee's location.

Awards reflect cultural expectations. This award was a North American initiative, deriving from countries that have a long tradition of making awards to individuals, honouring exceptional work or professional contributions. Social work's commitment to equality and social concern may generate an anti-elitist view that discourages people from seeking individual honours but rather rewards team efforts and cooperation. However, there is a growing trend to award titles such as 'social worker...' or 'team... of the year'. In those countries which do award such national titles there may be the potential for international awards to become more highly valued.

Networking is an important part of what IASSW offers its membership. Katherine Kendall's exceptional competence in networking became midwife to the networks and careers of several awardees, as we can read from their stories. No formal criterion favours people who have served on the IASSW board. Nevertheless, it seems that networking in IASSW has been important in achieving the board's acknowledgement. Does the award, at least partly, reward involvement in IASSW networks? Has it then become inward-looking? Should there be more effort to achieve a wider field of candidates?

Looking at the awardees so far, it seems that it is easier to get the award if you come from big, rich English-speaking countries, where resources are accessible for research, publication, travelling and exchanges. This may be because the criteria are based on a generalist and universalist view of social work and do not sufficiently take into account the fact that social work may draw on different cultures and so be differently constructed socially and locally. Social work takes varying forms and is based on diverse ways of knowing in various parts of the world. The biggest membership groups in IASSW are not English-speaking, as we saw in Chapter 1. Representing those factors in the selection process means asking how to secure an equal opportunity for nomination for people from smaller, poorer and non-English speaking countries. This is a challenge for IASSW, but such a change might bear dividends in the award's visibility.

We have seen in Chapter 1 that it is not always clear whether 'international social work education' refers to teaching social workers for international practice abroad or at home or to developing further social work education in areas other than the educators' home countries. Practising in either way means that educators transfer knowledge and ideas across national borders; as knowledge travels the context for local practice and how local social workers are taught to do their jobs changes. The global definition of social work (IASSW/ IFSW, 2014) implies that education needs to adapt transferred international knowledge in the light of local contexts and indigenous knowledge. This in turn implies that foreign educators should interact with local people in establishing social work education. The degree of involvement that they achieve may influence the sustainability of their knowledge transfers.

Three concepts help us to analyze international social work education:

- arena
- activity
- level (Askeland and Døhlie, 2006)

'Arena' refers to the reality that international social work education is carried out in social situations that are unfamiliar to international educators, and local people are experts in local contexts. Consequently, local people should be the ones to influence how transferred international knowledge should be adapted. We have seen in Chapter 2 that 'activity' varies from teaching or developing an educational programme to being a consultant. While international social work may be performed on the individual, group, community and structural 'level', international social work education takes place primarily on a political and structural level. It seeks to promote, through indirect means, social change for large groups of people.

Successful promotion of social work internationally requires participants to establish a cooperative endeavour to which each party contributes differently, complementing each other. International relationships vary in the amounts of time, commitment, mutuality, complexity and equality they display. We have argued elsewhere that the more effort expended in each of these factors, the more likely it is that international relationships will be successful and sustainable (Payne and Askeland, 2008: pp 129-130).

This development may be further stimulated by changes in IASSW itself. The three most recent former presidents are all from the Global South. This may recognize broader sources of social work education expertise and commitment, as IASSW moves from the twentieth century phase of extending social work education across the world. Future awardees might continue to come from a broader range of backgrounds. This suggests that activities in the arenas in which knowledge transfer takes place will be better informed by activity at the highest level of international interaction, a level which more consistently takes account of a wider range of sources of indigenous knowledge.

The regional and national associations affiliated with IASSW, for example, in Africa, the Asian-Pacific region, in India and the Caribbean, played important roles in developing social work education and its curriculum. In recent years, the largest membership groups in IASSW are, in decreasing order, the Japanese, Chinese and North American and Caribbean regions (Semigina, 2014). Regional and national groups are likely to be familiar with potential nominees from their own areas. Lack of language compatibility with the leading personnel and countries in IASSW makes it difficult to choose candidates who meet the formal criteria. This may mean that associations need assistance to present potential nominees in the award process, in ways that can attract other support. The 2005 language policy discussed in Chapter 1 might indicate that IASSW is serious in being more inclusive of different language groups. This would consolidate its position as a globally representative organization. Assessment of future nominations might therefore need to include regional exchanges and publications in different languages to a greater degree than in the past.

Only a few potentially eligible people will ever enter the nomination process and even fewer will receive the award. Many more social work educators than those who have received awards have played important roles in establishing social work around the world. Most of the awardees so far come from the Global North. Table 1.2 shows that several African, Asian and Latin American countries had established social work education before many European countries. In these regions, there have been farsighted people who promoted social work education with fewer resources for travelling and greater obstacles to publication than educators working in the Global North. A closer regional involvement might reduce the disproportionate number of awardees from the Global North.

Lieberman's (2010) biographies also raise the question of whether social work adequately recognizes, in awards such as the Katherine Kendall Award, the contribution of women. In both social work and education there is a high proportion of women, but a lower proportion of women in senior posts that are likely to command notice and recognition. Thus, although seven of the 13 awardees so far are female, gender is a topic to bear in mind in future selections.

International social work education

During the period of over 60 years in which the awardees functioned, it seemed important to get social work to every part of the world. Political, social and economic change made it possible to establish professional education worldwide. Social work education is now offered in every region of the world, if not every country. In the future, what will be required might be different. Exchanges and consultations will take new forms. We have already seen such visits start to become shorter. More mutuality between assisting and receiving institutions would sustain more extensive and creative collaboration. Not least, more people will visit other countries as travel reduces in cost, and technological development may enable more connections to be made via social media. The world is globalizing and increasingly interdependent, with international issues being shared. IASSW might well play a role in the resulting policy and service development.

In the future, knowledge transfer and educational travelling might reverse to come from the Global South to the North. Migration and the situation of asylum-seeking, refugees and economic migrants are all current issues for social work. Educators from the Global North might learn from colleagues in the South in order to teach the changed international social work courses that will result. Benefits to be gained from sharing competence and personnel in both ways will become more apparent.

There may be difficulties. Students from the Global North having their practice education in the Global South may be so steeped in their home country's definition of 'social work' that they may have difficulty in recognizing the local practice as such (Nimmagadda and Martell, 2008; Askeland et al, 2016). Students from the Global South studying in the Global North, and having their practice education in their home country, have shown difficulties in recognizing approaches based on local traditions they are familiar with as social work (Beecher et al, 2010). It may be alienating for social workers to use approaches and follow ethical norms that are developed for totally different situations and not applicable in a new setting (Kreitzer, 2012). Kreitzer also points out, from Ghana, how important being able to teach in a culturally appropriate language is for students to be able to grasp what social work is all about.

Nevertheless, we saw in Chapter 2 that the financial resources for international social work have mainly been accessible in the Global North, and there are no indications that this might change in the near future. The interviews show us that sources of finance have always waxed and waned. The UN and international development aid from the Global North has reduced its once heavy commitment to social welfare, and governments shift their aid objectives. The EU, which funded development of social provision in former Soviet states and enabled several awardees to do their international projects has withdrawn from much of this work. Foundations change their policies, or reduce their activities. For example, the Open Society Foundation, which, we noted in Chapter 2, supporting some awardees, has now been excluded for political reasons from several Eastern European countries.

In this book, we have concentrated on those who travelled with their knowledge and expertise to establish social work internationally. They were asked to go, and found it challenging; for many it had a profound effect on their lives. However, we do not know much about the countries that received these visits, and how the consultation approach to professional exchange was experienced by local colleagues in social work education and in the field. This might also be an issue IASSW should explore further.

Reviewing the interviews, the awardees' engagement and belief in social work and its education is obvious. Less clear is their analysis of potential future roles and tasks for the profession. Despite gradually poorer circumstances for social work in much of the Global North, social work continues its rise in the Global South. Several awardees draw attention to politically difficult circumstances, with decreasing financial resources. At the same time, they also point out how social work has had a positive influence in improving people's living conditions and empowerment.

If social work and its education are important for people's well-being – as the increase in educational programmes during the last few decades might indicate – why is social work politically invisible? Is it because its practitioners, agencies and educators are too modest in highlighting its importance? When the international community responds to disaster and conflict, medical and nursing professionals are in the forefront, while social workers are rarely mentioned. But, as the awardees show in their interviews, social work education prepares them well for working at individual, group, community and political levels of intervention. This is a combination that other professions do not have, and which conflict and disaster work demands (Askeland, 2007). Recent awardees identify disaster and crisis work as a priority for social work knowledge-building. In doing so, they are highlighting the value of the contributions that social work might make.

Social work knowledge that draws on the experience of the Global North has retained widespread influence – and has been both valued and criticized. The awardees and other educators have identified a need to develop further a theoretical basis for international social work and its education. This would be richer by voices being heard from various parts of the globe – from different cultures, traditions, religions and languages – and IASSW could be an instrument for such a development. Exchanges of personnel and expertise might then be enhanced by the processes of travelling knowledge (Harris et al, 2015; see also Chapter 1).

There are many more questions. Why has US social work developed more into counselling and psychotherapy than the public welfare provision of many European countries? Would we understand international social work education better, be more prepared for policy advocacy and other political action if we learned more about Marxist influences on social work in Latin America? Would our interpersonal practice be enhanced by Asian spiritual interventions? Would taking spirituality and religion as perspectives of holistic social work see body, mind, soul and the whole of creation integrated into our understanding and approaches to solutions? What are the merits or disadvantages of these different directions? Is international social work an irrelevant personal preference for a few educators? Will broader transfer of knowledge and expertise make social work and its education richer in all directions, instead of the largely North to South transfers we have explored in the careers of these awardees? IASSW faces the challenge of building the potential of a wider range of interactions in international social work.

IASSW in the future

The interviews show that few awardees had clear expectations and wishes for the future of IASSW. They pointed to how lack of funding restricts what IASSW can do for its members. It has to rely on officers and board members to initiate and organize activities, which is demanding on the few who can commit themselves and their resources.

The period in which IASSW flowered was when the association had a full-time staff. In more straitened circumstances, it cannot reach out to every social work educational programme around the world. Awardees pointed to the possibility of making efforts to recruit more members and the opportunities that may offer, as well as securing fees from existing members. Latin America is one region that has great potential, but there is an additional language challenge to growth there.

Good housekeeping might make permanent full-time administrative support possible, which would open up opportunities for more activities. Funding for projects might also be expanded to help IASSW's visibility; the family planning project and the smaller project funds are examples of this.

A repeated suggestion from Armaity Desai is to situate a permanent secretariat in a country where costs are lower instead of moving the operating base to the president's location. Awardees also shared a vision to increase member services in different areas beyond conferences and to engage more members in policy advocacy in the UN, the Global Agenda and other international organizations, using the internet and social media. Several awardees claim that, in order to have a stronger voice politically, it is important to cooperate and form alliances with the other international social work organizations and other relevant bodies.

Conclusion

The awardees whose careers are remembered and reviewed in this book were part of a generation that established social work education across the world, from relatively small beginnings at the end of World War II. It is now an international phenomenon. These successes demonstrate that a well-functioning international organization facilitates valuable work.

The next generation of social work educators needs to consider how they will draw on that established international position to benefit the many poor, vulnerable and troubled peoples that social work has always sought to help. We hope that understanding something of the process by which international social work education has become established will enable IASSW and the profession to plan and act to build knowledge, expertise and education further – and that this in turn will have a positive impact on the future troubles that social workers everywhere will face and try to help with.

International social work education: notable figures

Part 2 gives a clearer picture of the personalities of Katherine Kendall, the recipients of the award given in her name and the social work world that each was engaged with.

Chapter 4 presents a brief biography of Katherine Kendall. It outlines the career and achievements that led IASSW to create an award in her name to honour educators who have made significant contributions to international social work education.

Chapters 5–17 present the interviews with the thirteen awardees on which Chapters 2 and 3 in Part 1 are based. While Part 1 explored information about the awardees as a group, these biographical narratives give an opportunity to learn more about the people involved in these efforts. They grew up and received their education at different times, lived in different parts of the world and had different motives for engaging in social work and in advancing its international position. The hope is that, through their own words, they will emerge as the diverse and interesting people they are. The world of social work that they experienced during their careers and the possibilities that they see for the future are expressed more vibrantly in their own words than in any summary.

FOUR

Katherine A. Kendall (1910-2010): a brief biography

Introduction

This chapter provides a brief biography of Katherine Kendall. There are two main reasons for this. First, we think readers will be curious about someone who has had an award named after her. Second, as an important figure in the 'establishment' phase of international social work, her personal and professional lives are a source of the ideas and interests that formed conceptions of international social work and its education. This biography draws on: interviews with Katherine Kendall (Billups, 2002c; Watkins, 2010; Foxwell, 2014b); biographies and tributes (Beless, 2004; Healy, 2008d); and Kendall's own published accounts of some of her activities in her lifetime (Kendall, 1994).

Kendall's career-defining roles were a series of executive management posts at CSWE between 1952 and 1971. She always had significant international responsibilities. For most of this time she was also Honorary Secretary (1954-71) and then, after leaving CSWE, the first full-time paid Secretary-General (1971-8) of IASSW. In retirement, she was Honorary President of IASSW for over thirty years until her death in 2010. Her faithful service to IASSW and her time at the centre of international social work education thus spanned nearly 60 years. Her work with the UN, prior to her employment at CSWE and IASSW, meant she brought her understanding of international organizations, and the personal networks within them, into IASSW; this facilitated the development of its work with the UN.

Childhood, marriage and early career

Katherine Kendall was born in Scotland on 8 September 1910, the third of four children and the only girl. Her father, Roderick Tuach, emigrated to Canada in 1913, but joined a Canadian Scottish regiment and was seriously wounded fighting in France during World War I. He sustained a lifelong disability as a result. He returned to Canada doing war work, but then migrated to Chicago, to be joined by his family in 1920. Tuach and his wife returned to the family building and masonry business in Scotland when work in Chicago dried up in the 1930s depression, so Katherine maintained connections with Scotland for many years. Her letters show that she was in regular contact with her mother until the latter's death in 1980 (Klaassen, 2016a). In her early life, she experienced migration in search of a better life and the human impact of war and disability on families. This must have been an important foundation for her later contribution to international social work education.

Katherine, a studious child, grew up in Chicago, receiving her first (BA) degree in Romance languages, history and philosophy from the local University of Illinois in Urbana in 1933. Her Spanish teacher was an assistant professor a year older than her, Willmoore Kendall (1909-67), who was also a journalist and political philosopher. He was awarded a Rhodes Scholarship to study in Oxford and Katherine joined him. They married in London in 1935 and were divorced in 1950. Contacts with left-wing students and academics in London and Paris gave her experience of the social movements of that period, and coloured her 'pink' politically, she told Billups (2002b: p 146). This did not extend to communism, she emphasized to Watkins (2010: p 170). They moved on to Madrid, where her husband was a foreign correspondent for United Press, and experienced the period of turmoil just prior to the Spanish Civil War. She told Watkins (2010: pp 170-2) stories of winning a diving competition, unionizing kitchen workers, and working as a hat maker.

In her twenties, Katherine experienced the onset of a major disability: she lost her hearing. Throughout her life, she wore hearing aids, initially those operating by bone conduction and concealed in her hair. Later in life, she also lost her sight and was legally blind for period before receiving successful corneal transplants. She also had stomach cancer. This was diagnosed early so, although she lost some of her intestines, she continued to lead an active life in good health until her death, at just over a hundred years old.

Interviewed for a biography of her ex-husband in 1973 (Nash, 1975, n5), Katherine described his early left-wing views and said that his affinity for Trotskyism was because of his detestation of the oppression by Stalin and the Moscow-based communists. 'Militant, uncompromising hostility to Communism ... became one of the dominant features of his thought' (Nash, 1975: p 128), and he later became a well-known commentator on conservative causes. After a long and apparently fractious period at Yale University (Ealy and Lloyd, 2004), he occupied a chair at the University of Dallas until his death in 1967. On their return to Illinois from Spain in 1936, Katherine had two part-time jobs to keep them going, while Willmoore completed his PhD on John Locke's political thought (Kendall, 1941) financed by a teaching fellowship. Moving to Louisiana State University when Willmoore joined the Department of Government, she switched her career ambitions from law to become one of the first students of social work there (gaining an MA in 1939). Starting out committed to social action, her fieldwork experience led her to realize that personal help with 'unhappy and impoverished relationships' (Billups, 2002c: p 147) was just as important, a significant balance that she maintained throughout her career. She then became the first qualified social worker at East Baton Rouge Parish Department of Social Welfare. Taking up PhD studies at the University of Chicago School of Social Service Administration, with additional fieldwork experience in child welfare, she also worked as a teaching assistant and as a research assistant with Edith Abbott. She was taught by, among others, Sophonisba Breckinridge and Charlotte Towle. These people are all towering figures in the history of American social work education. Katherine became an American citizen in 1940.

When the US joined World War II, she delayed her PhD studies, working for the American Red Cross from 1942-5, first as a home service correspondent helping military families, and then as a regional assistant director of training in Virginia. Her husband was involved in the Office of Strategic Services during the war, staying on when it became the Central Intelligence Agency, working on Latin American affairs. He became a significant commentator on the role of intelligence in the US state (Olcott, 2009).

Partly because of Katherine's knowledge of Spanish, Abbott recommended her in 1945 for a post with the Children's Bureau, as Director of the Inter-American Unit. The Bureau was a redoubt of social work within the US government's Department of Labor. She was organizing study and travel for Latin American visitors to the US. Later, when it became the International Unit, she did the same for other international visitors, also organizing consultancy on social work education in other countries. Doing so, she built up contacts both in US schools of social work and internationally. This work was part of the 'Point IV Program', pursuing the fourth point of US President Harry Truman's inaugural address promoting international cooperation in developing better social conditions across the world.

Social welfare services and the social work profession were seen as significant contributors to these aims (Kendall, 1994).

From 1947, Katherine moved to the newly formed UN, conducting an international survey of social work education (United Nations, 1950), which also became the basis for her PhD, awarded in 1950. The study involved collating materials from 36 countries, analyzing differing definitions of social work and varying curricula and systems of social work education. Doing this work further developed her understanding social work education and her personal links across the world. These enabled IASSW to achieve NGO status as an advisor with the UN and its Economic and Social Commission, and this activity has continued to this day (Healy, 2008c). Katherine told Billups (2002c: p 148) that separation pursuing different careers was a factor in ending her marriage. While she was silent in the Billups or Watkins interviews on other matters of contention, it may be that other relevant factors included Willmoore's shift towards conservative political views and what Nash (1975: p 127) describes as a pugnacious and disputatious temperament that helped '... to explain the later troubled personal and academic life of this strangely driven man'.

At CSWE (1952-71)

In her early forties, Katherine began to move into the roles which were to form her life's culminating achievement: her employment within the coordinating and accrediting body for US social work education and, alongside this, her leadership roles in international social work education.

Having completed her PhD, she was appointed Executive Secretary of the American Association of Schools of Social Work (AASSW) in January 1951 (Kendall, 2002: p 81). AASSW was one of two associations of the American schools whose differing interests had led to conflict about the predominant mode of professional social work education. By the time she arrived in post, AASW was gearing up for merger with the competing organization, the National Association of Schools of Social Administration (NASSA), which resolved the conflict, forming CSWE. This led to the establishment of a post-graduate qualification with a significant focus on individualized casework and an important element of field or practice education as the recognized form of social work education at this stage in the US. Katherine later argued (Kendall, 2002: p 81) that her focus on international matters in the previous decade had insulated her from any personal animosities that still remained from pre-existing conflicts when she took up her post.

That focus on the international continued as Katherine took up her work in the new Council on Social Work Education, because she was already on the board of IASSW, and was shortly to become its honorary secretary. Ernest F. Witte (1904-86), a former dean of two social work schools, was appointed executive director of CSWE, with Katherine transferring initially as educational secretary (Social Welfare History Project, 2016b). CSWE had a small staff group with few resources, but this team managed rapidly to build an influential and effective organization in two important spheres: the development and accreditation of social work education in the US and international social work education. Witte's career included war service with welfare responsibilities in Europe and the Pacific so, like many of his generation, he had experience of both social distress and poverty in the US and of international affairs. It was natural that he supported efforts to pursue international social concern as part of the work of the new CSWE.

Katherine certainly needed his support. The first full-scale international social work conference took place in 1950, around the time of the publication of her UN Report on social work education internationally, and she was invited to be a keynote speaker. At the conference, the president, René Sand, 'tapped me on the shoulder' (Billups, 2002c: p 149) co-opting her to the Executive Board. When Sand died in 1953, Katherine was offered the presidency or the secretary role, taking on the latter alongside her CSWE work. Despite support from inside CSWE, however, Katherine assumed a huge burden of work in her voluntary IASSW role, much of which she carried out in her own time. She said: 'It also meant I always used weekends and vacations for IASSW business. Almost all the trips I took, lots and lots of them, I had to do on my own money and the only money I had came from my salary' (Billups, 2002c: p 156).

Calling on her UN experience, international standing, and being a Spanish speaker, Katherine was also invited to undertake international assignments for the US government. She wrote about an early one in Paraguay at length (Kendall, 1994). The Paraguayan government sought a social welfare consultant from the US government in 1954. The request came shortly before a state visit by President Peron, a controversial figure from Argentina, who offered Argentine social welfare experts. The State Department sought CSWE's help, apparently to forestall the prospect of Argentinian involvement. They offered Kendall for a short-term mission. She developed a seminar in which local experts presented a social problem or work area, and she contributed material on similar areas of concern in the US or other Latin American countries that she knew, using her 'serviceable

Spanish' (Kendall, 1994, p 5). After her visit the Paraguayan Ministry of Health, whose minister had been present throughout, had social welfare added to its responsibilities, and set up specialized sections for different client groups. All was in vain, though, because the dictator Stroessner came to power in Paraguay and dismantled many positive outcomes, although some training initiatives continued. In this piece of work, Katherine was developing an approach that contributed US expertise within a structure of active participation by local personnel. This stood her in good stead in later international projects.

During the remainder of her time at CSWE, Katherine undertook international assignments, often in concert with work for IASSW. For example, in 1956, she was a delegate and recorder for the UN International Working Party on Social Work Training in Munich, at the same location as the IASSW Congress in that year. She also made consultation visits to Greece, Iran, India and Hong Kong in 1961 and to Paraguay, Argentina, Chile, Peru, Jamaica, Honduras, Nicaragua, Costa Rica and Panama in 1962, all alongside international or regional IASSW meetings. Many other visits appear on her curriculum vitae (Social Welfare History Project, 2016a).

Most member schools and academics are familiar with the international congresses organized by IASSW, associated with its general assembly meeting, every two years. The work of bringing these together successfully is routine but important detailed administration. A major achievement of Katherine's years as voluntary secretary to IASSW was the extension of the membership and activities from a European and US base towards a global membership (Healy, 2008d). Katherine saw this as an important challenge, to which she successfully rose (Billups, 2002c: p 156). She also did a great deal of editorial work on the jointly sponsored journal, *International Social Work*, during its first ten years of life.

Katherine's role at CSWE was primarily to deal with educational matters, including curriculum development and accreditation of courses. Witte also continued with international links. In 1955, for example, he was a member of a team of three sent to India, Iran, Egypt and the Gold Coast (later Ghana) by the International Cooperation Administration of the Department of State to study community development.

CSWE's work on educational matters involved extensive contacts across the US and Canada (where social work education was accredited by CSWE until 1970). For five years, Kendall '... travelled the United States and Canada as a consultant, working with graduate schools on curriculum building ...' (Billups, 2002c: p 153). Many leading social work educators were members of CSWE committees or undertook curriculum development projects for CSWE. Katherine was, therefore, able to build a network of contacts throughout social work education and facilitate relationships between that network and colleagues across the world through her international work. Her experience later informed her involvement in curriculum building as a source of unity and cooperation within international social work education. She saw being in at the start of CSWE and the opportunity to travel throughout North America developing social work education as a highlight of her career (Billups, 2002c: p 153).

During the 1950s and '60s, Katherine also played an active professional role representing CSWE. For example, she regularly took chairing or speaking roles in the US National Conference on Social Work (NCSW), initially on general social work issues, and by the 1960s consistently in leading roles concerned with international links.

CSWE grew rapidly. Four years after its foundation, in 1956, it had 12 professional and 12 assistant staff. A contemporary account showed that its work included a nationwide recruitment campaign, expanded accrediting activities, a systematic consultation service to graduate schools, developmental work with undergraduate departments and a comprehensive curriculum study. In addition, it pursued intensive cooperative activity on educational matters with governmental and voluntary agencies and many other groups, promotion of scholarship and fellowships, and a host of other activities (Social Welfare History Project, 2016b). Witte needed greater executive support, and Katherine was appointed associate executive director in 1958, continuing with her educational and international roles, while he dealt with fundraising and management (Billups, 2002c: p 151). In 1960-1961, Katherine had a period as Carnegie Distinguished Visiting Professor at the University of Hawaii, Honolulu and she maintained her links with the university.

In 1963, Witte left the CSWE, and a search committee was set up to find a successor. The Council's president reported:

> It was clear from the very beginning that Dr Katherine Kendall was an unusually competent person in her role of choice as Associate Director, where she has so much to give to all social work education and especially the area of her great interest – international social work education. However, to our delight and gratification, the letters poured back to the Committee stating in many different ways that Dr Kendall was obviously the person of first choice as full Executive Director. (Social Welfare History Project, 2016c)

Katherine agreed to take on the post, and an administrative assistant was appointed to help with her international work (Billups, 2002c: p 151). By 1966, however, another opportunity arose: the US Congress passed the International Education Act which encouraged US support for education across the world, leading CSWE to establish a division of international education. Since this was her major interest, Katherine stepped aside from the executive directorship, and became Director of International Education, pursuing this role in tandem, again, with her secretary role in IASSW. Later, interest in international issues began to decline among CSWE's members. But (as Chapter 1 showed), with the opportunity of a large USAID grant for a project to develop education in family planning (also supported by Canadian and Swedish aid agencies), IASSW was able to set up a full-time secretariat. Katherine left CSWE in 1971 to become secretary-general of IASSW.

Katherine's UN work led to her membership of the IASSW board, for a period her CSWE role was adapted to enable her to function as IASSW secretary, and she also had, for a time, the international portfolio within CSWE. As well as this, she managed to fulfil some international consultation responsibilities. Building on this latter experience, she was later to argue for the importance of collegial relationships when offering international technical assistance from rich Western countries to developing countries (Kendall, 1979).

IASSW and after (1971-2010)

Katherine's work at IASSW fell into two phases: her full-time paid employment as secretary-general from 1971-8, a relatively short period in her life, and then her unpaid work as honorary president, a post which she took up on her retirement.

The major aspect of her employment at IASSW lay in the directorship of the USAID project on family planning (see Chapter 1 for more detail), since this funded her employment. In addition to Katherine, the project employed development staff in different regions, notably Angelina Almanzor (Philippines) and Maxine Ankrah (Uganda). The approach included curriculum development work in pilot schools, regional conferences to bring in technical expertise and international consultants and international workshops to share experience (Almanzor, 1974). The family planning project was at the centre of Katherine's work, alongside keeping IASSW going and consultation work with the UN and UNICEF, for much of her full-time employment with IASSW. She saw the family planning project as an important highlight of her professional career (Billups, 2002c: p 153).

In her retirement, Katherine undertook various roles associated with the Hunter College School of Social Work in New York. She continued to attend and contribute to IASSW board meetings annually, and became both a figure of continuity and a repository of the history of IASSW after World War II (Billups, 2002c: p 161). Her role was like that of a constitutional monarch: to advise, encourage and warn on the basis of her broad responsibilities, her long experience and her extensive networks within social work education and international bodies. In the middle years, she exercised her greatest sphere of influence through elected presidents, where she sometimes had close personal relationships. For example, in her personal papers, deposited at the Social Welfare History Archives, two presidents are described exceptionally: Huws Jones ('close friend'), Stein ('old friend') along with the British doyenne of social work Younghusband ('dear friend'). Others do not come within the category of personal correspondence (Klaassen, 2016b).

Katherine Kendall's publications

Throughout her career, Katherine published a wide range of papers, accurately described by the social welfare history archivist, as addressing '… issues in social work education and international social work, with many of them in the form of historical overviews and biographical tributes to individual leaders' (Klaassen, 2016c). Some substantial papers were collected in a valedictory collection issued by IASSW on her retirement (Kendall, 1978). This includes a paper presented in 1950 about the UN Report, and her account of the history of IASSW, often based on her personal recollections. Many of her publications are of this kind: the work of an important executive, reports on current work and accounts of 'what happened' with a degree of analysis, based on her recollections and personal papers. There were also editing tasks, often completed with CSWE or IASSW colleagues, including the two editions of the extensive *World guide to social work education* (Rao, 1984).

Her earliest substantial work is the UN Report (United Nations, 1950), an exercise in formulating complex information from international sources to facilitate important progress in the official recognition of social work as part of international social development. Later in her life, she completed two larger projects, drawing on documentary sources: the definitive organizational history of the formation and early years of CSWE (Kendall, 2002), which is rather neutral in tone; and a more personal account of early social work education, which aims to draw attention to the European roots of its development (Kendall, 2000). As histories, their credibility is blemished by her personal involvement in and commitment to both, though this is rather downplayed in the CSWE volume. They are largely descriptive accounts of heroic achievements, ignoring the political and social contexts of the flows of events she provides. Nevertheless, they will form useful starting points for wider and more critical analysis of the material she collected.

Conclusion: Katherine Kendall's contributions

This chapter has presented an account of Katherine Kendall's long and active life. How may we assess her contribution to social work and its education in the context of that life story? Anyone who, like Katherine, has been associated with a professional field for three-quarters of a century, and in leadership and developmental roles for more than sixty years, demonstrates extraordinary commitment and loyalty that commands admiration. Consequently, she has been described as 'a world-renowned icon of social work education' (Katherine A. Kendall Institute, 2016) and 'the founder of international social work' (Watkins, 2010: p 157), although this perhaps overstates the influence of someone whose involvement was only from the 1940s. However, her standing in international social work led CSWE to establish the Katherine A. Kendall Institute for International Social Work Education.

Brandwein (2005) summarized Kendall's interest for feminist scholars in social work as follows: 'Her early career and personal decisions reflect feminist values in the context of the Depression Era, World War II, and the postwar period. She is a powerful role model for women today and especially for active, positive aging.' Watkins (2010) identifies the UN project, and the resulting interest of UN and related bodies in social work education, the Paraguay consultation, the family planning project and her influence on IASSW as the main professional contributions of her career.

FIVE

Armaity S. Desai, 1992

Interviewed by Vimla V. Nadkarni

Biography

 Beginning as a lecturer, Armaity S. Desai (b. 1934) became Vice Principal and Principal, College of Social Work, Nirmala Niketan (NN) (1957-82). She was appointed Director of the Tata Institute of Social Sciences (TISS) (1982-95), then Chairperson, University Grants Commission (UGC) (1995-99). Her educational qualifications include: a BA (Hons) in sociology and anthropology, Bombay University, 1955; Diploma in Social Service Administration (family and child welfare), TISS, 1957; an MA, 1959; and a PhD in 1969 from the School of Social Service Administration (SSA), University of Chicago. Practice roles included casework at the Chicago Child Care Society, staff supervision at the University of Chicago Hospitals, and voluntary and leadership roles in Indian social work, focused on child, family and youth. While Director at TISS, she was President of the Association of Indian Universities (1992). International roles have included serving as Vice President, IASSW; President, Asian Regional Association for Social Work Education (later APASWE); work for the UN Economic and Social Commission for Asia and the Pacific in Bangkok and Manila, and with the Commonwealth Secretariat, London.

What has the award meant to you?

The award was not as important for me as the person I have cherished in whose name it was given. I value the award because Katherine has played a significant role in my professional development, and I was the first awardee to be selected, which I cherish. However, I do not talk about my awards. Your work speaks for itself and results in awards or positions.

Katherine knew me thoroughly and was familiar with my work. My relationship with her started while I was doing my PhD at the University of Chicago. As an international student, I wanted to take up a topic relevant for me, rather than an American issue. I decided to do a study on the relevance of social work education for international students who came to study in the US. My PhD supervisor directed me to meet Katherine, then Secretary-General of IASSW.

After completing my studies, on my way back to India, I met her again in New York to share my study with her. She was happy and took me for a meal in a restaurant. She loved good food and was a great cook. Over the meal, she discussed her plan to start a programme in Asia and asked me to arrange a seminar for IASSW. We were able to have the first South East Asian Seminar on development issues and social work curriculum, attended by Dr Kendall, Dr Herman Stein, then President of IASSW, Dame Eileen Younghusband, from the UK, and Dr Ruby Pernell, Social Welfare Attaché, US Embassy in India. It was a successful five days' programme at the College of Social Work, Nirmala Niketan. It sowed the seeds of an association for social work education in the region under the umbrella of IASSW focusing on regional concerns.

Katherine and I sometimes had strong differences but she was most gracious about it. We related to each other in an independent and yet a warm way. She was always a role model for me in social work education, a person with professional concerns, the capacity to put ideas together and move things, never static.

What activities were of major importance for your professional career and its impact on social work and educational development?

All my activities are based on social issues, social work education or higher education. One thing that was clear from my PhD thesis was that students who came from Western cultures and developed countries found social work education in the US relevant, but those who came from developing countries and non-Western cultures did not. After returning to India, I worked on rethinking the methodology and content of the curriculum, and how to develop and structure it. Being invited in 1972 to present a paper on curriculum development at an IASSW conference in the Netherlands helped me to begin developing a more country-specific curriculum at NN. Later, a lot of discussion took place in India on curriculum restructuring, resulting in the Association of Schools of Social Work in India (ASSWI) moving towards a social development thrust. Other schools started taking it up.

Again, when I moved to TISS in the 1980s, I suggested modifications and made it more development and community-oriented, balancing it with institutional and therapeutic focuses, and method-orientation based on the nature of problem solving. Both have a place, as we work with individuals and families in distress who need personal help, but we also need to focus on the larger picture of poverty, illiteracy, ill health, housing, land and water which affect the lives of millions of people, and develop strategies for community mobilization and social change.

I introduced two courses on teaching/training and field instruction having undertaken similar courses under Charlotte Towle[1] in Chicago. I introduced the course on field instruction at NN and TISS for the second year masters degree students, as a number of them became supervisors in their organizations almost immediately on graduation. I was also concerned that, while classroom teachers had a course outline and units for teaching, field instructors are left to develop their own ideas of what to teach. We spent considerable time evolving an outline for field instruction for each semester. It covered what generic inputs supervisors must do, tasks for students and expected outcomes of students' learning. The course on training met a felt need, as MA graduates were expected in their agencies to undertake short-term training and workshops for staff, para-professionals and volunteers and allied professional groups. The interaction and discussion in the classes between the students, faculty and agency field instructors who attended the courses, both at NN and TISS, was fascinating and instructive for everybody.

I was always involved in areas that were little known in India, such as adoption in 1962, in which I had sought work experience after completing the MA degree in Chicago. It has moved on a great deal since then. It was a steep hill to climb. Children were not given for adoption by institutions. It was not easy for Indian couples to adopt unrelated children. Only the Hindus had an adoption law, there was none among other communities. Both Hindu law and minorities who have no provision for adoption in their personal laws lacked procedures. I had to lay down procedures with the help of legal persons to give a 'legal' sanction to it. I also brought all the organizations together and drafted a Bill, which the Indian Council for Social Welfare promoted, and we presented it to the Minister for Law. However, in spite of many attempts, it has remained mired in politics with fears of alienating minorities, since family law is still based on the personal law of each community.

Several of us got together and started the Indian Association for the Promotion of Adoption to undertake advocacy on behalf of the child, especially on law for adoption. The structure we developed – to ensure that Indian couples had the first choice of adoption, before children are offered for international adoption – was finally adopted by the Indian government. With the Indian Council of Social Welfare, we also created the scrutiny of applications by foreign nationals, to aid decisions by the High Court of Mumbai. Other states followed. These institutions set up by us in the 1960s and '70s continue, but now with more government involvement. Another area was school social work, especially for disadvantaged children where dropout and failure were high. These two areas of children's work have been my interest areas in field practice and have been very satisfying for me, because it was pioneering something new and different in the field in India.

Social work in the US was more counselling when I was there, while here it requires different strategies, using all the methods. I taught a course in casework at the School of Social Work, Loyola University. Interestingly, student feedback was that my class was the only one where the clients' social and cultural context was discussed. I had pairs of students recording their home-visit interviews for discussion in class. This technique was unique at the time, and when I was leaving for India, they presented me with a tape recorder for use with students.

While I was there, they got a grant to set up a project providing social work based in schools. Because of my relevant experience in school social work in India, they offered me the job.

In which field do you think you made the biggest contribution?

When I was doing my doctoral studies in the US, I knew I wanted Indian students to learn more than one method of practice, both in the classroom and in the field placement. In India, it is appropriate to practice more than just one method with the kind of problems we face. Hence, I developed an integrated social work practice syllabus. I used students' practice experiences to promote classroom learning. In NN, we had a seminar where students presented integrated practice based on specific field intervention. It laid the foundation for me to move from looking at practice methods as separated and closed units to see what cuts through them. It was about slicing the cake laterally instead of vertically.

In India, I was the first one to introduce integrated social work practice. It was not even taught at SSA, Chicago University, although, at the time it was discussed by the Council on Social Work Education (CSWE) at conferences and in books.

Another unique contribution is field action projects, a very Indian concept, conducted by institutions for social work education. In the early history of social work education in India, we did not have a variety of organizations for student fieldwork, especially in group and community work. Hence, such programmes were developed for placements, wherein social work educators could experiment with innovative practices and demonstrate them for replication and policy making. Several pioneering projects demonstrated new practices, which were later absorbed by the government and local bodies. For example, Childline, a telephone and outreach service, made an impact at the policy level. A child protection component is in place in the Ministry of Women and Child Development. This all India service to children has come a long way from a field action project at TISS. These projects give faculty members a feel for grassroots realities and a base for integrating teaching, practice and research, and lead to practice-based literature. It provides quality placements for students, and spin-offs through students who start their own projects, after graduation.

Demonstrating school social work with disadvantaged children and communities was another project, later absorbed by the Greater Mumbai Municipal Corporation. All social work methods were utilized for intervention with the child, the family, the school and the community. It was a multi-pronged programme with teams of para-professionals, BSW and MSW students placed with the school system covering 80,000 children located in 17 large slums in Mumbai. After a decade of demonstration, it was handed over to the city administration.

If you do relevant work and demonstrate a tested programme with benefits to the disadvantaged sections of society, the local, state or national government is ready to absorb it within its system. However, you have to negotiate for it. Whatever we do has to become part of the system, because academic institutions should not run services but research and demonstrate new methods of practice. As soon as a project reaches a stage of regular service, one should seek for it to be absorbed in the system, despite the risk that it will not be run as well. My idea of field action projects is that they must be pioneering, demonstrating a new thrust on a theoretical base, and bringing out the basic linkages to social work, to society, to issues. Projects should be meaningful in demonstrating professional competence and educational content.

I realized the operation of the glass ceiling in higher education only after I was appointed Chairperson of the UGC, moving around the country and seeing the problems at first hand. I started talking about gender blindness to our Standing Committee for Women's Studies in the UGC. The focus was to sensitize and motivate female academicians and lower-level female administrators to see themselves becoming managers in academia and, thereafter, offering workshops to give them the necessary skills to become managers.

What did social work and its education mean to you personally and professionally? Why did you choose it?

I took up social work because my parents were both in social work. They lived through the freedom movement in India and its struggle for independence. Gandhi's constructive work and his philosophy such as *swadeshi* – prioritizing Indian goods and services – were part of our lives and stirred me to do something as I was growing up. My aunt was one of the early graduates of TISS. As a child, she was my role model. I was very clear that I wanted to go straight to TISS after high school. I grudgingly went to St Xavier's College for graduation since a bachelors degree was a requirement. Happily, I had opportunities there because I was in the Social Service League. When I was finishing school, my father insisted I had a vocational guidance test, which identified my strong areas as teaching and agriculture. I wanted to be a social worker. I realized only later that I was a teacher all my life, albeit at the professional level. Gardening is my hobby. I appreciated years later the relationship between my interests, my potential and what I would be doing.

To be a social work educator has been meaningful for me. It is fascinating to see what my own students have done after graduation, making reflective and relevant contributions in leadership positions. Life has been very meaningful if you have been able to start these people off in their careers and see them doing their own thing, feeling proud of their professional achievements.

What were the challenges of social work and its education?

The College of Social Work at NN and I grew together, as I came in the second year after the establishment of the College and left after its silver jubilee. I owe my professional growth almost entirely to the challenges of the College's work; it was where I spent some of the most creative years and tried out many experiments. In the span of 25 years, I had two periods of three and four years in the US.

When I moved to TISS, I was not sure whether I could do anything because it was a ready-made place. Then I found there were many areas that needed attention, besides the Trustees' brief to me to develop further the social work programme. No institution can remain static. To identify areas of intervention in my new setting, I used what I have been teaching all the time: integrated practice and the theoretical framework. Look at the system, get information, collect the facts, identify the gaps, the issue/s, and alternative strategies and begin the intervention for change, all with the participation of those concerned with the system. I started by meeting each department. From that came all the issues we needed to work on.

TISS as a university was too small with 29 academic staff and departments of two staff members each. I had to create positions, making departments more workable. We also started women's studies, family studies and labour studies during that five-year-plan period. I spent a lot of time on developing the Institute, the infrastructure, not only the curriculum and degrees offered, but recruitment, placement and orientation for academic staff.

I realized that the existing campus would be saturated in less than a decade and the Institute would not be able to grow further to meet new and emerging needs. Over the twelve years, I managed to get donations of ten acres of land for the Mumbai campus from a private donor, close to its existing campus, and 100 acres for the rural campus from the Government of Maharashtra, our state, plus some funds from the UGC and the Sir Dorabji Tata Trust for construction. This assured the further expansion of the Institute, and I looked to the rural campus as the future of the Institute. When I went to the UGC, I used the same process to understand the system better, although I knew it through my earlier contacts with committees and as a recipient of the UGC development grant and schemes.

I have appreciated my social work education because I have used it in administration all the time. As a head, you understand better all the people who work with you because you understand their personality, their way of dealing with things, and the systemic inputs they need to facilitate their work, helping them grow and derive satisfaction from their jobs. Our knowledge base is very good, along with our understanding of social dynamics and techniques in working with individuals or groups and seeing the organization as a community using democratic procedures.

What was the importance of international work in your career?

It gave breadth to my understanding of social work education around the world. Interaction with other educators stimulates one's perceptions and offers new ideas. The international perspective helps by broadening one's horizon, realizing that social work is many things to many people. The differences depend on the requirements of each country, which give the profession a localized colour. There is a core element, but the issues it addresses are not common to all. One has to relate the curriculum and education to the social reality. If I had not gone abroad, I would have been limited and would have taken for granted that what is in India is universal.

Reading the history of social work education in India, the common criticism is that we have been so influenced by the colonizers. We went through the entire phase when social work educators returned from the US and did not question applicability in the Indian context. They introduced the same methods and the same content, although some subjects were added. Later, we had the US Technical Mission to India supported by the US government, sending five social work educators to five schools of social work in India, and the trend was further reinforced. Their major contribution was to start the Association of Schools of Social Work in India. They had money to hold seminars and bring the schools together. In these meetings, we, the Indian educators, started to debate what is applicable, what not and what we needed to do. We began to challenge the focus on casework and human growth and behaviour. There was less emphasis on community work and political processes which were equally, if not more, important for us. However, this was not emphasized in the US, as I discovered when I was studying at Chicago. Casework and group work were offered but separately, you could not do both. I insisted on two field placements, with casework and community work. This was eventually agreed to, after some negotiations with the Dean of Students. She acknowledged that it was a successful experiment, but they attributed it mostly to my previous experience from India and did not replicate it. Similarly, in the adoption and foster care agency, I wanted to form a support system of a group of foster-mothers but was not permitted as I was supposed to be a caseworker!

The change in curriculum was discussed in the 1960s and '70s in all the Asian countries. Development activities became initiated in our countries by the respective governments and through the United Nations in the region. When APASWE came into existence in the late '70s, many of the educators in the region realized the need to contextualize the curriculum. It was a fascinating period. The curriculum had an urban bias and the vast rural populations were neglected. We needed to look at social development issues, and at human behaviour in relation to these issues.

I became much more involved in international social work as Vice President of IASSW and, subsequently, President of APASWE. Although I was the first President, Dr Angelina Almanzor, from the Philippines, did a lot of groundwork for starting the Association, especially involving the institutions that had already come together in a NN workshop. IASSW had employed her on a social development project for Asia developing a curriculum on family planning. We were proud of this collective effort of all the Asian schools of social work in shifting emphasis from a narrow focus on family planning to social development. Dr Kendall saw the importance of this shift and had the sponsors (USAID) agree to it. Angelina travelled to all the schools of social work, motivating everyone to join an association for social work education in the Asian region. As a staff member of the IASSW she could not be president, and therefore began pursuing me to become president. Finally, she made me give in. I also played an active role in IASSW policy issues concerning the Asian region and the developing countries, because at that time IASSW tended to be overwhelmed by Western representation, including all key officials.

What were the major obstacles that you faced in your career?

Funding was the major obstacle in appointing academic staff, providing adequate salaries in the early years of the College, and funding field action projects. I always wanted to develop audio-laboratories for speech and language, for students with language handicaps. In TISS, there were many needs, especially hostels for students as we expanded the programmes, and funding the rural campus. I was systematic in putting our social work graduates into the field action projects, supervising them on the job, giving them various experiences in the field, building on their innovative capacities and, subsequently, recruiting them as academic staff. It was very difficult to get staff with at least some field experience in those early years. In this manner, I was able to recruit people who started teaching after relevant field experience, which cannot be substituted by a PhD. A PhD should only follow adequate field experience. Once you recruit the right people, you create programmes for staff development so that they continue on the path of growth.

Developing indigenous literature requires time and facilitation. In a developing country, teachers' workloads are high, including field action projects. Writing becomes a casualty. Our social work practitioners are not writers, not used to conceptualizing. Therefore, development of indigenous literature takes a back seat.

How has social work education changed?

It has to change in view of all the new problems and issues that have emerged. Since social work relates to social reality, it will have to go on modifying itself, change its content, borrow from other fields and remain multidisciplinary. Moreover, as social workers, we are challenged to take up problems we discover in our country. Social work has developed its own skill base. However, it borrows theories from other disciplines because they contribute to understanding the individual, the social systems and the reality, on which our practice develops.

For instance, frequent disasters, natural and people-made, have led to developing social work disaster interventions by at least some schools of social work in India. Environment was never on the map, and has become an issue. HIV/AIDS has replaced concerns we had for sex-related diseases in medical social work. One of the messages I always gave my students was that we have no formulas and we must know how to work even in ambiguous situations. In India, social workers need to take up the challenge as various marginalized groups have begun to ask for their fair share: women, tribal people, displaced people, and those living on the margins of poverty.

What would you like to see happening in social work and its education in the future?

Social work needs to have a more pro-activist stand, which is what social work started with, as shown by the early history of Faculty at SSA, like the work of Edith Abbott.[2] This was also true of the social reformers in India. We have to concentrate on not only theoretical aspects, but also respond to emerging issues and strengthen the capacity of students to deal with ambiguous situations. Today's issues do not remain local, but take a global colour. Correspondingly, social workers have to look for the global influence in our national context, building linkages between the grassroots, the state and the national level. Issues like child labour and abuse exist in our society. Rescue and rehabilitation of such children is not a local task. It involves the governments of both the area where the child is rescued and where it is being returned to the family and, ultimately, advocacy for the national policy on child protection. Some of these children are trafficked across borders, and it becomes an inter-country issue. We have been dealing with such issues in Childline India Foundation. Paedophilia comes with tourism. We have taken cases to the courts, including the Supreme Court of India. Social work is not sufficiently addressing these kinds of issues. By being pro-active, social workers look ahead and do not wait for problems to happen. One should have a pro-active approach in dealing with social issues at the policy level, being concerned with policy changes and advocacy. We are not doing enough at that end. We are so busy with our agency, and our organization, we do not move beyond it to make an impact.

Activism where essential, we may have to stand up against the state, and be clear when working with communities that our obligation is to the community. If the state is against any aspect of the work, then we have to take a stand against the state's view.

What would you like to see happening in IASSW?

After IASSW had to close down in Vienna, I argued that the headquarters should be placed in one of the developing countries for two reasons. It would cost less to run it, and the perspective of the organization would become much wider. The majority of the people of the world do not live in the Western world. IASSW must consider social work from different perspectives, not only from the limited Western region.

A global thrust should secure that IASSW serves the varying interest of its members. Katherine Kendall made good efforts to bring specific activities to developing regions. Asia had the social development and family planning project.

When IASSW can have regular staff, it can stimulate and conduct activities as witnessed in New York and Vienna. That some activities are continued is encouraging in a global downturn. The same is true for APASWE, which has kept up its biennial conferences since the first one held in Australia when I was the President.

Selected publications

Desai, A. S. (2012) 'Transforming higher education for gender equality', in A. S. Kolaskar and M. Dash (eds) *Women and society: The road to change*, Oxford: Oxford University Press: pp 60-85.

Desai, A. S. (2007) 'Disaster and social work responses', in L. Dominelli (ed) *Revitalising communities in a globalising world*, Aldershot: Ashgate: pp 297–314.

Desai, A. S. (2009) 'Catalyzing higher education and school education linkages', in M. Mukhopadhyay (ed) *Quality school education for all*, New Delhi: Educational Technology and Management Academy: pp 47–65.

Desai, A. S. (2003) 'Value orientation of higher education', in M. M. Luther (ed) *Building a vibrant India: Democracy, development and ethics*, New Delhi: Tata McGraw Hill: pp 271–88.

Desai, A. S. (1985-86) 'The foundations of social work education in India', *Indian Journal of Social Work*, 46(1), pp 41–57.

Notes

[1] Charlotte Towle (1896-1966), Professor, SSA, University of Chicago, where she worked from 1932-62; author of *Common human needs* (1945) and *The learner in education for the professions* (1954).

[2] Edith Abbott (1876-1957), first Dean, SSA, University of Chicago, first female dean of any postgraduate school in the US, a major influence on the development of US social work curricula.

SIX

Herman D. Stein, 1994

Author: Katherine A. Kendall[1,2]

Herman Stein, President of IASSW (1968-1976), has for more than sixty years excelled as an educator, scholar, internationalist, university administrator, and leader in a variety of professional associations. From almost the beginning of his career, the world has been the stage on which he has played those many roles, all of them with an abundance of talent. In fact, while he was in the graduate programme of what is now the Columbia University School of Social Work, he had to decide whether to become a social worker or an actor. As an undergraduate, he became involved in student theatrical productions, where he teamed up with the famous comedian, Danny Kaye, who became a life-long companion and friend. At the end of Stein's first year in the social work programme, he was invited to join an off-Broadway variety show that helped to launch Kaye on his meteoric rise on both stage and screen. 'If I´d joined,' Stein has said, 'the theatre probably was going to be where I would make my career as a character actor.' Fortunately, for social work and social work education, he chose instead to continue his studies at the School of Social Work, from which he received his masters degree in 1941 and the doctoral degree in 1958.

While the world has been his stage, education has been at the heart of his manifold activities. Following a period of direct service practice as a caseworker in a well-known private agency in New York City, he was recruited by the Columbia School of Social Work in 1945 as a faculty member. With an interruption for a significant overseas assignment from 1947 to 1950, he continued at Columbia for another fourteen years, rising through all professorial ranks to Professor and Director of the School's Research Centre.

Educator and university administrator

During his years at Columbia, Stein became well-known throughout the profession for his talents as a teacher, his ground-breaking work on curriculum development, his remarkable international achievements, and the breadth of his vision for social work education. It was not surprising that he became a prized target for deanships in other schools, but it was not until 1964 that he was persuaded by Western Reserve University to become Dean of the School of Applied Social Sciences. His rapid rise as a university administrator began only three years later when he took on an additional assignment as Provost of Social and Behavioural Sciences. This was when Western Reserve merged with the Case Institute of Technology to become Case Western Reserve University. He then moved from the School of Social Work to serve as the University Provost and later as University Vice-President. All of this was climaxed by his designation as University Professor, a high academic status held at the time by only one other faculty member, a Nobel Prize winner. This position enabled him to take leave without pay whenever he wished, which greatly facilitated his international work.

Against that background, it is interesting to assess his impact on social work education in the US. Research, his initial field of interest as a teacher, remained significant throughout his career, but he is best known for his introduction of entirely new areas of study, inspired by international experience. Upon rejoining the Columbia faculty in 1950, following an eye-opening experience in Europe and North Africa with displaced persons and Holocaust survivors, he saw that there was something missing in the American social work curriculum. Let me quote here from my introduction to a recently published collection of his papers.

> In this collection of papers, we see the beginnings of his successful campaign to strengthen professional education for social work through a more fruitful and reciprocal relationship between social work and the social sciences. He makes it quite clear that while he regards concepts drawn from the social and behavioral sciences as indispensable in education for social work, he does not consider social work an applied social science. What he stresses as a pivotal concern is the relevance of social science content to practice. Again and again he underlines the importance of testing relevance within the acknowledged social work functions ... The social science concepts he outlined and taught as central, the connections he built with related disciplines, and the research he stimulated all contributed

to the enrichment and clarification of the knowledge base
of social work practice. (Kendall, 2003, p x)

The courses he developed in this area along with a well-received
textbook co-authored with Richard Cloward (Stein and Cloward,
1967) led to widespread adoption of a new emphasis on socio-cultural
content in the social work curriculum. The impact was actually much
broader than curricular enrichment. In the 1940s when Stein joined
the Columbia faculty, the mission of many, although by no means
all schools of social work was to prepare social workers skilled in
psychoanalytically-oriented casework to work with individuals and
families. To make socio-cultural content truly relevant to practice, not
only casework teachers, but fieldwork supervisors along with teachers
of human behaviour, group work, and community organisation needed
to come on board. The seminars Stein conducted for that purpose
at Columbia and for educators at other schools led to lasting change.

His early years at Case Western Reserve coincided with the
turbulence on college campuses provoked by the war in Vietnam and
the civil rights struggle. His performance during a period of student
protests at Case Western Reserve is still recalled with admiration. In a
recent review of his service to the University, it is told how, as Provost,
he insisted on meeting with unruly students and dealing directly with
their protests and demands.

A colleague described his actions as a choice reflecting 'integrity
and honesty and humanity that is rarely equalled in people in high
office' (CWRU, 1998). In tandem with the President of the University,
he helped to build lines of communication with student groups and
arranged regular meetings for continuing dialogue. He listened and
heard their motivations, he learned what prompted their protests, and
advocated patient reasoning with them. His Solomon-like wisdom
was seen not only as a tower of strength but as the major reason Case
Western Reserve University, after an initial period of disruption,
'avoided the violent conflicts and arrests that were so damaging in many
other campuses'. In writing about how to combat racism, poverty, and
all forms of injustice, Dr Stein urged educators to capture the zeal of
demonstrating students into constructive channels for change.

His success in dealing with minority students and civil rights issues
stemmed in part from his experience as a senior advisor to Carl Stokes,
the first black mayor of Cleveland. As Chair of a Commission on the
Crisis in Welfare in Cleveland, he brought together a wide range of
community leaders, many of whom had never met a welfare recipient.
In a personal history interview, Stein describes what happened when

they actually met welfare families and learned how they lived. 'The elite members of the commission,' he wrote, 'were often flabbergasted at the knowledge they gained just through direct exposure' (Billups, 2002b, p 267). The final report of the Commission, while much acclaimed, did not lead to the change in the welfare system that was hoped for, but did lead to a better understanding of the problems to be solved.

International beginnings

In 1947, he left a promising career as a faculty member at the Columbia University School of Social Work to join the American Joint Distribution Committee (AJDC) in Europe and North Africa. The call to work with displaced persons and victims of the Holocaust following World War II could not be ignored. In Europe, he witnessed the unspeakable tragedy of lives tortured and destroyed. In North Africa, he experienced at first hand the sights and smells of mass poverty. Those years can be seen as a defining time in his life. His work with displaced persons took him to every country in Europe where he saw how desperately social work service was needed. Upon his recommendation to AJDC, a social work training centre designated as the Paul Baerwald School of Social Work was established in Versailles, on the outskirts of Paris. A former professor at the Columbia University School of Social Work was recruited to direct the programme, which gave priority to the training of social workers for service in Eastern Europe. With the fall of the Iron Curtain, that objective could not be achieved. The programme in Versailles was closed and then reconstructed as the Paul Baerwald School of Social Work at Hebrew University in Jerusalem, Israel.

Soon after his return from Europe to the Columbia faculty, he became involved in the work of the Division of Social Affairs of the UN. This led to his appointment as Senior Advisor to a landmark international Conference of Ministers of Social Welfare sponsored by the UN. Almost 100 countries were represented by ministers or other high-ranking officials with responsibility for social programmes. The objectives, as projected by the UN Economic and Social Council, included examination of the role of social welfare programmes in social development, proposal of principles for social welfare programmes, and arrival at recommendations for the training of social welfare personnel. Professor Stein helped to plan the Conference and drafted many of the findings and conclusions. A major outcome was strong support for a reorientation of social welfare toward a developmental approach, including attention to training for preventive and developmental functions. This coincided with Stein's perception, based on his first international experience, of what was missing and needed to be developed in professional social work education in the United States. Working with like-minded colleagues, he developed international courses and, also, advocated better preparation for research, planning, and administration, cited as priorities in the ministers' conference.

The years at UNICEF[3]

Over a period of twenty-one years, Herman Stein served UNICEF with dedication and distinction. His appointment as University Professor gave him the privilege of taking leave without pay to pursue other interests. This made it possible for him not only to accept part-time assignments but to devote some years to work with UNICEF as a full-time staff member.

His long association with UNICEF began in 1962 when he was recruited as an advisor to the Planning Commission of Tanganyika (now Tanzania), a newly independent nation in Africa. He enthusiastically joined the young Tanganyikans, who were taking over responsibility from the departed British to build a new nation. The productive relationships formed with the Ministry of Community Development in this first visit led to his returning every year for twelve years. This was the first of a series of missions to developing countries. In the course of his long career, he has conducted similar missions on programme development in more than thirty developing countries in Africa, Asia, Latin America, and the Middle East.[4]

While such missions made important contributions to the work of UNICEF, even more significant over the years was his work on organisational policy, structure, and management. At an international conference held in Bellagio, Italy, in 1964, a group of high ranking government officials from developing and industrialised countries along with outstanding economists and planners came together to plan for the needs of children in the developing countries. Dr Stein edited the report which led to a complete change in the way in which UNICEF operated. Previously, all decisions by UNICEF field staff had to be routed through a bureaucratic maze involving WHO,[5] FAO,[6] and UNESCO. The requirement of working through all the UN specialised agencies also prevented staff in the field from making direct contact with high-level government officials. As a result of the Bellagio Conference this was all changed and one of the outcomes, which Stein initiated, was an annual three-week interregional staff seminar. After serving first as a resource consultant, he assumed direction of the seminars and carried that responsibility for eight years.

Much of his work on organisational policy and programme development took place in his continuing role as Senior Advisor to Maurice Pate, Henry Labouisse, and James Grant, the first three Executive Directors of UNICEF. Two of his full-time appointments and his final association with UNICEF occurred during the tenure of James Grant. At a farewell party for Herman, Grant described the seminars as 'a process of re-education and rededication' (CWRU, 1998, p 17). The discussions and training had the purpose of keeping the field staff vital and on board with UNICEF concerns. They also encouraged UNICEF staff to examine agency policies, raise their own questions, and engage in debate without fear of reprisal. Understanding other cultures and how to work in teams with people with different values and perspectives also emerged as important programme objectives. Herman's performance at these seminars has been likened to that of 'a world-class virtuoso musician' (CWRU, 1998).

He left his mark on a number of UNICEF programmes. He advocated an integrated approach to child development to ensure adequate attention to the many and various factors that affect the health and welfare of children and was instrumental in launching in India the first major child development project with UNICEF support. His advocacy of mental health considerations in work with children, which had been largely ignored in UNICEF programmes, led to a connection with the International Federation of Mental Health and a prominent place as a speaker at one of their World Congresses. For Herman Stein, the long journey with UNICEF was replete with promises for the betterment of children, promises that he helped to fulfil. And he regards his assignments with UNICEF as among the most rewarding experiences, both personally and professionally, of his entire career.

Leader in the social work profession

With his many talents and breadth of vision, Dr Stein early emerged as a leader within the social work profession. He has served on countless boards, commissions and committees, research projects, and study groups. He has visited many schools of social work as a lecturer and consultant. For more than ten years, he managed to find time to serve on the summer faculty of the Smith College School of Social Work. As President of CSWE from 1966 to 1969 and President of IASSW from 1976 to 1980, he made outstanding contributions to both national and international social work education.

My close association with Herman began in the late 1950s when I was in charge of the educational services of CSWE and he assumed responsibility as chair of its first Curriculum Committee. The charge to the Committee involved review of 13 volumes of a controversial curriculum study (Boehm, 1959) and the production of a new Curriculum Policy Statement. This was no ordinary assignment. Each of the volumes of the curriculum study had to be analysed for policy implications and use in curriculum building. A previous move in the direction of a generic curriculum called for the elimination of all specialised sequences in the American social work curriculum. This represented a radical change, accepted with the understanding that the generic programmes would include key concepts from each of the established specialties in effect at that time in the US. Practice statements produced by the organisations representing the nine different specialisations also had to be analysed. Surveys of curriculum trends, issues, and concerns expressed by graduate and undergraduate educators along with suggestions from practitioners added to the mountain of material that somehow had to be gleaned for the new official statement of curriculum policy.

Herman Stein was the perfect fit for this Herculean task. He brought to the assignment his comprehensive knowledge of social work history, changes and trends in curriculum development, the characteristics of professions, and the place of social work in the academic world. His talents as a chairman were well-established. He knew when, what, and how to delegate responsibility for review of the source material. It had already been noted that he was a past master in handling conflict and listening to differing points of view. The Official Statement of Curriculum Policy that was produced and adopted in 1962 by CSWE represented the most thorough-going and broad-based review of educational and practice issues yet experienced by the profession. It could not have happened without the creative and disciplined leadership of Herman Stein.

When he was elected President of the Council in 1966, I had the privilege of working closely with him again, initially as Executive Director and then as Director of International Education. The powerful forces for change at work in this period had a far-reaching effect on American social work education. The Council had to encompass a new range of activities arising out of the anti-poverty programmes, the civil rights struggle, student demands for participation in governance and curriculum policy, and the need for priority attention to the recruitment of minority students and faculty. It was fortunate for the

Council that Herman Stein carried the heavy responsibilities of the presidency in this tumultuous time.

His experience with student unrest at Case Western Reserve University helped the Council deal positively with student demands and the disturbances that occurred during his time in office. He was equally helpful in the development of a variety of programmes to meet minority concerns and underline the importance of social justice as a central value in social work and social work education. Perhaps his most significant contribution was an amazing ability, when acting as chair of diverse groups, to turn spirited and sometimes acrimonious discussions into channels for positive change. This talent was instrumental in bringing about structural reorganisation of the Council, new opportunities for minorities, and strengthened curriculum offerings related to inner city problems.

Stein's international experience also contributed significantly to CSWE. He assumed the presidency in the same year that President Lyndon Johnson in 1966 asked for the passage of legislation that would greatly expand cooperative and interdisciplinary work among universities on international education. When John Gardner, US Secretary of Health, Education and Welfare encouraged wide participation in this promising nationwide activity, the Council responded by establishing a Division of International Education, for which I then assumed direction. Unfortunately, the failure of Congress to appropriate funds to support the legislation severely limited implementation of an ambitious programme.

Nevertheless, a number of significant international and interprofessional conferences, sponsored or cosponsored by the Council, were successfully organised in this period. Herman brought to this activity the benefit of his long international experience as well as his connections with UNICEF and other international organisations. He was particularly helpful as the chairman of an international conference held at the East–West Centre in Hawaii in 1967. Leaders in social work education from all around the world along with selected representatives of related disciplines participated in examining universals and differences in social work values and practice across cultures. The many different points of view and the cultural differences made this a challenging assignment for Dr Stein, which he met with his usual striking success.

While still very much involved with CSWE, Dr Stein took on the additional responsibility of leading IASSW. Elected President in 1968, he continued to serve in that role for eight years and continued as a member of the Executive Committee for another four years. Those were years of notable achievements, largely because funds had become available to establish a secretariat with salaried staff. How that came about is an important part of the Herman Stein saga.

From its conception at the legendary International Conference of Social Work in Paris in 1928, IASSW was managed by volunteers until July, 1971. As an elected secretary, I carried that responsibility, with the consent of the Council, for 20 years. The successful outcome of a joint CSWE-IASSW conference in 1970 dealing with population questions and family planning led to the production of a project to prepare qualified social work personnel for effective participation in family planning and population policies, programmes, and services. The project, to be carried out through pilot schools in every region, was designed to emphasise indigenous curriculum building, interdisciplinary involvement, and population services as a significant component of social development. Stein's international experience was especially helpful in shaping the project and moving it through a series of demanding reviews within the US Department of State. In the end, the project was authorised for five years, with sufficient funding to underwrite an office and a salaried international staff. That was when I left the Council to become Secretary-General of the IASSW.

The organisation of an independent secretariat in a building in New York across from the UN was one of the most important events in the history of the IASSW. The official opening on 1 July 1971, celebrated the culmination of years of hope and months of planning. Many legal problems had to be resolved, particularly the problem of acquiring an incorporated legal status as a non-governmental organisation. The involvement of board members around the world in this new endeavour, the recruitment of professional and supporting staff, and appointment of expert groups to advise on the implementation of the project were demanding tasks made easier with the help of Herman's organisational experience and management knowledge and skills.

Throughout his years as president and member of the board, the name of Herman Stein appears again and again as a major speaker at the International Congresses of Schools of Social Work, as a summariser of seminars and expert groups, and as the chairman of a variety of special committees and meetings. One of his most memorable contributions, however, falls again in the realm of diplomacy. With the adoption of a new constitution containing a specific reference to the principle of non-discrimination as stated in the Universal Declaration of Human Rights (United Nations, 1948), the membership status of South African schools of social work came under review. The Joint Universities Committee on Social Work of South Africa, with which all the schools were affiliated, was represented on the Board of Directors. At a meeting held in Trondheim, Norway, in 1973, the Board set conditions that had to be accepted by the Joint Universities Committee and its member schools in order to remain in membership. In essence, this was a form of probation, requiring plans for implementing the stipulated changes along with regular reports of progress.

The problem was compounded by the potential loss of IASSW consultative status with UNESCO if the South African schools remained as members. Dr Stein travelled to South Africa, ostensibly as a guest lecturer, but with instructions to obtain first-hand information from educators and others relevant to the questions faced by the IASSW in charting future action. Appeals from South African colleagues who were fighting the system to support their efforts against apartheid made a strong case for remaining connected. On the other hand, strong abhorrence of apartheid and racism in any form made it difficult for Board members to reach consensus on a course of action. The conditions set continued to be monitored through regular reports of progress, but the issue remained contentious until the end of apartheid. There was one immediate positive outcome of Herman's trip to South Africa. In testimony at a meeting with officials at UNESCO, his description of the actions taken by the IASSW Board were sufficiently compelling to remove the threat of loss of consultative status, which would have had an adverse effect on IASSW's relationship with other UN organisations.

Many other examples of leadership in the social work profession could be cited. Some of a different order than those already mentioned include his association with Mayor Carl Stokes of Cleveland, with a prominent industrialist on management problems, with fellow scholars at the Center for Advanced Study in the Behavioral Sciences at Stanford University, and in numerous endeavours with representatives of other professions. Those activities along with the public lectures he arranged with outstanding speakers on global issues projected a strong image of social work competence, thus enhancing the status of social work as a profession.

Honours and awards

Dr Stein's outstanding service and qualities have been widely recognised. Among his many honours, he particularly prizes the University Medal awarded by Case Western Reserve University – the highest honour the University can bestow. Given only once before to a faculty member, the award recognises leadership, service and dedication. The Columbia

University School of Social Work, at a celebration of its Centennial, inducted him into its hall of fame, honouring illustrious alumni. Smith College, where he also served on the faculty, recognised his achievements with a named award.

Professional organisations have been equally appreciative of his contributions. He was one of the early recipients of an annual lifetime achievement award established by CSWE. NASW followed with its lifetime achievement award. He was also one of the early recipients of the Katherine A. Kendall Award, established by IASSW for distinguished lifetime contributions to international social work education. ICSW bestowed on him its prestigious René Sand Award for his contributions to international social welfare and social development.

Final word

Fortunately, Herman's surpassing achievements and outstanding qualities have been seasoned by a quick wit and a robust sense of humour. His talents as an actor, carried over from his early flirtation with the theatre, were on display whenever he could be persuaded to declaim one of the side-splitting monologues that he created in his lighter moments. It was my good fortune to have the help of his wit in fashioning skits that gently satirised curriculum concerns or other issues of the day that became a feature of the annual meetings of CSWE in the 1950s and 1960s.

This portrait of Herman D. Stein can be summed up in a few final words. He has brought honour to the social work profession, not only in the USA but throughout the world. His intelligence and creativity together with his knowledge and experience have had a lasting impact on social work and social work education. His world view and lifetime of international service have made a significant contribution to many programmes that make this a better world for scores of men, women, and children. In sum, Herman Stein represents, at home and abroad, the best that social work has to offer in commitment to social justice, positive social change, and in competent professional performance.

Selected publications[7]
Stein, H. D. (ed) (1966) *Social perspectives on behavior: A reader in social science for social work and related professions*, New York: The Free Press, 1966.
Stein, H. D. (ed) (1968) *Social theory and social invention*, Cleveland, OH: Press of Case Western Reserve University.

Stein, H. D. (ed) (1969) *The crisis in welfare in Cleveland. Report of the Mayor's Commission* (Mayor's Commission on the Crisis in Welfare), Cleveland, OH: Case Western Reserve University.

Stein, H. D. (ed) (1981) *Organization and the human services: Cross-disciplinary reflections,* Philadelphia, PA: Temple University Press.

Stein, H. D. (2003) *Challenge and change in social work education: Towards a world view, selected papers* (edited by N. D. Aronoff), Alexandria, VA: Council on Social Work Education.

Notes

1. (GAA&MP) First published in 2005 in *Social Work & Society*, 3(2): 273-281, www.socwork.net/sws/article/view/103/392. We have added some explanatory footnotes, designated by our initials (GAA&MP). Katherine A. Kendall's original footnotes are designated by her initials (KAK).

2. (KAK) In addition to the sources cited, material for this portrait has come from my personal papers and a variety of documents related to Herman Stein that I have written.

3. (GAA&MP) UNESCO: A UN organization, operating as a charity in many countries, providing humanitarian and developmental assistance to children and mothers in developing countries. It was originally founded in 1946 to provide emergency food and healthcare in countries affected by World War II.

4. (KAK) Here, I must insert a personal note. As Secretary-General of IASSW, I was responsible for managing the biennial International Congress of Schools of Social Work held in Nairobi, Kenya, in summer 1974. Herman, our President with a heavy schedule of assignments, was in Tanzania on his annual visit. Unfortunately for him and for IASSW, he was hit by an automobile, sustaining injuries that prevented his joining us. Such are the hazards of international work!

5. (GAA&MP) UN public health agency.

6. (GAA&MP) UN agency concerned with defeating hunger.

7. (GAA&MP) Katherine Kendall's original article did not include selected publications. We have selected documents that represent a range of Professor Stein's interests, including a posthumous edition of selected papers.

SEVEN

Robin Huws Jones, 1996

Author: Katherine A. Kendall[1]

Robin Huws Jones, President of IASSW from 1976 to 1980, lived a life of challenge and change. Born in Wales in 1909, he often remarked that learning to speak Welsh at age two was such a challenge that he didn't bother to learn English until he was six. The death of his mother when he was three led to the first of many changes in a life that was not easy in the formative years. Robin remained in the care of his father while his sister became the ward of two aunts. With his father, a draper's assistant, he left Wales to live in a crowded boarding house in Liverpool.

Learning English did indeed pose a challenge. He managed the spoken language, but his efforts to apply the very different phonetic principles of the Welsh language to English spelling led to his undoing at age 15 when the time came to be considered for education beyond the required minimum. His headmaster would not let him sit as a candidate, far less take the examination leading to higher education. However, a job in the library of the Central Young Men's Christian Association in Liverpool fortunately gave him the opportunity to read widely and begin a successful programme of self-education. It was in this position, too, that he began to display the talents and temperament characteristic of his life work in forging social policy and promoting social action. He organised discussion groups and summer camps for unemployed young dock workers who turned up at the library, and befriended the homeless old men who came to get warm and read the newspapers, often visiting them when they ended, ill and alone, in hospitals.

Academic achievements

Omnivorous reading in his idle hours at the library finally prepared him to take examinations that led to a BSc external degree from the University of London. This was just the beginning of his self-directed academic achievements. With the encouragement of the Director of

Statistics at Liverpool University, who recognised his potential, he embarked on a three-year course leading to an MSc in social science, while maintaining himself through part-time teaching at the University.

His masters thesis on the nutrition of north country schoolboys revealed a shocking discrepancy in the medical assessments of malnutrition that were used to establish eligibility for free school meals. The painstaking care of his research and its surprising results created a sensation. He was invited to read a paper on its findings before the Royal Statistical Society, which awarded him its Francis Wood Memorial Prize. At age 27, the little Welsh boy who at age 15 was not regarded as eligible for higher education was elected the youngest Fellow of the prestigious Royal Statistical Society. His research made possible the development and use of scientific standards for measuring childhood malnutrition.

After several years on the research staff of Liverpool University, where he lectured in the social science department, he was invited by Oxford University to serve as an extra-mural tutor in eastern and northern England. In addition to teaching adult education courses, he was involved in organizing cultural activities in the communities he visited. During World War II he went to the airfields surrounding his base in Lincoln to hold discussions with young pilots in training from many countries. He particularly enjoyed talking about social policy proposals for the post-war world, particularly the Beveridge Report (1942) with its recommendations for a national health service. His interest in social policy and social reform became linked to education for social work when, in 1949, he accepted the position of Director of the Social Studies Department of the University of Wales, Swansea.

The Swansea experience

University courses in social studies and social administration in this period served as an academic base, both for further professional education or immediate employment in social work. Each university made its own decision as to the content, within a generally accepted framework, but most often the curriculum included social administration, economics, philosophy, psychology, and sociology. While there was no agreed-upon content relevant to social work, social administration courses usually provided an introduction to the various branches of the profession and required some form of practice experience.

It was at Swansea that Robin displayed a singular quality already suggested in the struggles of his early years and distinctly evident later throughout his career. No obstacle was too great to be overcome.

If there was an unmet need, something must be done about it. The Swansea experience illustrates the way in which he responded to a need in social work education and a challenge in social reform.

It was also at Swansea that he formed a partnership with Dame Eileen Younghusband, whose friendship had a significant impact on his career. He invited Dame Eileen, who was involved with the Social Affairs Department of the United Nations, to serve as an external examiner for the Swansea course. She told him of the urgent need for a qualified faculty for the emerging programmes of social work education in the developing world and for leadership of newly established social welfare programmes.

Huws Jones responded with the first and only course in the early 1950s devoted entirely to the further training of social work teachers, practitioners and social welfare administrators from third world countries. With only one additional staff member but with considerable help from other university departments in Swansea and staff support from the University of Wales, Cardiff, he launched a highly successful programme. By the time it ended, some 60 countries had participated, ranging from Portugal and Greece in Europe to countries in the Middle and Far East, southeast Asia, the Caribbean, and Africa.

Upon hearing about the course, Julia Henderson, Director of the Bureau of Social Affairs of the United Nations, was sufficiently interested to visit Swansea personally to check it out for possible use in their technical assistance programme. A significant UN activity of that period consisted of fellowships to produce teachers, trainers, and practitioners in social work and social welfare programmes. Her positive impression of his leadership and the content of the international course resulted in UN support of many of the overseas students. Challenged by the educational and cultural diversity in each new class, Huws Jones made a special effort to broaden the training beyond academic study. The students not only interacted as a group but learned to appreciate difference through a brief period of living with families in Welsh villages. They also participated in local community events, ranging from political meetings to attendance at soccer matches or, if so inclined, at the chapels that gave religion a special Welsh flavour. A brief period in London was arranged to observe new developments in the social services, and to visit the Houses of Parliament, where they sometimes had discussions with political luminaries. Dame Eileen Younghusband proved extremely helpful in the conduct of the international course and indirectly contributed to Robin's second notable achievement in Swansea.

In 1955, Robin Huws Jones was named vice-chairman [sic] of a prestigious working party established by the Ministry of Health to make recommendations for the staffing of the welfare services provided by local authorities. As it was chaired by Dame Eileen, it became known as the Younghusband Committee. On his frequent trips to London for Committee meetings, Robin became more and more aware of the appalling scenes of industrial devastation in the lower Swansea Valley. He described it in these words:

> There were great hillocks of toxic waste, poisoning the earth and the atmosphere so that not a blade of grass or even moss grew. This grim landscape was strewn with the ruins of industrial buildings. A lifeless river wound through the valley. (Billups, 2002b, p 137)

Despite the failure of earlier attempts to revive the area, Robin took on the challenge of restoring the Valley to its former beauty and he succeeded. His faith in the positive outcomes of research took the form of a proposal to the University College to sponsor an interdisciplinary study of the Valley with a view to finding a means to its rehabilitation. With significant backing by the University, including eight of its departments, and financial support from government, foundations and industry, an ambitious programme of research, social action, and public education was launched.

Although Robin did not remain in Swansea to complete the lengthy and complicated process of restoring the Valley, he left the project in capable hands with committees representing a broad range of interest and support, including the University, national and local government, industry, and the press. The final report produced a host of recommendations that led, some 20 years later, to the transformation of what was a toxic desert into a parkland of trees with a clear river and green meadows. Some slag heaps remaining as a symbolic reminder of former industrial devastation highlighted the contrast with new industry that brought in modern factories and contributed socially as well as economically to the surrounding community.

While credit for this positive outcome can be spread in many directions, it was Robin who saw the need and acted to meet a seemingly impossible challenge. His role as the creator of the project was fittingly recognised by the University of Wales when it conferred upon him in 1984 the honorary degree of Doctor of Law. His work with overseas students was also deemed highly successful. In a letter recommending Robin Huws Jones for an IASSW award, Julia Henderson wrote:

> At the United Nations, we were impressed by the results of this course as seen in the successful careers of our fellows upon their return to their home country. (personal correspondence, Henderson, 1995)

With a grant from the Ford Foundation in 1958, Robin visited former students in Burma, India, Malaysia, Singapore, and the Middle East to assess the outcome of their educational experience. It was a gratifying relief to find that most of them had become leaders in social welfare and social work education in their countries. He remained in touch with a number of his former students throughout the rest of his life. The Huws Jones 1996 Christmas letter described his attendance at the International Congress of Schools of Social Work in Hong Kong which was followed by a visit to one of the former Swansea students in Malaysia. He said: ' ... then to Kuala Lampur [where] we found the same warm friendship and astonishing hospitality as eight years ago. We got to know Penang even better than last time' (personal correspondence, Huws Jones, 1996). Robin added to a natural talent for making friends a special gift as a correspondent whose newsy letters kept friendships warmly alive.

National Institute of Social Work Training (NISWT)

Robin Huws Jones' next challenge came in 1961 when he was asked to serve as the Principal of the newly established NISWT in London. Britain had long been shackled by a fragmented approach to the training of social workers. Basic social studies courses in universities and specialised training for specific fields of practice did not begin to meet the need for the vast majority of social workers required for burgeoning health and welfare services throughout the UK. To remedy what was called a crisis in the staffing of those services, the Working Party established by the Ministry of Health produced a series of innovative recommendations that strongly affected the structure and content of British social work education.

The Younghusband Report (1959), named for Dame Eileen who chaired the Working Party, proposed two avenues to the preparation of qualified social workers, plus systematic in-service training for welfare assistants. Courses in universities would be continued, to provide professional education, but additional two-year courses related to but outside the universities would be established to provide a general training for more competent service in the local branches of health and welfare programmes. With later developments, the apparent distinction between professional and general social work training disappeared. At the time, however, the two-year courses were launched as pilot programmes in colleges of further education.

The daunting problems involved in starting and staffing the new educational venture were to a degree resolved by another recommendation that created the National Institute of Social Work Training, informally described as a 'staff college'. Robin Huws Jones refused the first invitation to head the Institute. Besides being heavily involved with the international training course and the Swansea Project, he did not think he had the right academic qualifications to lead a social work organization. Others disagreed and prodded by foundations interested in funding the new organization, he finally was persuaded to serve as the first Principal of NISWT.

This new challenge took him and his family to Tavistock Place in London, where, thanks to purchase by the Nuffield Foundation, the Institute was centrally located in the Mary Ward House, the former residence of a well-known Settlement. The Joseph Rowntree Memorial Trust also contributed with the Nuffield Foundation in underwriting support for the first ten years. Robin noted the importance of assured financing in giving NISWT '… a degree of independence, the chance to experiment, the opportunity to respond quickly, the feeling that one didn't always have to play safe' (Huws Jones, 1971: p 95).

He enthusiastically embarked on this new venture with his wife, Enid, an important partner in all his activities, and their three children. The family was installed in a flat on the top floor of the Institute. With the warm hospitality that emanated from that household and the myriad activities underway throughout the building, NISWT soon became a haven for international visitors and a centre for the exploration of new ideas. In fact, a key objective was stated as '… progressively becoming a centre of information, for research, and for meetings, discussions and conferences between senior administrators, social workers, academics and members of other professions' (Younghusband, 1978: p 87).

Two major objectives were given immediate attention. The terms of reference for NISWT called for pioneering the new two-year courses in colleges of further education and organizing a course within the Institute to prepare social work faculty for those courses. Eileen Younghusband signed on as a consultant with development of the educational programmes of the Institute as a major responsibility. The partnership they developed as a team requires a brief description of Eileen's contribution to the NISWT programme. With her expert knowledge of social work education and his skill in dealing with broad issues involving challenges and change, the two were ideally suited to the launching of a new and possibly controversial endeavour.

As a first order of business, consultation visits were scheduled throughout the United Kingdom to educate the profession and health and welfare officials in the local social services on the benefits of the new approach to social work training. As noted, Robin excelled at this kind of activity. Radiating commitment and enthusiasm, he had a way of making any project seem exciting and achievable with everyone involved in it highly valued as a participant. Sir Peter Barclay portrayed well this characteristic in the obituary published in the *Guardian*. He noted Robin's strong commitment to 'citizen participation' and described his tenure at the Institute in these words:

> From 1961 to 1972, as principal, Robin was at the height of his influence, a smiling quietly-spoken manipulator, whose energy, charm, and persuasiveness it was hard to resist. (Barclay, 2001)

For Dame Eileen, setting up the courses was a golden opportunity to put into practice her ideas on the differing levels and content of social work education as presented in *Training for Social Work: Third International Survey* (United Nations, 1958). This landmark study, which she conducted for the UN, outlined the rationale for several levels of social work preparation in developed as well as developing countries and described in great detail the basic body of knowledge, and skills to be incorporated in educational programmes, regardless of the academic level. The different courses developed within the Institute as well as the two-year courses in the colleges of further education all reflected her guidance on essential content, teaching methods, patterns of learning, field practice, use of supervision, and relations with students. It is not surprising that the NISWT training offered by the colleges became known as the 'Younghusband Courses'.

Robin's interest in research guaranteed a strong emphasis on enquiries into a wide range of topics bearing not only on questions of education, but on fields of practice, the effectiveness of social policies, the organization and administration of services, and much more. Throughout his career, Robin complained about the lack of objective evidence of the positive outcomes of social work practice. His commitment to objective and systematic studies also attracted highly-skilled staff members who undertook action-research projects to demonstrate the value of new methods of social work practice. In every research project, emphasis was placed on using and testing the findings in social work education and practice.

Group work and community work as social work methods, for example, were not well-developed in British social work education. Robin saw the need and found the resources to demonstrate their value through an action-research project involving services for old people in the London Borough of Southwark. The interest generated and the results achieved led to the employment of community workers with salaries paid from funds raised for that specific purpose. Publication of the findings of NISWT projects had the desired result of focusing more attention on research in the programmes of professional social work education.

Given Huws Jones' experience with the Swansea course for overseas students and Younghusband's global connections, the Institute inevitably became a vibrant international centre. Visitors, students, and scholars came from every continent, but senior Fulbright teachers and researchers may have been the most deeply involved in NISWT programmes. Robin and Eileen had both visited the United States and found certain aspects of American social work education worthy of adoption. The two-year courses developed for the colleges of further education and the special courses for potential teachers both reflected approaches to curriculum building and teaching methods that Eileen, in particular, found useful. The Fulbright scholars had the privilege of teaching in the new courses while gaining new insights from a different educational experience. The international atmosphere at the Institute contributed to Robin's involvement with IASSW.

The IASSW experience

Robin attended his first International Congress of Schools of Social Work in 1956 while still at Swansea. On a personal note, I must describe our first meeting in which he revealed many of the qualities that foretold future leadership. As the recently elected Secretary with responsibility as a volunteer for administering the Association, I found the task of organizing my first International Congress rather overwhelming. The German schools, purged of Nazi staff and content, had been readmitted to membership in the IASSW. Although not overtly stated, holding the Congress in Munich carried a message of reconciliation. Awareness of the ambivalent feelings of some of the European delegates called for diplomatic handling of certain group activities. Robin, with his greater knowledge of European educators, took charge as I struggled with different combinations of leaders, secretaries, and participants to ensure harmonious teamwork in the workshops following plenary sessions. He helped to organize the groups, ushered the participants to their appointed places, and, in general, saved the reputation of the new and inexperienced Secretary.

His influence at that meeting helped to bring about the postwar restoration of the IASSW after World War II as a fully functioning international organization. It also marked him clearly for future leadership roles. At the General Assembly of school representatives, he spoke from the floor with such enthusiastic conviction about the need for a strong and effective international voice for social work education that the delegates unanimously accepted a series of Board proposals. Important changes included a revision of the By-laws, a substantial increase in dues, and a membership campaign. His appointment to chair an international membership committee followed almost immediately. In 1970, he was elected Treasurer, which he wryly noted was probably due to his reputation as a 'beggar with charitable foundations' (Billups, 2002d, p 139). His major contributions to IASSW, however, came during his tenure as President from 1976 to 1980.

All of the presidents with whom I worked from 1954 to 1978 were immensely talented, but Robin Huws Jones excelled at chairing meetings and encouraging the kind of discussion that ends in consensus. Personal qualities of charm, decency, and a ready wit had much to do with his performance but most important were his understanding of the issues under discussion and a genuine desire to hear and consider all points of view. To arrive at what was best for all concerned, which was always his goal, every voice must be heard. He also knew when to set limits to keep discussions from becoming gabfests.

During his tenure, he faced a serious problem that divided the Board and derailed his usual push for consensus. Even his special talent in handling controversial subjects could not produce general agreement on how to deal with the issue of apartheid in social work education in South Africa. The schools of social work had a long history of membership, having joined through their national association shortly after the founding of the IASSW. In the 1960s and 1970s, abhorrence of apartheid and all forms of racism led to an examination of membership criteria.

Herman Stein, who preceded Robin as President, obtained first-hand information in a visit to South Africa on positive efforts by certain schools and educators in outflanking discriminatory policies and working toward abolition of the system. The Board had to decide whether to expel all South African schools from membership or find a way to work with those that were struggling against heavy odds to rid their country of a national evil. A majority vote establishing a probationary status with conditions to be monitored through regular reports of progress kept the IASSW connected with the forces for change. However, that did not satisfy certain Scandinavian countries, whose representatives demanded that all the South African schools be excluded from membership. The issue remained contentious until the end of apartheid. Robin dealt with other serious controversies during his four years as IASSW president, but this was the only one that jolted his equanimity.

Robin excelled as an administrator and made substantial contributions as an educator, but he always regarded social policy as his major area of expertise. This made his involvement in a population and family planning project directed by the IASSW a source of tremendous personal interest and satisfaction. From 1972 to 1978 he served as the chairman of an Interdisciplinary Resource Group consisting of 25 outstanding experts in all aspects of population policy and its implementation. With representation from the United Nations Fund for Population Activities (UNFPA), the UN Commission for Social Development, International Planned Parenthood (IPPF), other leading non-governmental organizations in the population field, and a variety of disciplines, the meetings demanded a high level of skill in the chair. The Secretary-General of IPPF voiced the general opinion when she described his performance as 'brilliant'.

Designed to prepare qualified social work manpower for a more effective contribution to population and family planning activities, the project involved a close working relationship with pilot schools in 13 developing countries and a less formal connection with cooperating schools in seven countries. In addition to chairing the Resource Group, Robin played an active role, particularly in Asia, in monitoring progress and evaluating results. His visits to participating countries usually followed the provision of consultation by interdisciplinary teams on curriculum building. He was in his element, helping to establish new working relationships with health services and organizations concerned with social and economic development. At its final meeting in 1977, the Resource Group judged the results, especially in Asia, as highly successful. Robin's belief in the programme, his skill in relating school programmes to community needs, along with his enthusiasm and talents as an advocate, made a major contribution to the positive outcome.

It was during Robin Huws Jones's tenure as President that I retired and IASSW was faced with the necessity of vacating its long-time base in the United States. Invitations from Belgium and Austria set in motion a complicated series of negotiations involving site visits and discussions with possible sponsors. With substantial help from the Austrian representative on the IASSW Board and Robin's skill in working out a mutually satisfying agreement, the secretariat moved to Vienna in 1978. The lengthy process involved frequent visits to Vienna to meet with industrialists, possible financial backers, and officials at the highest level of government. It also involved linking the work of IASSW to the mission of the United Nations Department of Humanitarian and Social Affairs that had been relocated from New York to the newly established United Nations City in Vienna. Robin Huws Jones's ability to inspire confidence in the worth of IASSW as an international force in promoting social justice was a major factor in the successful relocation of the secretariat. He often referred with delight of his pleasure in signing the agreement with the Austrian government in the famous room with seven doors where the celebrated Treaty of Vienna had been signed.

Relations with foundations and ministerial committees

The personal qualities that made Robin Huws Jones so effective in the chair and as an advocate led to his appointment to a number of power-packed committees appointed by various ministries concerned with the structure and staffing of the social services. The Younghusband Committee appointed by the Ministry of Health, which produced NISWT, was the most important in terms of his career. From 1965 to 1968 he served on the equally prestigious Seebohm Committee (1968), which was likened to the Beveridge Committee for the breadth of its vision in promoting social well-being.

Appointed by four ministries to review the organization and responsibilities of the social services provided by local authorities, the Committee produced a landmark report that led to revolutionary change in meeting the social needs of individuals, families and communities. The Local Authority Social Services Act passed in 1970 authorised the establishment of new social service departments to provide unified community based and family oriented service to be available to all. Robin's message on citizen participation and the need for research with interdisciplinary involvement if services are to be effective came through clearly in the Seebohm Report. The *Guardian* obituary described his major role in these words: 'It was Robin who briefed the chairman [sic], held the ring, negotiated, supported and acted as advocate to ensure a good outcome' (Barclay, 2001).

His pioneering work at NISWT and in Swansea together with his leadership in the two national committees that reorganised social work and social work education led to his nomination for a CBE, an honour awarded by Queen Elizabeth in 1969.

The pioneering work that marked Robin's career could not have been undertaken and carried through to success without private as well as public financial support. The Swansea initiative early earned him a reputation for visionary leadership that appealed to foundations and other donors with social causes. Indeed, it was pressure from the Nuffield and Rowntree Foundations that persuaded him to change his mind about accepting the position as Principal of NISWT. The many research, demonstration, and other projects launched by the Institute were financed by grants that Robin was able to obtain from governmental and non-governmental sources.

The Joseph Rowntree Memorial Trust became a major source of help throughout Robin's career and a close association continued to the end of his life. He joined their staff as Associate Director when he left NISWT in 1972 and was retained as a consultant upon his retirement in 1978. Much of his work as President of the IASSW from 1976 to 1980 was made possible with help from the Trust which also brought to fruition a visionary plan he and Dame Eileen had shared about how to live happily in retirement.

The retirement years

Moving from the noisy bustle of London to the quiet beauty of the Lake [District] introduced Robin and Enid to a new life of rural pleasures. Their retirement house had all the charm of a centuries-old cottage but with the added conveniences of the modern age. Robin became an avid gardener, producing an amazing assortment of vegetables, fruits and flowers. The considerable bounty was shared with neighbours, who also looked forward to the strawberry festival that became a Huws Jones annual tradition.

Although cultivating a garden and exploring the hills and valleys of new surroundings offered an enjoyable experience, Robin continued in retirement to pursue a busy schedule of activities. This was the period when, as President of IASSW, he travelled extensively for the population project and exploration of a new home for the secretariat. He also continued to serve on committees, national and local, with some major assignments, such as membership on the Chief Scientist's Committee of the Department of Health and Social Security.

This was also the period when he had time to work on a proposal, initiated originally by Dame Eileen, for a new type of retirement community. On several visits to the USA, they both had occasion to visit retired friends in continuing care retirement communities, a model of supportive living very different from traditional homes for the aged. Designed for independent living with an abundance of amenities, they also offered the security of health care to the end of life. For Robin and Eileen, a special virtue lay in the contribution to positive ageing made through social interaction with fellow residents, involvement in every type of learning activity, attention to physical fitness, and participation in communal events.

Robin faced his final challenge in this effort to launch a British version of the American model he and Eileen so much admired. He again found a sympathetic response in the Rowntree Memorial Trust,[2] which with his help established the Hartrigg Oaks Continuing Care Retirement Community in York, the first of its kind in Britain. Robin and Enid Huws Jones promptly entered the new community that, to their delight, lived up to expectations. And that is where their long and productive lives both came to an end in 2001.

Final word

Robin Huws Jones will long be remembered for his able and inspiring leadership in a period of transition for IASSW. His endearing personal qualities along with his ability to work with change as a positive force and his dedication to the highest values of the social work profession enabled the Association to advance social work education worldwide, to introduce innovative approaches, and to promote social justice. Those talents, so abundantly shared, were recognised by the IASSW at its Congress in Hong Kong in 1996 when he received the Katherine A. Kendall Award for a lifetime of outstanding achievement and distinguished international service to social work education.

Selected publications[3]

Huws Jones, R. (1970) 'Social values and social work education', in K. A. Kendall (ed) *Social work values in an age of discontent*, New York: Council on Social Work Education: pp 35-45.

Huws Jones, R. (1971) *The doctor and the social services*, London: Athlone.

Notes

[1] (GAA&MP) First published in 2006 in *Social Work & Society*, 4(2): pp 341-350, www.socwork.net/sws/article/view/163/223.

[2.] (GAA&MP) Renamed the Joseph Rowntree Foundation in 1990.

[3.] (GAA&MP) Katherine Kendall's original article did not include selected publications. We have selected documents that represent Robin Huws Jones' publications.

EIGHT

María del Carmen Mendoza Rangel (Mariacarmen Mendoza), 1998

Interviewed by Bertha Mary Rodríguez Villa

Biography

 María del Carmen Mendoza Rangel's (b. 1947) career-defining post was as Professor of Community Development, Social Work Theory and Practice at the National Autonomous University of Mexico (ENTS-UNAM). She grew up in Uruapan, Michoacán, México. Her education led to a bachelors degree in social work and a masters in pedagogy. Her community and social work experience included rural, indigenous and urban settings. Important parts of her professional career were devoted to education, to work in local and regional community development projects within civil society organizations and civic education within Mexico City's government. For international use, she prefers her surname to be presented as Mendoza, and her preferred forename in interpersonal contacts is Mariacarmen; these names are used in the remainder of the book.

What has the award meant to you?

At the time, it was highly significant, especially because I was the first social worker in Latin America to receive it, the first Mexican and the first woman. It was something, which made us really proud, also because I was awarded the prize for Mexican social work. I have always said that I am part of a social work movement in which a group of colleagues constituted the *Asociación de Trabajadores Sociales Mexicanos* (ATSMAC: Mexican Association of Social Workers) in 1982. Since then, we have somehow taken on another professional dimension.

It was also very important that the recognition was assumed to be a university prize, and there were lots of different reactions to it. It was widely publicized around the university. They interviewed me and published the interviews in the university gazette and in a few national newspapers. At the time, I was working for Mexico City's *Asamblea Legislativa* [legislative assembly] as social policy advisor to the Democratic Revolution Party's parliamentary group. Through ATSMAC, I achieved recognition among colleagues and friends.

Congratulatory letters on the award arrived from people I did not know, especially women, notable in some branches of science or public administration. They were heads of department, or government secretaries, who have to show their recognition of equal opportunities. Merely by being a woman, people are obliged to recognize you, especially in university media. The award is often mentioned to social work students and has been widely publicized as one reason for Mexican social work pride.

Within the family, too, it was wonderful.

What activities were of major importance for your professional career and its impact on social work education?

I had a key international experience, by writing a booklet on methods for systematizing social processes published in Peru and El Salvador. It was an in-house publication illustrated with little dolls, using all the methods of system development. It became widely used in the field of people's education.

Later, I published the book *Una opción metodológica para trabajadores sociales* ['A theoretical approach to community practice'], which *Editorial Latinoamericana* published in Argentina. This text had considerable impact in Latin America. It also came into the hands of a college of storytellers in Argentina who began writing to me, and I maintained contact with them for a long time.

While I was secretary-general of ATSMAC, we were invited by the Latin American Centre for Social Work (CELATS) to organize the Latin American Seminar for Social Workers in Mexico in 1983. We decided then to call a meeting of trade unions within the Forum. At the meeting, the decision was made to promote the *Federación Latinoamericana de Trabajadores Sociales* [Latin American Social Workers' Federation], and to go ahead and form regional organizations. We, as members of ATSMAC, together with the Nicaraguan Association and colleagues from Venezuela and Costa Rica, filled the roles of regional co-ordinators of the social work organizations in Mexico,

Central America and the Caribbean. I was chosen secretary-general for the Second Management Committee, so I had the opportunity to promote organizational work in the region and to organize regional meetings in Mexico and Cuba.

Another area of my international work was adult education. It is one area to which I have become attached and committed myself. Within the *Consejo de Educación de Adultos de América Latina* [CEAAL: Latin American Council for Adult Education], I was the regional director for Mexico from 1997 to 2000, a role which gave me a whole host of duties, including producing texts and plans for community education.

What were your biggest contributions to social work and its education?

I think community social work influences two areas of adult education: civic education and popular education. My view is that social work gives a strong methodological support to adult education.

When tropical storm 'Javier' affected a large part of the south of the country in 1998, a foundation arrived in Chiapas to support aid projects in devastated areas. They commented that projects were not at all fully planned, neither regional projects nor a complete plan had been proposed, and no one was sure whom to work with. As the whole of the Chiapas coastal region was affected, we, a local organization, had asked to work on a complete, multi-dimension project. We were prepared for it, told them we were ready and agreed to embark upon it immediately. We started working through the civil organization *Servicio Desarrollo y Paz* [SEDEPAC: Service for Progress and Peace] on regional development processes. These included aspects of production, health and home affairs, as well as working with sponsoring organizations on training and extending intervention methods, which we as social workers had worked so hard to develop.

What has social work and its education meant to you professionally? Why did you choose it?

It is what I have spent my whole life doing. I have been giving classes for 43 years now. I have never left teaching, but have gone away to work elsewhere. For 15 years, I worked in civil society organizations and then in public administration, within the government of Mexico City. We were launching the project *Escuelas Ciudadanas de Educación Cívic* [Civic Education for Citizens] for adults' and educational experience that crystallized wonderfully at that time. This was because social workers have a different approach to how to deal with problems of real life. Since we carry out practical work throughout our training, it helps us not to separate theory and practice.

Putting all together, I might say I have devoted my profession to what is now called life education for adults, meaning civic education and education for critical consciousness, closely related to my links with the university.

I began to teach while still at the social work school. I was in my final semester, and a person came to ask someone to organize a group for working in the Valle del Mezquital. The school practice office recommended David Basurto. He then said to me, 'Help me, because I cannot go every week'. He was a painter, and exhibited his work every fortnight. So, I would supervise the students in the practice group instead of him.

That was how I got immediately into teaching, and I loved it. In 1973, they called upon me, and since then I have been fully involved with social work teaching.

The other area, adult education, I decided to devote my life to it because I liked the work I had begun to do within civil organizations and the social work association. It was then that we decided to make our marks upon social work. Under our motto, 'Serving the community sector through scientific social work', we began to work frequently with community groups and with organizations. Maria Luisa Herrasti (1943–2003) [social work teacher and urban community development expert], Martin Longoria [social work urban community development expert and legislator] and I embarked upon a community school project, reflecting Friere's ideas, together with colleagues from other civil organizations. We have since worked on that basis. We opened adult education centres, schools set up on behalf of municipal sponsors, to facilitate citizens, human rights organizations, law centres and anyone with an urge to train people. Their aims are to help people in identifying requirements and drawing up plans and projects, getting them off the ground and assessing them.

What were the challenges of social work and its education?

At the time I received the award, attention to emergencies was very important. I was in the US when Hurricane Mitch struck, because the American Friends Service Committee had invited me to form a forum on methods for adult education. The background was that we had created a forum in Nicaragua and another in Mexico, which had some very good results. They then invited civil organizations to the US and sought me out to work with them.

There we were during the hurricane, people from Venezuela, Costa Rica, Panama and from the affected area. We could reflect on what was happening, and what was about to come. Then with the experience of Chiapas, we brought in people who, following Mitch, had signed agreements and set up bases for education during the emergency process.

It was then that I decided on environmental issues as my major goals since, every day, disastrous effects are going to be seen in communities, especially in the poorest ones. It is an area that requires attention. You have to provide education on caring for the environment and ensuring that projects and processes concentrate on the world around us.

In Chiapas, we divided the SEDEPAC project into two work areas. In one, we conceived an interactive method, in which committees were appointed by the community, by the geographic area and by the region. The committees from the entire coastal region came together and became involved with devising the project, from initial assessment onwards. We met with them every month to assess the work. The process was put together jointly and was fundamental for its success.

Two sponsors for each community helped us sustain the project, and that was extraordinary. We got there one day, high up in the mountains and someone asked us: 'Where have you come from?' We told him, from Mexico City. He then said: 'I am the SEDEPAC sponsor', which touched us because that was the organization we represented.

The other work area was training in civic affairs. In Chiapas, processes for community elections were advanced, like those in the government elections. In those areas, political parties had become less credible over the previous decade. Community groups that were aware of democratic election processes had independent candidates, but were not political groups. Neither had they experience, so it became clear that there was a real need to train people for government participation. With Maria Luisa Herrasti, from the *Centro de Estudios Municipales* [CESEM: Municipal Study Centre], and from *Centro Operacional de Vivienda y Poblamiento* [COPEVI: Action Centre for Housing and Population], a lot of training was done, another area in which I was involved.

What was the importance of international work in your career?

It really opened up my career prospects. I consider myself fortunate to have had so many opportunities in social work. Initially, I was invited to the *Centro Latinoamericano de Trabajo Social* [CELATS: Latin American Social Work Centre], to take part in the workshops it was organizing in Peru and Brazil. Then, as the professional organizations' coordinator, I had the opportunity to get to know the region: Venezuela, Nicaragua and Costa Rica. I was in Cuba, where I was responsible for organizing the *V Encuentro Regional de Trabajo Social* [Fifth Regional Social Work Forum] in Havana. I met with the whole cabinet of the Cuban government, who constituted the organizing committee and were included in the whole event, which lasted for four days. They remained seated in the presidium, gaining much respect.

It was a great chance to get to know and work in the region, acknowledge requirements and find differences between Mexican social work and that of other countries. We were a region with underdeveloped social work. In Cuba, I told my colleagues: 'Your social work task is very easy because what they ask you, is what you have to do. Elsewhere, capriciously, they ask for something, hoping that we will do somewhat else, and that makes life very difficult'. What we saw in Argentina, Uruguay and Brazil, and the theoretical work they have done and their degree of discussion and debate, even now surprises us.

When I was secretary-general of SEDEPAC, a German foundation, Bread for the World, financed a tour to present SEDEPAC projects. I had the opportunity to go to ten countries and spread the goals and prospects of Mexican organizations in the field of international cooperation. This experience was very good because, focusing on social work, we were able to have transparent discussions. There are alternative perspectives on what might be done. We were not going to ask for any financing and merely sought to explore understandings of poverty. I do not believe we have made further progress yet, because what we have to do is find solutions and seek alternatives that will really help. The German foundation liked the projects, and they were especially interested in the educational options.

I believe that the different areas and capacities in which I have worked have been highly significant and have enabled me to find out what is relevant and see things from a professional perspective.

In 2002, I was invited to the UN's *Programa de Gestión Urbana* [PGU: Urban Environmental Management Programme] to go to Ecuador, supporting the development of systems for drawing up a regional development plan for Cuenca. I was a system advisor and worked with a Latin American team. They would analyze information from the area and create the projects, and I would devise a structure for the whole experience. The project was crossdisciplinary as others were specialists in their fields. For them, it was surprising that someone from social work was going to establish a system for them, but people accepted it. Not everyone gets that experience and the capacity to make progress and devise a system for generating information. It was a great experience!

What major obstacles have you faced in your career?

Maybe I did not take them into account. I see obstacles as part of the job and always try to direct my energy in productive directions. When I began teaching social work at the National Autonomous University of Mexico (ENTS-UNAM), I knew that I would not want to leave teaching ever, no matter that I had a full-time position within the government of Mexico City. For me, for both my tasks, linking theory and practice were important for my professional development and my ideology.

In fieldwork for adult education for citizens, I do not think I have encountered any obstacles. That is because we learn to teach, like Paulo Freire,[1] with what was there, under a tree, with a twig drawing everything on the ground. That has absolutely no meaning when thinking, I need a cubicle, a projector, a large screen. We have to find a make-or-break point; what we need in that situation is always to achieve something.

I have never felt any pressure when working with women, or men not allowing them to work, never, because I have always worked through organizations. With an organizational agreement, I draw up a training plan for women, and the husbands are not there to put the pressure on either of us. I have worked with a lot of respect from the organizations, and I cannot say that I have had any shortcomings in terms of resources or capital.

When I worked for the government, the main obstacles were of a political nature and I had to go against the flow but with the support of the manager, who is an adult education professional. We pioneered nearly two hundred schools in Mexico City working with COPEVI. Obstacles are part of a project, something to overcome in the same way as opportunities are there to be taken.

How has social work and its education changed?

As manager of the Publications Department at the *Escuela Nacional de Trabajo Social* [National School of Social Work] at ENTS-UNAM, I have been involved in coordinating reforms of the last two curriculum plans and reviewing the history of social work training. The two plans we have implemented have met the requirements of the time. However, I have told my students that a social work curriculum does not last more than ten years because the reality is changing very fast. Therefore, it is essential to include new content.

However, in social work schools we have not managed to go deeper into the idea of collective teacher efficacy (Ramos et al, 2014). One area we have worked on is practice, as practice teachers usually meet and organize themselves. They have four meetings each semester discussing content and methods, and thus they achieve something. Nevertheless, we have not managed to integrate the content from other areas. It is now important to get together those things that have not been taught properly in social work.

In 2003, when I was responsible for monitoring the progress of fulfilling the international commitments on adult education for the *Conferencia Internacional de Educación de Adultos* [CONFITEA: International Conference on Adult Education], an international comparative assessment was made in 20 countries. I was responsible for the Mexican one. In Mexico, the assessment was run by the *Consejo de Educación de Adultos de América Latina* (CEEAL). It was unbelievable, you arrived at government secretary level, you interviewed the secretary or a manager. The secretary would assign you someone to interview, but only when the word CONFITEA was mentioned. The managers did not know anything, and I believe that the international commitments are very important. They ignored in these international agreements the issues of human development. For example, in the case of older adults, we were asked not just to help them have a good death, but to encourage them to live well, a life exercizing their faculties and rights.

In the international commitments, there were a few suggestions which were alternatives to working with older adults, like working with women, with basic education, for example, basic literacy. Other commitments were also signed, including some on environment and gender. You can see how important social work is. If I had not been involved in the process, we would never have gained information about the international agreements, which have to be met. It would be great if we could implement them in the curriculum.

What is most important in social work is accepting that there are still lots of empty spaces that have not yet been discussed directly. The university where we devoted our lives to discussions in the square, in the full lecture theatres, that does not happen any longer, and the student community misses a lot of life. You have students who may score 10 because, with education as IT-oriented as it is, they know the formulae, but nothing else.

Here at the school, some workers from the *Sindicato Mexicano de Electricistas* [SME: Mexican Electricians' Syndicate] came to show the film *Viento negro* ['Black wind'], a very striking film about the railway workers' fight to build communication pathways and introduce them as a means of transport. The most striking expressions of collective experience were in such everyday, personal matters that, in a lecture theatre full of university students, you could not extract a target for public policy so it could be debated. Thus, there are social work students who do not see themselves in such human experiences. Of course, there are some in-depth discussions. You bring together a social work group and they do not leave for three hours, but it is rare.

The education system seeks to produce a subject, that is, someone who knows how to do things, who is not just a spectator, but who does not think, does not reason, and does not know how to distinguish one thing from another, and consequently, knows far less about how to deal with problems in real life.

Education brings this risk with it, because they want to set general university criteria on skills-based education, and unify the baccalaureate at a technical level. If that is permitted, it will be very serious for us. To date, the Rector of the University has rejected it.

As I said earlier, most people are what we call subject teachers. This means people who have another job and teach only one subject, which prevents them from devoting their time to interacting with their peers. Full-time professors are dedicated to their individual research projects, not taking part in integrating the content and pointing out the links between theory and practice. Researchers are in the corner on the third floor, and practice educators are in the perimeter on the first floor, and there is no way they can meet up; not merely a question of geography, but lack of connections.

What would you like to see happening in social work education in the future?

I would like the education to be in the hands of social workers. It will do no harm to other disciplines; we can cooperate with social scientists and professionals in other areas. However, cooperation means that, if I were to give classes in medicine, I would have to get involved in the doctors' training process. It does not depend on what I believe it should be like, but I would have to commit myself to their vision in their curriculum, its prospects, and what type of professionals they want to train.

Similarly, I would like to see social work education managers being at the helm of social work. That does not mean that others should be excluded, but we only accept managers who are committed to social work. That is not the case here because there is not much respect for the profession, as the belief is that social work is not important.

As I was saying earlier, we do have many goals, and the major goal for me is being able to bring about efficacy in teachers working together. At this university, for example, we have teachers' meetings, social work areas, practice, but there is no clear path to achieving the goals, which requires a lot of coordination. The activities are normally coordinated by teachers who do not even have any respect for social work. It is difficult, but that is the main goal. At the moment, we have more goals than strengths as teachers.

I would like experiences to be written down. Since the last director at ENTS-UNAM, the publishing process has changed completely. The possibility that any professor could publish has opened up and that selection should no longer be subject to administrative or political decisions. Now anyone can present an article or a book for editorial consideration. This change is helping us to provide different journals with social work material. A journal on migration, published at the school, has only one article on social work. All the others are by different specialists, who write about their field, and we want to avoid that.

Something else I wonder about is that we have so many opportunities to write, and yet there is nothing on social work education. There is hardly anything published, even though people directly involved in the field of practice have huge opportunities to retrieve information about social processes. That is why I proposed an edited book, written with practice supervisors, which is now published, to put all this information together to be shared.

I would like to see social work taking its place as an important discipline and being highly recognized in the social sciences, having an authorized voice and that voice being visible in publications. We always see ourselves as social workers only concerned with direct relationships with humans and working with the individual and the community. I am convinced that we can contribute a lot more to the major emergency we currently have on our hands, the building of humanity. This is certainly what I reiterate wherever I go.

I did not mention it particularly, but our discipline is a contribution towards building humanity. I consider training in this subject has stood out in adult education and in social theory. This is just the beginning of social work's future. Some time ago, someone from Argentina spoke at a conference about how a merely economic problem devastates all humankind because their whole world is in conflict, and we will then have to work with distressed people.

Many years ago, social theory studied how to direct work with individuals and groups towards the construction of collective subjectivity, working together to empower people. In Latin America too, there are people who are saying that now, this is more important than resolving a housing or health problem, to which we have devoted our lives. The housing problem might be a lower priority when the human being involved is being destroyed. I think we have to change lenses. We have conceptual frameworks and methods available, that is why we proposed the construction of the subject, the human being with capacity to act for themselves, as the primary purpose to lead us to build a new humanity. We have to incorporate this in social work training.

Selected publications

Mendoza, M. C. (1986[2006]) *Una Opción Metodológica para los Trabajadores Sociales* [*A theoretical approach to community practice*], Buenos Aires: Editorial Humanitas.

Mendoza, M. C. (2001) 'Popular education and the politics of identity: women's and indigenous peoples' movements', in L. Kane, *Popular education and social change in Latin América*, London: Latin American Bureau: p 146.

Mendoza, M. C. (2003) 'ICAE report: Agenda for the future' in *National researchers for México*, Montreal: International Council for Adult Education/UNESCO.

Mendoza, M. C. (2005) 'Social work in Mexico: towards a different practice', in I. Ferguson, M. Lavalette and E. Whitmore (eds) *Globalisation, global justice and social work*. London: Routledge: pp 22-33.

Mendoza, M. C. (ed) (2012) *Contribución del Trabajo Social a la Construcción de Sujetos Sociales: Sistematización de Experiencias de Práctica Comunitaria* [*The contribution of social work to the construction of social subjects: Systematizing experiences of community practice*], México City: Escuela Nacional de Trabajo Social de la UNAM.

Notes

[1.] Paulo Freire (1921-97), eminent Brazilian community educationalist, author of *Pedagogy of the oppressed* (Freire, 1972).

NINE

Harriet Jakobsson, 2000

Author: Pia Aronsson[1]

Harriet Jakobsson (b. 1926) passed away just after she had celebrated her 84th birthday, and could look back on a long and interesting career. She gained a degree in social work from the Social Policy Institute in Stockholm in 1949, and completed the Erica Foundation's programme in child psychotherapy in 1956. Harriet Jakobsson received numerous awards for her contributions to the field of social work. In 1987, she was awarded an honorary fellowship by the Central Union for Social Work (CSA) in Sweden. In 2000, she received the Katherine Kendall Award in Montreal, Canada. The prize was awarded for:

> ... her pioneering achievements in social work education and practice, not only within the relative calm of the Nordic and Baltic countries but, most notably, in some of the world's trouble spots.

In an interview after the nomination, she says that she 'was surprised, humbled, and gladdened when I received the news' (Josefsson, 2000, see Selected Publications). The following year, she was granted an honorary doctorate in social work at Örebro University, Sweden.

Activities of major importance for her professional development and career

Harriet Jakobsson worked as a lecturer on social work methods in the social work programmes at Lund and Örebro from 1964-91. She was recruited to Örebro in 1967 to establish the fifth school of social work in Sweden. The work was done from the ground up. When teaching materials were lacking, she translated British and US texts and gathered materials from the social work institutes in other Nordic countries.

> We were teachers of social work methods and worked a lot together. We designed case studies and group projects for our students together.

During the years 1975-6, Harriet Jakobsson worked as assistant professor in Social Work at Trondheim University, Norway and took part in the development of a masters and doctoral programme in social work.

In interviews, Harriet Jakobsson emphasized three important areas of her activity:

- the voluntary sector (NGOs)
- training social workers
- her own practical work in the field

She described the importance of being curious, creative, and persevering. She enjoyed facing challenges, even if she sometimes doubted her own ability. Her driving force was to work for the best interests of the child as she worked with them and for the rights of the child in society as a policy aim. She had originally intended to become a paediatrician, but the social work programme attracted her more strongly, especially as her older sister was already a student at the Social Policy Institute in Stockholm University. She never regretted her choice of profession.

> I found my niche, and there have been children around all the time.

She was a strong supporter of field placement in social work education; one of her internships while training at the Social Policy Institute was as the child welfare office in Örebro.

In working for the best interests of the child, Harriet Jakobsson emphasized the need to take each child's situation as a starting point and to use local, context-bound knowledge. She based her teaching in social work on emancipatory principles and on the participants' practical experience, drawing in part on the pedagogy of Paulo Freire. She came into contact with Freire's pedagogical principles through her involvement in the Swedish scout movement, which was inspired by his teaching. Freire further developed his ideas while serving as a consultant at the World Council of Churches in Geneva.

The training Harriet received at the Social Policy Institute made it possible for her to begin working with children as she had wished, first as chief guidance counsellor at the children's psychiatric clinic in Örebro in 1956 and, later, as a consultant for Save the Children. In the field of social work, she deliberately developed a child-centred perspective and was informing the public about the UNCRC (United Nations Convention on the Rights of the Child).

Importance of international work in her career

Harriet Jakobsson was elected to various programme committees in IASSW and served as vice president from 1980. She often told social work students that the commitment to IASSW was very inspiring for her in her professional development as a social worker and a lecturer:

> I gathered impressions, experiences, contacts, yes, all kinds of things from the various trips and study visits. We were in Jerusalem, in Manila in the Philippines, in Brighton in the UK. I mean, there were things big and small, close and far away. I have experienced natural disasters, a super-flood in Manila where people lived in small huts that drifted on the water. (Interview, 2005)

These experiences have all been especially important for the international social work that Harriet Jakobsson pursued. In connection with IASSW's conference in Kenya in 1974, she agreed to work with refugees in Nairobi on behalf of the UN. She had several non-Nordic placements abroad for both the Office of UNHCR in Geneva and the Swedish International Development Cooperation Agency (SIDA). However, it was not until 1979 that she departed on the first mission to Indonesia to work with Vietnamese 'boat people'. During the years 1979-80 she was director of a refugee camp in South East Asia on behalf of UNHCR. Together with a team of UN employees, she contributed to returning 11,000 refugee children scattered across South East Asia to their home country, Vietnam. Following that, she investigated the situation for refugees in the Horn of Africa on behalf of SIDA. The following year, 1982, she received a commission from UNHCR in Djibouti. During the years 1983-7, she worked on the development of a social work programme in Beirut University College, Lebanon, as a professor of social work with the support of Save the Children.

Harriet Jakobsson took the experience and knowledge of international social work gained in her travels to develop social work theory with an international dimension.

Theory and practice

Within the subject of social work methods, Harriet Jakobsson taught casework, crisis intervention and counselling skills.

> There were no textbooks in social methodology, but our bible at that time was 'Casework Notebook'.

As a social work methods lecturer at the School of Social Work in Örebro, Harriet Jakobsson defended the strong link between theory and practice. She considered both casework and community work to be social work and was convinced that there is no conflict between them:

> The more you have been out and worked in other parts of the world, the more you see the importance of community work. Now, even the UN's social welfare officers have been renamed community workers, which is what I think you should be doing; you should be rebuilding shattered communities.

Harriet Jakobsson stressed the importance of practice and that aid efforts must be grounded in the actual reality that people face. She said:

> I was in the Philippines and there were some officials with a textbook, and they drew up an organogram on the wall. But this did not reflect the true situation because they had refugees from Cambodia and refugees from all over the place. I asked, what do you know about them, what are you doing, and what do they need? It is more important to see that you have 5,000 people here, now, who need help than to walk around with a book in your hand.

Harriet believed there is no contradiction between theory and practice. Theory and practical action are equally important, though in different ways. She stressed that, in disaster areas and refugee camps, action comes first because it is important to create a functioning everyday life for the children. Therefore, it is good to begin by organizing effective preschool and school provision. Through these measures, society can become organized and start functioning. At school, the children are given the opportunity to talk to each other and with teachers about their experiences. About 50 per cent of the people in the camps are children and they experience the greatest hardships.

Global, local, and individual

Harriet Jakobsson was interested in the practice of social work and the importance of the context of the client's world and the social realities in societies. Social work is practical action in a complex world. The context and the individual's situation determined the conceptual tools she used to understand the social reality. Her theoretical foundation started with the individual, not society. This foundation was made up of psychodynamic theory and crisis intervention. She had a threefold perspective on social work: the global, the local, and the individual. She had the ability to describe world events and disasters in a comprehensive manner, and illustrated these by telling the story of a particular child she had met, with a striking sense of involvement and empathy.

The perspective of the child permeated her choice of placements and also her theoretical principles, which she conveyed to the young students through her teaching. Knowledge for social action has been developed on the basis of practical experience and theories. Harriet Jakobsson emphasized that experience is the main source of knowledge. She contributed to developing social work teaching by asserting the need to translate theoretical knowledge into practical action. In education, it was important to convey the latest findings with reference to national and international research. She worked at an overall structural level by creating an Institute for Social Work in Lebanon, Beirut University College. She fought for the rights of children in poor and war-torn countries.

In this way, it can be said that Harriet Jakobsson, in her practical work, shifted from efforts oriented towards individuals to working for structural and international change. She emphasized the irreplaceable value of practical training in education, and the importance of a child-oriented perspective in social work and international solidarity efforts. With her international involvement and her commitment to developmental efforts, she appears more as someone who combined theory and practice in social work than as a researcher. Her action-oriented work was guided by a social development perspective and a paradigm of action. She did not have time to write and publish her own articles or books on the subject. Instead, she was involved in participatory development efforts and the dissemination of knowledge about social work, both nationally and internationally.

The challenges of social work and its education during her career

Harriet Jakobsson described a problem that affected her during her career, namely the tension between practical knowledge and academic knowledge. Because of her international assignments, she developed unique intercultural skills and unique experience of international social work. She worked with tasks requiring international cooperation, and she participated in various international forums to share experiences and exchange knowledge. The training of social workers has become more academic, with the result that it is now more important that teachers have a PhD than practical experience of social work. It has become more important to study users and their circumstances than to conduct practical work with the clients.

For Harriet Jakobsson personally, this meant that her competence and skills did not lead to professional advancement within the university. She developed her knowledge and methods based on her experience of meeting people and working with people who found themselves in extremely difficult situations. She revealed this in her teaching and in her lectures. However, because she did not write any academic articles based on this knowledge, the potential for her to pursue an academic career in Sweden was limited: only research qualifications lead to a professorship.

Harriet Jakobsson was highly appreciated as a lecturer, both in Sweden and internationally. She was especially committed to the situation of children in war-torn countries and gave several talks on this subject under themes such as 'A lost generation: children as victims of war and refuge'.

Her vision for social work and its education in the future

Harriet Jakobsson believed that an important change in recent years is that children have received their own platform, including the UNCRC. Children's views must be taken into account in all matters affecting them, and any administrative decision should be preceded by a child impact assessment. She was, however, concerned that in Sweden we live in a consumer society, and so:

> A kind of relative poverty emerges, especially among single, low-paid mothers. I am also thinking of all the immigrant children growing up in families where the parents understand neither the society nor the language,

and where the children in a consumer society more or less demand that their parents get them the latest mobile phones and designer clothes. (Örebro County Council, 2005)

From a global perspective, it is important to combat poverty, war, and violence. What Harriet Jakobsson found particularly disconcerting was that at least half the victims of wars in the world are children. Children who are orphaned are most vulnerable; they become homeless and lack protection. Children are being exploited as child soldiers, and children who experience war are at risk of serious injury and of being afflicted by severe psychological trauma and suffering.

Harriet Jakobsson stressed that children in Sweden are generally doing quite well but there are many vulnerable groups, such as the hidden refugee children. These children may not get the protection and assistance they need; they should be provided with both education and health care. Unaccompanied refugee children are put through a protracted asylum process. The rights of children under the UNCRC must be guaranteed.

It is important that social workers and other government officials see social work from a global perspective. Jakobsson suggested that future social work education should help students to develop intercultural skills. Social work needs to be more international and based on human rights, she stressed. The child's rights, according to the UNCRC and a child-oriented perspective, must be emphasized in future social work education. She believed that students studying to be social workers in Örebro must be given sufficient practical training to be able to apply their knowledge among the people in the community; otherwise they may not get an adequate education.

As a friend of children, Harriet Jakobsson hoped that the UNCRC would be respected both in Sweden and the rest of the world, that all the rights of children will be respected, and that their living conditions will be improved.

Selected publications

(GAA&MP): As the text notes, Jakobsson did not publish extensively. This chapter includes information previously published as follows:

Aronsson, P. (2007) 'På spaning efter ett mönsterbildande inslag i socialt arbete' ['In search of a pattern-forming element of social work'] in E. Brunnberg (ed) *Socionomutbildningen i omvandling 1967 till 2007: En Jubileumsskrift [Social work courses in transition 1967 to 2007. A jubilee exchange]*, Örebro: Örebro University.

Aronsson, P. (2008) 'Från fattigvårdskvinnor till moderna socialarbetare' ['From poor women to modern social workers'], In H. Swärd and M.-A. Egerö (eds) *Villkorandets politik. Fattigdomens premisser och samhällets åtgärder – då och nu [Conditioning the conduct of the policy: Poverty and premises of society – then and now]*, Boras: Egalité.

It also draws on the following publications:

Josefsson, C. (2000) 'Det sociala arbetets pris gick till en svenska' ['Social work prize goes to a Swedish woman], *SSR-tidningen*, 6: p 16.

Josefsson, C. (2001) 'Porträtt Harriet Jakobsson' ['Portrait of Harriet Jakobsson'], *Socionomen*, 2: pp 55-8.

Örebro County Council (2005), *50 år – Ett halvt sekel med barn- och ungdomspsykiatri, 1955–2005, [50 years – Half a century of child and adolescent psychiatry, 1955–2005]*, Örebro: Örebro County Council.

Notes

1. (GAA&MP) Prepared for this volume by Pia Aronsson after Harriet Jakobsson's death, based on an interview in 2005 and personal communications between 2006 and 2009.

TEN

John Maxwell, 2002

Interviewed by Lynne Healy

Biography

John Maxwell's (b. 1934) career was defined by his 35 years at the University of the West Indies (UWI) Mona Campus, Kingston, Jamaica. This was his base for wide involvement in professional social work and community organizations in the Caribbean, as president of NACASSW and Vice-president of IASSW. His qualifications include: Diploma in Social Administration, LSE; MSW, McGill University: Advanced Diploma in Social Work, University of Toronto; PhD, Cornell University. He had sabbatical periods in the US, England and Zimbabwe. His last position before retirement was Senior Lecturer in Social Work and Deputy Dean, Faculty of Social Sciences, UWI-Mona. Among his achievements, he took a central role in starting and editing the *Caribbean Journal of Social Work* and in publishing about Caribbean social work.

When did you receive the award, and on what basis?

I received it in 2004, but it was a belated award for the 2002 year. I understand it was particularly for my contribution to the development of social work education in the Caribbean region, and the role I played in making links between the region and the international social work education community.

I taught at the University of the West Indies from 1971 to 2004, during which time the social work programme developed from a two-year certificate course to an undergraduate degree and then to a masters degree. I played a major role in developing the curriculum from the 1970s until the 1990s. At the same time, I was involved in developing links to IASSW and the international community, in particular the US and Canada.

I remember first meeting Katherine Kendall when she was with CSWE. I had to discuss with her what was necessary for social workers having done their training at the University of the West Indies to receive accreditation in the US. Subsequently, I met her at conferences, became aware of her impact on the international social work community and I recognized what an amazing woman she was, certainly the dominant personality of the age.

What activities were of major importance for your professional career and its impact on social work and its education?

Prior to joining UWI, I had ten years' experience – four years of teaching and six years of youth development – which, collectively, helped me develop a sense of commitment to influence the lives of others, especially the more vulnerable in society.

Concurrent with my university career, I served on various social welfare and social development committees and boards. The most significant one was the Social Development Commission, responsible for government youth and community development programmes nationally. I had two appointments as a board member for a total of ten years, between 1972-93, and was deputy, sometimes acting, chairman for the last two years.

I was involved with the Jamaican Association of Social Workers (JASW) from its inception in 1968. I was one of the founding members, and served as president for two terms. I was also actively involved with the Council of Voluntary Social Services, which is the coordinating body for all voluntary agencies in Jamaica.

The exposure and range of experiences through these activities prior to and during my years as a social work educator have all contributed to shaping my values and attitudes, and indeed my overall identity as a social worker.

In my principal role as a social work educator, the years that I worked at the UWI gave me the opportunity of contributing to the evolution of the social work programme from a pre-baccalaureate through to a masters degree. Thus, I was able to help professionalize the work force throughout the region, especially as the UWI-Mona campus was initially the only one and, until the 1990s, the principal centre of training.

In my efforts to achieve those goals, in addition to the benefits of my education at institutions in the UK, Canada and the US, the opportunity for active linkages with the international social work community contributed greatly to my professional career.

In the early 1990s, when we had just celebrated 30 years of the UWI's social work programme, I was involved in developing ties with CSWE and the Canadian Association of Social Workers. In 1992, what had until then been the North American Region of the IASSW was reconstituted as the North American and Caribbean Association of Schools of Social Work (NACASSW), which became one of the five regional groupings of the international body. This led to our becoming significantly involved in this wider professional community, and I had the opportunity to serve as the president of NACASSW for one term from 1992-96.

Under this umbrella, I was able to play a significant role in a number of joint initiatives, such as the establishment of a biennial Caribbean regional conference, facilitating colleagues' attendance and presentations at international conferences and the development of a special relationship between our UWI-Mona campus and the University of Connecticut (UConn) School of Social Work in Hartford. The presence of a large West Indian immigrant population there provided the opportunity for a mutually beneficial exchange of programme expertise with faculty from UConn. It was helpful for launching the Mona MSW degree, and our faculty were assisting UConn in reaching out to the West Indian community in Hartford.

In relation to all that I have mentioned, I must specially acknowledge your mentoring role, Lynne. You not only facilitated the partnership of your university but were integral to every aspect of the Caribbean region's international involvement since 1992, so that you are popularly regarded as an 'honorary' Caribbean social work educator.

In what field do you think you made your biggest contribution?

I would probably say the evolution and development of the curriculum of the social work programme, because I was formally involved with it from the end of the first decade (1971) when I was appointed as a lecturer. I had earlier served as a research and teaching assistant from 1966-68. I had then been responsible for formalizing an orientation for beginning students, which involved study visits and observations at a range of social service agencies and related seminars.

Initially, there was a two-year professional Certificate in Social Work and then a third year was added with related social science courses to complete a baccalaureate level programme. I was asked to restructure the curriculum for a more conventional bachelors degree in social work, was engaged in subsequent modifications especially after becoming social work unit coordinator in 1986, and then had the lead role in drafting the curriculum for the masters degree that started in 1993.

I was there at the right time to be significantly involved in developing the regional and international links, because there was a gradual spread of social work training throughout the Caribbean. The University of Guyana in the 1970s was the first to develop a programme after UWI-Mona. Then the College of the Bahamas followed in the early 1980s, and the other two campuses of the University of the West Indies, Cave Hill Barbados in 1988 and St Augustine in Trinidad in 1990. The University of Belize was the last to join the fold in the later 1990s before I retired. It was gratifying to be able to liaise with and advise as requested these newer regional initiatives and, in a number of instances, to see graduates of our 'parent' programme at Mona appointed to leading positions in those institutions.

What did social work and social work education mean to you professionally?

I would say the opportunity eventually to achieve a level of recognition in an accredited discipline, and exposure to the wider international community. Social work, while practised in several less developed countries, had from its inception not been given status equal to a number of other professions. Thus, at the university, social work education was certainly in the 1960s regarded as a poor relation. To be involved in its evolution to a programme that offered a full undergraduate degree and then a masters degree, and which was eventually given 'parity of esteem' alongside other disciplines in the social sciences, was a rewarding experience.

It undoubtedly provided me with a great measure of personal and professional satisfaction, not least that I subsequently served as head of the Department of Sociology and Social Work, which afterwards became Sociology, Psychology and Social Work, and then at a later point became deputy dean for four years in the Faculty of Social Sciences. It did mean that, as a social work educator, I had been able to achieve a measure of recognition for my professional service and academic standing within the university community.

Since you had been so involved in community development and service work, how did you make the decision to move into social work education?

Originally, after I left high school, I intended to become a history teacher and actually started out in that role. However, in what I intended as a mere diversionary experience, I went to work at a new experimental youth development camp which was opened in Jamaica in the late 1950s, but with the intention of going back to qualify as a teacher. However, I was then asked to take up a position as director of Boy's Town in Kingston. It was a non-residential centre that offered a youth and community service programme in a very difficult, depressed area of the city. I served there for six years and developed a strong commitment to serving the less privileged and to advocating for social justice.

My movement into social work education was a matter of the opportunities presented to me. I left Boys' Town in 1963 as a relatively mature person at age 29 and did my undergraduate studies on a Commonwealth scholarship in the UK at LSE and Moray House College in Edinburgh. I assumed I was returning to Jamaica to a position in youth and community work. However, the job opportunities were rather limited. At the same time, the relatively new social work programme at the UWI was looking for someone to teach in group and community work areas. After a two-year temporary appointment, I was sent on a Canadian International Development Agency scholarship to do my MSW at McGill University in Montreal. Subsequently, I did an Advanced Diploma in Social Work at the University of Toronto and then came back to my scheduled appointment as lecturer in social work.

My role to teach group and community work method courses provided some balance to the existing heavy orientation towards social casework. However, I was also appointed as coordinator with responsibility for developing practice education – a role which I carried singlehandedly for much of the 1970s and 1980s.

Given how my career had proceeded, my eventual move to become a social work educator was, I suppose, the ideal merger of my two affiliations – teaching and social work.

What were the challenges of social work and its education during your career?

Significant challenges were to help both the social work profession through JASW and also, through being involved in teaching social work at the university, to achieve a greater level of professional recognition.

In the community at large there was a failure to distinguish between practice that required special training and voluntary community welfare service. A move that I spearheaded was to have the designation 'social work' removed from the award of national honours for persons without any formal training. They were, indeed, deserving of recognition but, it was agreed, for their contribution to community service work.

As the number of trained workers – largely from our local university – increased, agencies which had not necessarily appointed staff with social work degrees previously, became more selective. In the early 1990s, the Public Service Ministry engaged with a group of us from JASW to develop what was designated a 'social work service' in a reorganized classification of civil service jobs. This represented a real improvement on a somewhat ad hoc system of job assignment. While formal certification of the profession has not yet been achieved, there has been slow progression towards greater professionalism.

In the area of academic training at the university, there was no independent department but rather a programme unit, which functioned alongside the sociology and later psychology degree programmes. It benefited from a selection of relevant courses in those subjects, which underpinned social work practice. There was, therefore, the challenge for the specific social work courses to have equal recognition with those of the traditional disciplines.

While classroom offerings in practice methods and agency administration could be readily equated to other courses and research training was largely an area to be shared, the challenge posed was with regard to field practice. The assumption within the other disciplines in the department and the wider Faculty of Social Sciences was that you simply sent students out for some experience and had them submit a written report. The realization of all that went into structuring student placements with competent agency supervision and detailed evaluation of student performance in order that they could be graded in a manner comparable to written coursework and exams, was not easily represented to colleagues whose experience was largely with conventional classroom teaching. And the case for crediting the fieldwork coordinator with recognition equivalent to that of a classroom teacher was one for which I had to advocate strongly.

The almost complete dependence on social work literature from metropolitan countries (US, UK, Canada) was not surprisingly a notable shortcoming and affected the image of the programme, especially in the setting of the university. It also contributed to a reluctance to critique the relevance of the curriculum for preparing Caribbean social workers (Williams et al, 2001, see Selected Publications). The need to encourage the production of indigenous writing was therefore a real challenge, and it was a special privilege for me to begin playing the role as co-editor of an annual peer-reviewed *Caribbean Journal of Social Work*, which had its first publication in 2002. I also contributed the first piece giving an overview of the development of social work in the English-speaking Caribbean (Maxwell, 2002, see Selected Publications). This journal has subsequently provided an opportunity for both educators and practitioners from the region, the diaspora and other areas to publish articles that address substantive social work topics and social issues confronting Caribbean people.

How has international work been important in your career?

Certainly, it has significantly expanded the horizons of social work and social work education for us in the field in Jamaica, especially through participation in conferences.

From 1976-78, I served as a member of the board of IFSW when I was president of JASW. Subsequently, identification with the international community was with IASSW activities and, under the umbrella of NACASSW, special features have been linkages with CSWE, in particular attending annual programme meetings. The relationship with the University of Connecticut, School of Social Work has been particular significant. Highlights of that connection, in which I played an active role, included faculty exchanges, assisting with outreach, organizing field placement of UWI students, shared presentations at conferences and joint authorship of published articles (Healy et al, 1999, see Selected Publications).

During my sabbatical year, 1994-95, I spent the first semester teaching two courses at the University of Connecticut, and then three months at the National Institute of Social Work (NISW) in London. Thereafter, I went on to the Harare School of Social Work in Zimbabwe for two months. I did a comparative study of the Harare Field Practice programme with those of the University of Guyana, and the UWI Mona campus in Jamaica. It led to an article in the *Journal of Social Development in Africa* (Maxwell, 1999, see Selected Publications). That year, I made presentations at all three institutions where I spent my sabbatical, on aspects of Caribbean social work and on interagency coordination, the theme of my doctoral dissertation at Cornell University (Maxwell, 1990, see Selected Publications).

At the level of Caribbean regional involvement, an early experience soon after my joining the teaching staff was a four-year secondment to the then UWI Department of Extra-Mural Studies to serve as coordinator of a UNICEF-sponsored Caribbean child development project. This involved encouraging regional governments to establish or to extend services for preschool children beyond the standard maternal and child health provisions as well as the establishment of a centre on the Mona campus for short-term training of childcare workers and research. This included a demonstration preschool day-care unit. My role as coordinator was principally to lobby with the relevant government agencies in 12 countries of the region to get this commitment. This was aided by small initial inducement grants provided by UNICEF, as well as the facilitation of regional training programmes. The experience offered me invaluable familiarity with the social services of the region and served me well on my return in 1976 to teaching students from across the Caribbean.

The most enduring engagement for me in Caribbean regional activity has been the developments promoted since the formation of NACASSW in 1992. The Association of Caribbean Social Work Educators (ACSWE) started in 1997 and picked up an earlier initiative, a biennial Conference of Caribbean and International Social Work Educators (1993); this has now become a regular feature. It has been a matter of pride to have between 150-200 social work educators and practitioners from the Caribbean, the North American-based diaspora and other international participants assemble for presentations of special relevance to that community.

What major obstacles have you faced in your career?

As I have implied or stated before, the earlier limited recognition for social work locally as a helping profession and, concurrently, what was the low status of social work education at our university. I would like to think that – through the increase in trained personnel and our efforts to improve the curriculum in the education programme – I contributed, along with other colleagues, to changing this perception to some extent.

There is also the shortage of males in almost all areas of practice, with this being all the more consequential in a largely post-slavery society with a predominantly matrifocal household composition. As males – whether children, juveniles or adults – are the ones presenting the highest incidence of behavioural problems, the limited male role models among the would-be 'change agents' is all the more unfortunate.

How has social work, the profession and education changed over the course of your career?

I would comment on this with reference to the Caribbean region. The primary focus of some social service agencies, and the bias given to social work education when it started in the early 1960s, was very much a clinical orientation. The social work curriculum was definitely weighted towards treatment and rehabilitation and, indeed, most students came for training from the major government agencies, such as the childcare and the correctional services. Few staff from principally youth and community work agencies came to the university for degrees. They did short in-service programmes and were more likely to attend a residential four-month course offered by the then extra-mural department of UWI. Community workers were largely seen as requiring only lower-level training.

That definitely has been turned around, and there is now much more equal recognition, at least in training at the university, for equal attention to casework, group work, and community work. Preparation for macro-level practice with the requisite skills for policy development and programme planning has also been given much more emphasis, especially at the masters level. Graduates are now better recognized among the community of human service professionals. Here I recognize in particular the great contribution of colleague Peta-Anne Baker, the current coordinator of the Mona programme, for much of this improvement.

What changes would you like to see in the social work profession in the future?

At the local level, as indicated earlier, I would like to see the development of an active national association that would strengthen advocacy for professional standards and for better recognition. A recently agreed code of ethics and proposals towards certification are encouraging steps in that direction. Similar recommendations are applicable across the Caribbean region.

At the field practice level, there is a need for specializations to address particular challenges to the Caribbean community. In relation to natural disasters, there is a high risk of hurricanes and rare but severe instances of earthquake, particularly in Haiti, and of volcanic eruption, particularly at Montserrat. The role of social workers in disaster mitigation and management is especially important in dealing with household dislocation, as well as mental health problems.

Regrettably, high incidences of crime and violence have been alarming features of social disorder, particularly in Jamaica, and, while there is a need for extending poverty alleviation programmes, peace management initiatives in the most crime-ridden areas are also activities which can benefit from the application of specialist social work skills.

The improvement of standards and professional recognition will also be attained through greater support offered to the ACSWE's biennial conference. Similarly, the annual publication of the *Caribbean Journal of Social Work* should nurture an increasing body of academically respected indigenous literature.

At the international level, I would welcome a spread of engagement between the practitioners and educators of the more developed and less developed countries. All possible attempts should have linkages as mutually beneficial as possible, rather than the traditional top-down relationship, while command of material resources and longer experience will necessarily give the richer countries a great advantage as we move towards a more globalized world. Every effort should be made to foster exchanges that accept universally applicable knowledge and practice and also respect culturally relevant variations.

Selected publications

Maxwell, J. A. (1990) 'Factors influencing the process of inter-agency coordination: A Jamaican case study', PhD dissertation, Cornell University.

Healy, L., Maxwell. J. A., and Pine B. (1999) 'Exchanges that work: mutuality and sustainability in a Caribbean-USA academic partnership' *Social Development Issues*, 21(3) pp 14-21.

Maxwell, J. A. (1999) 'Student assessment of supervision in social work field practice in the Caribbean and Southern Africa: A comparative study and commentary', *Journal of Social Development in Africa*, 14(1) pp 85-100.

Williams, L. O., Maxwell, J. A., Ring, K. and Cambridge, I. (2001) 'Social work education in the West Indies with special reference to the programmes of the University of the West Indies', *Social Work Education*, 20(1): pp 57-72.

Maxwell, J. A. (2002) 'The evolution of social welfare services and social work in the English speaking Caribbean (with major reference to Jamaica)' *Caribbean Journal of Social Work*, 1: pp 11-31.

ELEVEN

Terry Hokenstad, 2004

Interviewed by Andrea Bediako

Biography

 Merl C. (Terry) Hokenstad's (b. 1936) career was defined by professorial roles at the Mandel School of Applied Social Sciences, Case Western Reserve University, Cleveland, Ohio, USA. His education at Augustana College, South Dakota (BA), Columbia University (MSW) culminated at Brandeis University (PhD). At various times, he served as president of NACASSW and CSWE, chaired NASW's International Committee and was also treasurer and secretary of IASSW. He served on a number of important UN bodies concerned with ageing, and led delegations and gave workshops on a variety of subjects across the world. He has authored nine books, co-edited journal special editions and books, published many articles and papers, and served as editor-in-chief of *International Social Work*.

When did you receive the award and on what basis?

I received the award at the IASSW conference in Adelaide, Australia, in 2004. Thinking about it, there were three different reasons why I received it. One certainly was my role and leadership in IASSW over the years. I was actually on the board for 16 years in all. I was elected treasurer of IASSW in 1978, and I held the office two terms until 1986. In 1986, I became president of CSWE, a position I held until 1989. During that time, I represented the US on the IASSW board as president of the council. Both president and executive director of the Council have always represented the US. After a hiatus, I came back on the board of IASSW from 1996 to 2000, as secretary of the organization. Hence, I held leadership roles in the organization for a number of years.

Another reason is that I have served as one of the representatives of the IASSW at the UN since 1996. I have been one of the five-member IASSW team, involved in the Social Work Day planning. I became actively involved and have been serving on the NGO Committee on Ageing at the United Nations for this entire period. My work with the UN, which started out because I was active in IASSW, leads to the second reason why I might have been chosen for the award. As a member of the NGO Committee on Ageing, I was asked to co-chair the United States celebration of the International Year on Ageing in 1999; we had a number of big events in the US. The planning committee consisted of people in leadership roles in the field of ageing in the US. Thereafter, I was asked by the UN to be a member of the NGO committee to work with the Secretariat in planning the Madrid International Plan of Action on Ageing in 2002. The UN Secretariat was asked by the Commission on Social Development to develop the first draft of this document, and the Secretary-General appointed an expert committee. We were 15 members from 14 different nations who worked over a period of two years. Our first meeting was in Frankfurt in June 2000, and then we met in Santa Domingo, Dominican Republic, and in Vienna. We worked with the Secretariat to develop the document, which went to the UN Commission on Social Development for further action, before taken to Madrid for the World Assembly on Ageing in 2002. I was fortunate enough to be appointed as a member of the US delegation to participate in that meeting in Madrid, following on my prior work. The appointments came from the Secretary of the US government Health and Human Services, representing the private sector, the non-profits, and the State Department as well as the Department of Health and Human Services. In Madrid, the final document was approved by the 150 nations present, and it is now called the Madrid International Plan of Action on Ageing.

The third reason would have been my involvement in promoting the international dimension of social work education, both in the United States and on a broader level. Over the years, I have been very active in this role. My latest contribution has been as member on the Katherine A. Kendall Institute (KAKI) advisory board [an educational initiative of CSWE, see Chapter 4]. Prior to that, in the early '90s, I chaired the Council on International Activities for CSWE, now called the Commission, and participated actively as a member for many years. Another way of promoting international social work education is that I have spoken on international themes to 56 universities in 32 different countries around the world, talking about the internationalization of social work education and the importance of the international dimension of social work education. For example, one of my subjects was 'The realities of global interdependence: what role for social work education?'.

What has the award meant to you professionally and personally?

Obviously, the award has provided me with added clout in forwarding the international dimension of social work education, particularly in the US, because there are only two Americans who have received this award, and I am the only living American now [Lynne Healy received the award after this interview was conducted]. Herman Stein was the other American who received the award. It is a very prestigious award, which is given to social work educators in different countries throughout the world, so it is very gratifying to receive it. My selection indicates that the US does have an important role to play in international social work education, and it gives me greater influence in communicating that within my own country.

It is amazing that both Herman Stein and I are from the same institution, Case Western Reserve University, which I think is without question one of the US leaders in international social work education. We have a history of strong commitment to the international dimension of social work and social work education, and a number of other members of the faculty and alumni also have made major contributions.

Another point is that it is given in honour of Katherine Kendall, and I worked with Katherine for over forty years as I stated at her hundredth birthday party. This makes it a special honour for me, because it recognizes Katherine as well. Katherine influenced the careers of many social work educators. She had a magnificent career in her own accomplishments and also serving as a role model, confidante and consultant to many of the rest of us in this field. I met her when I was a relatively young social work educator and, throughout my career, she had an important impact. I co-edited a book with Katherine. She was instrumental in getting me involved with IASSW, in fact encouraged me to run for treasurer in 1978. She was also a role model of how social work might be effective at the United Nations, because of her role at the UN in the 1950s, where she had a significant impact. We could have a whole other interview about Katherine Kendall, her impact on social work education and more specifically on my life and work.

What activities were of major importance for your professional career and its impact on social work and its education?

The first would certainly be organizational leadership; we have already talked about IASSW, CSWE and my involvement with the UN. I also chaired the International Committee for NASW and was active in that arena as well.

Another area in which I have been active, both in my writing and my international activities, is policies and services for older people. In the 1990s, I led a team of professionals from medicine, nursing and some of the allied health professions as well as social work to Central and Eastern Europe, where we helped develop home- and community-based care for older people. We had professionals from 18 former Soviet bloc nations participating in this three-year project. Therefore, I would say the focus on global ageing and the development of care for older people certainly is very much part of my career. That was a very significant activity for me, which combined the international and the ageing components of my interest.

I became interested in the field of ageing as a young social worker on the Lower East Side in New York City, after I had graduated from Columbia University School of Social Work. This was in the 1960s, a period of major social change. One of the big issues at that time was poverty among older people and the need for social policy for older people. I was involved in advocacy for Medicare and the Older Americans Act, both of which were enacted in 1965. When I went back for my doctoral education, I concentrated on the field of ageing and, ever since, it has been a very important focus of my research and writing.

After I graduated from college, I spent a year abroad studying in the UK and became very interested in the international scene and international cooperation. However, it was not until 1975, when I was invited to give an address at an IASSW European regional seminar in Nottingham, England, that I really started focusing on international social work education. My interest in ageing started out more on domestic issues in ageing policy. I have always been interested in policy, so I became involved in that a bit earlier than my international engagement. Nevertheless, the interplay of those two has been a focal point of my career.

Another activity in which I have been involved is the development of doctoral education in social work. I provided leadership in our own programme at Case Western Reserve in developing and then chairing an innovative doctoral programme. I have been invited to the University of Hong Kong, to Eotvos Lorand University, Hungary, to the University of the Philippines, and Stockholm University, Sweden, in each case to help them set up doctoral education in their countries. So that has been a major area, to consult on the development of doctoral programmes that fit the needs of different countries.

Another international role is my participation in the Citizen Ambassador Program that is part of People-to-People International. I have led delegations of social work educators and practitioners to Cuba, China, Russia and South Africa. This exchange programme has contributed to international good will. I also have had two Fulbright grants, one a research Fulbright at the Institute for Applied Social Research in Oslo, Norway, and the other a teaching Fulbright at Stockholm University, Sweden. Those have given me opportunities to do research as well as participate internationally, offering leadership and consultation.

I have either authored or edited nine books. The most recent book is a co-edited volume entitled *Teaching human rights: Curriculum resources for social work educators* (Hokenstad et al, 2013, see Selected Publications). Also, recently I have been a co-editor of *The Sage handbook on international social work* (Lyons et al, 2012), working with editorial colleagues from the UK and Australia. Other books include one for IASSW, *Participation in teaching and learning* (Hokenstad and Rigby, 1977, see Selected Publications). It was actually the first book that I did in the 1970s, and was directly related to a project that IASSW had to strengthen teaching in social work education. That one was well received in a number of countries. I co-edited a book with Katherine Kendall on ageing and social work internationally (Hokenstad and Kendall, 1988, see Selected Publications) and I have co-edited several books with Jim Midgley that profile international social work, including *Issues in international social work* (Hokenstad and Midgley, 1997, see Selected Publications), and *Lessons from abroad* (Hokenstad and Midgley, 2004, see Selected Publications), focusing on international innovations in social work. I have done quite a bit of writing in the area of ageing as well. Much of it relates to crossnational comparisons in programmes for older people. The United States certainly has a lot to learn from the rest of the world. *Lessons from abroad* reflects this commitment that we need to learn from other countries to improve our social welfare system in my country.

Because of my very strong commitment to the international dimension of social work education, I endowed the Hokenstad International Lecture given at the annual programme meeting of

CSWE. It enables us to bring outstanding social work educators from other countries and have them speak to US social work educators.

What does social work education mean to you professionally and personally?

Social work education has been the major focus of my total professional career, and that is reflected in many of the activities that I have mentioned. It has meant making many friendships around the world, and those friendships have enriched my life. On a professional level, having the opportunity to visit other countries and learn from others around the world has been incorporated into my writing. Those friendships are professional friendships, but they have become personal friendships as well, which have meant a great deal to me.

More than that, my teaching as well as my research has been enriched by my international experiences and my international commitments. For many years, I have taught a course on international social work, but I also incorporate international dimensions into my other courses, for example, in my courses on American social policy and policies and programmes in the field of ageing.

Why did you choose social work?

I chose social work because I was interested in service to disadvantaged populations. After college, I considered going into the Episcopal ministry here in the United States. I studied Anglican theology for a year at the University of Durham in the UK on a Rotary Foundation Fellowship. Then I decided that my vocation was perhaps secular rather than sacred, but still meant service. Along with service, I have always had a strong commitment to social justice. I was very active in the civil rights movement in the 1960s, participating in some marches that took place during that period and being active in a group called Lower East Side Social Workers for Civil Rights. We thought that our own profession should be at the forefront of working towards integration. Thus, a combination of service commitment on the one hand and the social justice commitment on the other hand, together with experiencing the commitments my family had in those areas, had a major impact on why I chose social work as a career. It also influenced my emphasis on the social policy and action part of social work.

What were the challenges of social work and its education during your career?

At the beginning of my career, social work education was moving towards a more active macro role. When I was in graduate school in the early 1960s, social work had been a predominantly casework profession. Even community organization was more related to local community services and planning, and not so much to grassroots action. The social science part of social work, as differentiated from the psychology and behavioural science part of social work, was entering the knowledge base of social work at that particular time. The Lower East Side of New York started a major organization called Mobilization for Youth. This was during the time of the civil rights movement, as I mentioned, and of the 'war on poverty' and the 'great society' [policies of the US government during this period], so it was a time of activism and of social change. Social work became an active participant in the era of social change. It does not mean that social work was uninterested in social action before that, but it became more of a major part of social work, at that particular time in the 1960s. We had social workers such as Whitney Young[1] taking on major leadership roles in the civil rights movement; we had social workers becoming very active on the war on poverty and projects set up related to that war.

Two decades later, a great expansion of international exchange in social work education took place with the growth of internationalism in social work education. We used to have annual meetings at CSWE with a couple of international sessions, and we would be lucky if half a dozen people attended. After the fall of the Berlin Wall in 1989, the following decade witnessed a major move forward for the international dimension of social work education.

International work was important in my career because we do live in a shrinking world, which has been created by economic globalization and by technology, so that we are all more interrelated. That factor has been a theme that has run throughout my career. I would say that is a really significant theme. A second major theme of course is population ageing, and the fact that this is a worldwide phenomenon. The third theme relates to both of those, and that is the increasing international migration. People are moving all over the world. The immigration into the United States this decade is the largest one since the 1920s. Again, we are becoming a country of immigrants, which calls for the need to include in social work education understanding other countries and cultures from which people come.

What were the major obstacles that you faced in your career?

One major challenge was the difficult financial situation at CSWE when I was elected president in 1986. Along with other members of the executive committee, I worked to bring financial stability to the organization. A new set of bylaws to simplify the structure was also enacted. We recruited a new executive director, Don Beless, who effectively carried out the reforms.

Another one of the challenges I faced during my career occurred after the opening up of the former Soviet bloc and the fall of the Berlin Wall that occurred in 1989. How could we best contribute to the transition, in helping these countries develop social work education and social services? Many of the Eastern European countries had had some social work education before World War II, but not during the communist time. The Soviet Union itself – including Russia but also Ukraine, Armenia, Azerbaijan, and a number of other countries – had never had social work education, because the communist revolution in 1917 came before social work education had really taken hold. Therefore, that was a real challenge for all of social work education.

It was also important for me personally, and I travelled to a number of different countries in the Soviet bloc in the 1990s, helping them to get social work education solidified and underway. Then, starting in 1996 with a sizable three-year grant from the Open Society Foundation, I led a group of social work, medical and nursing educators from the United States to work with educators and programme administrators from eighteen different countries in that part of the world. We provided seminars, workshops and consultation, helping them to develop home- and community-based care for older people. There were other challenges, but those two are probably the most significant.

In the current decade, I have spent considerable time in the People's Republic of China, both consulting and teaching as that country builds and expands social work education, in particular now at the graduate level. China has recognized the value of social work for its society and the current challenge is to provide quality education at all levels so that social work becomes an increasingly effective helping profession in that country. I and many other internationalists in social work education are assisting our Chinese colleagues in addressing this challenge.

How have social work and social work education changed?

In addition to increased international exchange, social work has expanded its knowledge base, making more effective use of empirical studies. Also, social and community development has become an essential component of the social work curriculum. It is a major topic of social work education in many developing countries, which I think is appropriate. Social work education has changed over the years, and I am sure will continue to change because we are a contextual profession. That is, we need to not only respond to but also influence the environment in which people live. Thus, social work and social work education must change as the environment around us changes.

What do you see happening in social work, social work education and IASSW in the future?

One important new development is the Global Agenda by the international organizations (IASSW, ICSW and IFSW, 2012). I have long been a proponent of the international organizations working closely together. During my final term on the board of IASSW, I wrote a position paper indicating the reasons why it was important for the international organizations to work together, and proposing a working committee to coordinate this effort. That working committee now has become a standing committee, which is focused on the action plan that was discussed in Hong Kong at the joint conference in 2010 and adopted in Stockholm in 2012. International social work vitally needs all the components of social work, social work education, and social welfare and social development, to work together. We do that now at the UN in other areas in addition to the Social Work Day, which includes IASSW and IFSW. We are also cooperating more with ICSW.

Incidentally, I did want to mention one other thing that exemplifies this cooperation. Another part of my career was being editor-in-chief of the journal, *International Social Work*. We brought together the three organizations to be co-sponsors, and signed a contract with Sage in 1986. A plaque on my office wall commemorates this transition, which is still operational 30 years later. It is a tremendous plus on the international scene that those three organizations are working closely together. As individual organizations, they can do something, but they can do much more in a coordinated effort. I see that as a continuing challenge for social work internationally.

Selected publications

Hokenstad, M. C. and Rigby, B. D. (1977) *Participation in teaching and learning: An idea book for social work educators,* New York and Vienna: International Association of Schools of Social Work.

Hokenstad, M. C. and Kendall, K. A. (eds) (1988) *Gerontological social work: International perspectives*, New York: Haworth.

Hokenstad, M. C. and Midgley, J. (eds) (1997) *Issues in international social work: Global challenges for a new century*, Washington, DC: NASW Press.

Hokenstad, M. C. and Midgley, J. (eds) (2004) *Lessons from abroad: Adapting international social welfare innovations*, Washington, DC: NASW Press.

Hokenstad, M. C., Healy, L. and Segal, U. A. (eds) (2013) *Teaching human rights: Curriculum resources for social work educators*, Alexandria, VA: Council on Social Work Education.

Notes

[1] Dean of the School of Social Work at Atlanta University, who became Director of the National Urban League and President of NASW.

TWELVE

Sven Hessle, 2006

Interviewed by Darja Zaviršek

Biography

 Sven Hessle (b. 1941) is now Emeritus Professor of Social Work, Department of Social Work, Stockholm University, having been appointed Professor of Social Work there in 1993. His education led to qualification as a clinical psychologist (1968) and a PhD in pedagogy (1975). Research and leadership roles include work in family and child welfare in areas affected by poverty as well as in international social work in Europe, the Middle and Far East, Latin America and other parts of the world. Publications include 40 books as author, editor and co-author, articles, mostly in Swedish, but some translated into different languages, and many research and consultancy reports. He was the founder and editor-in-chief of the *International Journal of Social Welfare* for more than two decades.

When did you receive the award and on what basis?

I received the award in 2006 during the Santiago de Chile IASSW World Congress. Lots of Latin American, Spanish-speaking Marxists were at the congress, reminding me of what it was like in the late 1960s in Sweden. Latin America might still be one of the last bastions of Marxism, I think.

I guess the award was given to me for my international engagement in different parts of the world, for example in the former Yugoslavia since the peace agreement in December 1995 after the terrible war, maybe also for the engagement in the *International Journal of Social Welfare*. I have been writing, lecturing and doing research in different parts of the world.

What has the award meant to you?

For me personally, it meant a lot to have been given this award. It is the most honoured recognition internationally in our discipline, but I am afraid that only a few people in Sweden know about it and its merits. I would put it like this: one of the challenges I had in social work has been to persuade my Swedish colleagues that this award is one of the most important international ones we can receive in social work. This kind of challenge in turn shows how rudimentary the level of international social work was at that time in Sweden. I had to persuade people to understand that this is a kind of Nobel Prize in social work. This is our most important international acknowledgement in social work ever since Jane Addams received the Nobel Peace Prize 1931. I like to think of solidarity and peace making as fundamental to social work.

On the international level, I guess that the award opened up invitations to different prestigious lectures abroad, for example, the Friedlander Lecture in Berkeley (2008); the Terry Hokenstad International Lecture in Atlanta (2011); the Herman Stein Lecture at Mandel School of Applied Sciences (2013); as well as leading to me receiving the Harald Swedner Award from ICSD in 2014.

What activities were of major importance for your professional career and its impact on social work and its education?

Working in the region of the former Yugoslavia, I would say, was one of the most important decisions in my life. Just before Christmas in 1995, UNICEF called me in Stockholm from the former Yugoslavia and asked me to go to Sarajevo to take part in reconstruction of the civil society and social work education in Bosnia. The first step was to dare to say: 'Yes, I will come'. That was the start of it. I arrived in Sarajevo in February 1996 just after the end of the peace negotiation in Dayton. The whole country was so materially destroyed, but not socially due to the fantastic engagement of the social workers for the poor residents during the war. From then on, lots of projects developed, including what I consider to be a peace project: establishing the Department of Social Work at the University of Banja Luka together with my Swedish colleagues and colleagues from the former Yugoslavia. The final document from that collaboration was to write two books simultaneously, one in a regional language, that colleagues from the

Balkans could understand, and another in English (Hessle and Zaviršek, 2005, see Selected Publications).

When I reflect back on the work I have done, there are three important areas of my activities. Psychosocial work is the first and main field of specialization. I started my career originally as a clinical psychologist, and back in the 1970s, I was the director of a therapeutic community for people who were misusing drugs heavily. I learned then in my analysis to change perspectives from individual to group and to community level and back. For me having worked to begin with as a psychotherapist, this was an entry to working with the clients' social world. That change from psychotherapy to psychosocial work was my first important activity in the beginning of the 1970s and onwards.

My second area, child welfare, goes back to the middle of the 1970s. Then I was working both in practice and in research with very psychosocially vulnerable multi-problem families in a unique village for client families and personnel living together, Barnbyn Skå, a unique treatment centre, now closed. Since then, I have been working within child welfare practice and research, both on national and international levels. I have learned to look at the child on many contextual levels, like the Russian dolls about which Bronfenbrenner (1979: p 3) writes.[1] There is always another layer for interpretation of children at risk. This is a very important discovery.

The third area I have already mentioned, my international engagement, which was triggered when UNICEF called and asked me to go to Sarajevo. I remember that, when I arrived, the professors in the ruins of the university said that we came too late and they were angry with us for that. Then they were telling us that we took all the human capital away from them by accepting all the refugees in Sweden! We had accepted around 60,000 in Sweden. Professors of social policy had counted how many million dollars we had stolen from their country by accepting the refugees in Sweden. That was the beginning. We stayed for more than ten years in former Yugoslavia. Many projects developed from the Sarajevo ruins into the regions of former Yugoslavia, and a new university department of social work was established, located in the campus in Banja Luka. This enterprise was made possible through the formation of a network of schools of social work at the universities in the former Yugoslavia. My idea was based on an observation that voluntary or non-governmental international organizations invade nations during crises and leave shortly afterwards to another catastrophe. Also, politicians seem to come and go, sometimes very often. Maybe we would expect that the academy or universities to be essentially stable, and they provide a soil of continuity to grow from and trust in the long run. I think this is the basic concept when we build collaboration between universities over national borders.

This was the starting point for my engagement in development programmes in many countries after former Yugoslavia – for example, Kurdistan (Iraq), Vietnam, China – and guest lecturing in all corners of the world. The Swedish Government appointed me to a position on the board of SIDA, the Swedish International Development Agency. Sweden then had a voice to argue for the social perspective in the international development programmes in countries with less developed medical, economic and industrial sectors.

The activities in these three areas played crucial roles in my development, both as university lecturer and researcher: psychosocial work, child welfare and international engagement. My writings are essentially within these three fields, in Swedish and in other languages.

Usually I act because someone asks me. In the same way that UNICEF asked me to go to Sarajevo, in the case of Banja Luka, the Social Workers' Union in former Yugoslavia got together and expressed a need for social work education in that part of the country. We had a long, ongoing discussion whether we should start or not, and in what way. We were convinced it should not be ethnically homogeneous or based on a somewhat nationalistic movement evident in civil society in the *Republika Srbska* at the time. We wanted to establish an internationalist corner of Europe, a multi-ethnic university in fact. I do not know if we succeeded, but my fundamental principle was in this case that I do not want to colonize people. However, if they ask me to come, I do. Everything had to start through a dialogue, and continue as such. I cannot tell if there is another possibility, but if somebody had had another idea, we might have considered it. We did what we could with the resources we had. I must remind you that the University of Banja Luka was probably one of the first among university departments in social work that tried out the global standards that were established by IASSW. We tried them out before they were introduced in Sweden.

In which field do you think you made the biggest contribution?

I would consider as my most important contribution the work we did in the former Yugoslavia. There, I think social work could be viewed as peace work.

Another key piece of work was that I started and was the editor-in-chief of a scientific journal, the *International Journal of Social*

Welfare (IJSW), which aims to open the communication among the international communities and colleagues in social welfare research. In 2016, we are publishing the twenty-fifth volume. It became a really highly rated journal in social welfare; we are among the 'top 10' in the world. I resigned from the chief editorship in 2014. Nowadays, I might be visiting colleagues or PhD candidates in a university to run a workshop on 'How to get published in a scientific journal – recommendations from a former chief editor'.

What did social work mean to you professionally?

I think I was able to enter the world of psychosocial work, going from the inside of the clinic to the outside world, both in my practice and in my publications. I had to, because I was the director of a therapeutic community, and I could not hide my clients in the room, and then throw them out and wait for the next patient. I had to consider them being in a community. I was forced to take a holistic view of them.

I moved back and forth between professional work and academia. I started as a practitioner, and then I was hijacked to the university, where they supported me to do a PhD. After the dissertation, I went out into the field again. I started working with heavy drug users that you could find at the railway station, usually in big cities. Then I was working with and doing research on children and families at the well-known Barnbyn Skå in Sweden. Then again, I went back to the university. I was back and forth, like in a dialectical circle.

When I came out as a social worker from the darkness of psychology in the beginning of the 1970s, social work was defined as a discipline searching for solutions for the social problems of our society. Sweden had quite a homogenous population, of which one million had migrated to the US at the end of the nineteenth century. The context changed dramatically. We became an immigrant country with one million migrants during the 1970s and '80s. Not to mention the current challenges of the 'invasion' of asylum seekers to Europe! If I may make a comparison, we are now living in a global society, which demands exchange of knowledge across borders. Increasing migration demands improved knowledge of social welfare and social work, as well as knowledge of the contextual premises in the countries of origin, from which the migrants are pushed or pulled, to knowledge about the premises of the receiving country. We have to understand the social welfare models or the social work premises of the countries where the migrants came from to understand how we should encounter them in

Sweden. I am not sure, but I hope that education nowadays in social work considers these changes.

In the 1970s, there were only a few schools of social work in Sweden and only a handful of full professors. Since 1979, when the first university professor got his chair, we have increased to 15 university departments or schools of social work in our country. Quite a lot of the social workers are professionally trained, but we may question what they are doing. Many social workers have become administrative workers and managers in municipalities. This happens in spite of the development of lots of methodology in social work practice that is taught in the schools of social work, and which we might think would attract them to working directly with clients.

What major obstacles have you faced in your career?

During my work and my career, I have had two difficult obstacles to deal with. One is the attitude that we have nothing to learn from other countries: why should we learn from others, they should come here and learn from us? This attitude has delayed the development of the Swedish social work towards internationalization. This obstacle is always challenging the importance of a dialogue. For more than 20 years, I have been involved in the appointment of professors or people in higher positions in other countries. I can therefore make comparisons between where different countries stand when I see their applications and the level of Swedish professors when they send me their applications. I have also been participating in international expert committees for establishing social work in different countries, for example, China, and committees for evaluating social work education, for example, Israel. It is obvious that we are in a stone age, because most Swedish people would avoid doing international social work, but now we are forced to because every university requires us to become internationalized.

The second obstacle I have encountered is within my own field of expertise, child welfare. Sometimes I meet colleagues and others, both at national and international levels, who think that they can handle child welfare cases considering the child only, without taking into account the context within which the child is living. This was the subject of my first important research project, and now when I turn to an international perspective I can see this as an international dilemma as well. I could see these obstacles as challenges because 'obstacle' is something standing in the way but 'challenge' is something you can go into dialogue with.

What were the challenges of social work and its education during your career?

When I look at my working life, I can see that I have done quite a lot of things. However, the most important challenge I took on during my time as professor was to fight for social issues in an international world where only economics, medical, technical and natural sciences count. I have been involved in SIDA and have been fighting for social issues to be included, which is difficult against the dominance of the other sciences. I go out into the world and I see the African dilemmas for instance, and then have to struggle to persuade people to invest in social welfare issues. Everywhere I go, I am triggered to try to convince my colleagues that there is always a social perspective to add to any other subject. Everything happens among the members of a society.

The EU Bologna Agreement[2] streamlines or puts the same costume on all college and university education in all subjects in all European countries and is another challenge. Since it is a costume that looks the same, when it comes to social work, we also abide by these standards. This is a good thing, on the one hand, for exchange of students and teachers and even courses. On the other hand, in my opinion, there is a risk that the practical aspects of social work will drown in this streamlined academic costume. I have been travelling around in all parts of the world, and I would say there are many differences according to history, tradition, welfare and state model. Social work practice must always be context bound, even if academic education is costumed and something you can choose to study everywhere. There is a risk that academization will diminish the value of practice, even make it disappear sometimes. If it does not disappear, it might be streamlined in all parts of Europe. That is a risk because we should emphasize the contextual part of social work.

I ask myself, what is the future role of the social worker? I think that the professional identity of the social worker is quite uncertain for the time being. Ethical questions have become urgent. How we see it depends on whether we are leaning to the right or to the left politically, but I would say that people are becoming more conservative. Then more responsibility will be taken over by churches and voluntary organizations, because social workers are becoming highly professional and may be seen as too expensive to employ.

Maybe the most important challenge right now and in the future is to add the social perspective to the climate change discourse. As in all other global issues, the losers of the climate change are poor people, mostly in the Global South, and women and children are in the high-risk categories. If social workers could be among the first soldiers in the front line of the army fighting against the consequences of climate change, it is possible that social work might climb the ladder to become the most important future social experts, and not be viewed as secondary to other professionals. I think we have to be in the front line. I quote Zygmunt Baumann,[3] who defined social workers as the army of front-line soldiers of solidarity. I like that! This is why I chose social work in the first place. I always have some kind of spur that pushes me to say 'Yes', when it comes to supporting people who are being excluded or at risk of being excluded. I think that is the vital responsibility of the social work discipline.

Selected publications

Hessle, S. (ed) (2001) *International standard setting of higher social work education* (Stockholm Studies of Social Work 17), Stockholm: Stockholm University, Department of Social Work.

Hessle, S. and Zaviršek, D. (eds) (2005) *Sustainable development in social work: The case of a regional network in the Balkans*, Stockholm: Stockholm University, Department of Social Work.

Hessle, S. (2013) 'Child welfare development in Sweden' in P. Welbourne and J. Dixon (eds) *Child protection and child welfare: A global appraisal of cultures, policy and practice*, London: Jessica Kingsley.

Hessle, S. (ed) (2014) *Social work – social development*, Vols I–III, Farnham: Ashgate.

Hessle, S. (2015) 'Child, family and the external world – establishing policies in a dialogue with increased migration' (Plenary speech at the Finnish Congress of Social Work, February 2015) *Tutkiva Sosiaalityö 2015* pp 5–9, http://www.talentia.isinteksas.com/mag/tutkivasosiaalityo2015.php.

Notes

[1] The ecological environment is conceived as a set of nested structures, each inside the next, like a set of Russian dolls' (Bronfenbrenner, 1979: p 3).

[2] The Bologna declaration (1999) by EU education ministers aims to ensure comparability in the standards and quality of higher education across EU countries: http://ec.europa.eu/education/policy/higher-education/bologna-process_en.htm.

[3] Zygmunt Bauman (1925-2017), eminent Polish sociologist living in England since 1971, Professor Emeritus of Sociology, University of Leeds; author of *Liquid modernity* (Bauman, 2000).

THIRTEEN

Shulamit Ramon, 2008

Interviewed by Brian Littlechild

Biography

 Shulamit Ramon's career culminated in academic leadership roles at the London School of Economics, Anglia Ruskin University and Hertfordshire University. Her education led to professional qualifications in clinical psychology and social work, including a PhD on defects in communication and cultural change in families where the index client had experienced schizophrenia. Significant professional contributions include experience and research in mental health, leadership in developing social work education in Eastern and Central Europe and the former Soviet Union, and work on practice in areas of political and social conflict. Her publications include work on innovations in mental health internationally, on community care in the UK and the policy of normalization, and on social work in the context of political conflict internationally. She has also created innovative postgraduate courses in mental health. Since the interview, she has continued her work in areas such as mental health, user participation, political conflict and international social work education, as well as in participatory action research focused on empowering marginalized groups.

When did you receive the award and on what basis?

I received my award in 2008 for my international work rather than for my work in any particular country. Some of it was for work on political conflict in the context of social work. That was international from the very beginning, and the other part was for the focus on involving users in social work.

What has the award meant to you?

It was nice to get and obviously an ego boost and wonderful to know that some people thought I should get it. It was not my idea, so that was pleasant. It is about professional recognition, though nothing happened afterwards to celebrate it. It became a personal thing, although my employer at the time, Anglia Ruskin University, was very pleased, and so was my Dean, and that was about it. I have not come across anyone mentioning it to me in professional circles, in England or in other countries.

Maybe it makes a bigger difference for award holders in other countries. I have to say that people, including professionals, who heard that I received it said, you well deserve it, which was nice to hear.

What activities were of major importance for your career and its impact on social work and its education?

A lot of my work is in mental health. However, I do not distinguish much between social work and mental health because most of my mental health work is about its social aspects. Before I became engaged in the work on political conflict, a lot of my international work was in mental health, looking at different contexts to make sense of the direction in which those mental health systems have gone. I have worked with people from Australia, Canada, Italy, Portugal, Slovenia, the US, Israel, as well as in the UK on reforming mental health services.

When I came to the UK, I thought I was coming to a community mental health system and discovered that this was not exactly the case. Then I heard about Italy, and I started to invest quite a lot in researching the Italian psychiatric reform. I learnt the language, and for years I was going to Italy about twice a year, each time to a different place for a couple of weeks to observe, get immersed and understand what was going on there. One of my first books was a comparison of the Italian and the British system (Ramon and Giannichedda, 1988). That certainly was international in the sense of a two-country comparison.

I was then at the London School of Economics (LSE). Many people there could not for a long time understand why I am interested in Italy. Italy was seen as a fairly 'uncivilized' country; therefore, it was a waste of my time from their point of view. What could be learnt from the work in Italy? I found reactions to it both funny and enraging. Well-known experts in the UK referred in writing to this 'opera buff' enthusiasm for Italian reform. It was interesting to experience this condescending approach to another country's radical innovation. Italy is after all in Europe, not very far. We share a history with Italy, and both the UK and Italy are[1] members of the EU.

Therefore, it was quite interesting to come from that side. In addition, the assumption was if I speak Italian, I must be Italian. I think people could not contemplate the idea that you would learn a language for research even though you had no ties otherwise to that country. Italians of course would ask me, would you not like to come and live in Italy? When I was honest, I said I would not. There are aspects I like about Italy, but I do not think I could live with the mentality of 'clientelism', which does exist in Italy.

I worked on social work a lot in Eastern Europe, especially Ukraine, Russia, Slovenia for a very long time, a bit after that in Azerbaijan and also visited other countries. Azerbaijan is not a European country, but was part of the Soviet bloc. That made it interesting because there was a different perception of what social work could be about. Professional social work was not really recognized, so some people said: 'Of course, we've always done it'. However, there was a lot of interest when the Soviet Union ceased to exist, in trying to develop this new profession.

I did pioneering work, always with others. These were huge projects, which the European Union funded. The Azerbaijan work was funded by the Open Society. The Open Society and the Eileen Younghusband Fund from LSE funded the initial project, which I did in Armenia. It was fascinating to observe who wanted to develop it and who was keen on sabotaging it. I tried to continue developing it, even though I was phenomenally disadvantaged by not being part of the social cultural scene. Therefore, I strived very hard to develop the local leadership in each of those places, cooperating with schools and departments that were ready to do so.

I found it interesting that they developed it much better in the smaller than in the larger countries. Ukraine with 50 million people is a small country compared to Russia. It was much easier to develop social work education in Ukraine than in Russia. I think I was up against the Russians' mentality that they were the pinnacle of the empire; especially in Moscow, where they thought they knew everything. This was so, even though I had much support in Moscow from a group of people interested in developing social work; this was partly for personal reasons, as my partner works there. He was a social worker when we met, and he is well connected.

We did manage to develop more in Ukraine and Armenia, even in Azerbaijan, than in Russia, and especially in Slovenia. I was not in Slovenia to develop social work, as it existed already. Nevertheless, I think social work has changed partly because of the exchange with the

UK. The programme, which was focused on introducing community mental health to a multidisciplinary range of professionals, started in 1991 and lasted for six years, which is a long time for such a programme. Most of the Slovenian participants spent six months in the UK, so they had quite a lot of opportunities to learn about the UK.

In addition, I visited many other countries, carrying out evaluations. I evaluated the masters programme in social work run by the Open Society, which brings a small number of people, from each of the former Soviet Union countries to prestige universities in the US for two years. However, the key issue is the relevance of that training to what they can do when they return to their own country.

I did insist on having someone initially from Armenia, and who knew Armenia and Russia well, to carry out this evaluation. She was not allowed to enter Azerbaijan because of the political conflict between Armenia and Azerbaijan, but we went together to Kyrgyzstan, Kazakhstan, Georgia and Mongolia. I do not think they liked our conclusions, that money is much better spent inside these countries. Bringing people from the US and other countries is more productive than taking people away for two years.

INDOSOW is a European PhD and social work programme, which has four partner countries, led by Professor Darja Zaviršek, from Ljubljana. The other partners are from Austria, Finland, Germany, Italy and the UK (Anglia Ruskin University).

INDOSOW has been another core feature of my international work between 2006 and 2015. Three books have come out of the programme. The project was developed as a curriculum-building programme, funded by the EU (2006-09), which was very helpful in enabling us to develop a full curriculum with the participation of PhD students and social work educators from each partner country.

The programme includes an annual summer school, and students have to spend a semester in another country within the programme, and be co-supervised. PhD work is very important in the context of developing social work, because in some countries it is the only existing research in social work. Doing a PhD gives more time, and freedom, to explore things, even if on a small scale. Being supervised within your country and outside it enhances the richness diversity brings, but is likely to raise the question of differences in standards among different research cultures. This emphasizes the comparative perspective.

We want to make sure that the lives of clients are improved with our input, and therefore must have some universal standards in addition to local ones, which may be a source of conflict, thus raising yet again the level of complexity. You may be accused of being egocentric or, as I was in INDOSOW, of bringing in an Anglo-Saxon hegemony; a funny assumption given my background, and my expressed criticism of the English system.

Coming from a different background, it was interesting to be exposed to this type of accusation. I was not sure for what I was supposed to apologize, nor was I particularly apologetic. The English system is not less good than others are. It has its strong points and its weaknesses. However, I cannot deny that each of us comes inevitably with our own inherent standards.

An important area is my work on involving users in social work, in teaching and in research. In teaching, it is easier for people from other countries to understand and to do. I think in research it is much more complex because there are issues of standards and assumptions that only well-trained people can do research. I think it is essential that users will be more involved in social work research.

User involvement happens a lot more in education in the UK than in practice. Even so, social workers are all the time involving individual service users, but I am concerned about a lack of collective perspective of users in social services. Involving users in practice has been quite complicated, and I do not think English social services want to develop it. They may say so, but their actions do not reflect that. I see my role as continuing to work with users wherever it is possible.

I have now (in 2009) two additional projects on user involvement. One, which compares students' views on involving service users in social work education in England and Israel, where older people are the co-researchers. The other one is more concerned with mental health, in Niza Monferrato in Italy, where I have been invited to prepare service users to interview other service users about the issue of employment. The people in Niza Monferrato have been mental health service users for some time, while the co-researchers in England and Israel are older people who have had a professional life. They are now retired, and use more health and social services. The UK group had a four-month training course in research, specifically designed for older people who want to know more about research, and organized themselves into a research cooperative, titled Why Not?

The final project in social work is the context of political conflict. This obviously comes from my autobiographical background. What has been happening in Israel, especially since the second intifada, has been very difficult to accept and has made me think about what I can do living in England. During the first intifada, I demonstrated every week against the Israeli government. I was living in London at the time and with a group of others, primarily women, we demonstrated near the Israeli embassy. It was not particularly easy, and no Palestinian women wanted to join us. Most Israelis thought we were traitors and most Palestinians thought we were not to be trusted.

When I moved to Cambridge, it was during the second intifada. I was against any suicide bombing from the Palestinian side. I cannot justify it in any form, not even against soldiers, and certainly not against civilian populations. Therefore, I could not find myself publicly demonstrating for the Palestinians. Nevertheless, I could not agree with what the Israeli army was doing and with the Israeli government policy. Therefore, I thought maybe I could look at how social workers work with victims of that type of violence, and sometimes also with perpetrators. How does this type of traumatized cultural context affect their work, being aware that it is not just the work? They are citizens, with their life experience and views about what is happening.

For me, this first research project on the impact of the second intifada on Israeli Arab and Jewish social workers was quite important, and also brought together the political and the personal. This is something that English social work hardly wants to know about. It is much easier to see yourself only as a professional. I am not the only one thinking that such an approach does not work in either health or social work. Iain Ferguson, from the University of Stirling, started his talk at the conference of EASSW in 2009 with a quotation about the relation between the personal and the political from my book on social work in the context of political conflict (Ramon et al, 2008). The second intifada project partly led to other Israelis doing similar research. Most of them were frightened to touch the topic, but ready to help me, and I brought in the necessary funding. However, one or two people are not frightened, and have done some interesting work. I was successful in convincing Jane Lindsay, from Kingston University, UK, to do a replication study in the occupied territories using the same questions (Lindsay, 2007; Lindsay et al, 2011).

In 2003, I organized a successful study day on this issue in Belfast, because I did not think anyone in England would be interested, unlike colleagues in Northern Ireland. We had some people coming from South Africa and Bosnia. A Palestinian came with Jane Lindsay and an Israeli colleague came with me. The two did not speak to each other, which was a bit complicated. Some Northern Ireland politicians attended, and that led to wanting to do a project, which IASSW supported, to develop more awareness within social work of the issue of political conflict (Duffy et al, 2013).

The second project that we have attempted, unsuccessfully, was to create a curriculum that, with some modification, could be used internationally (Duffy et al, 2013). It is important to understand why we were unsuccessful; the 80+ responses we got to an international survey highlighted that the need for such a curriculum exists, but the will to prioritize it does not. We did publish a book where we have contributions from 12 countries, very international and comparative of different aspects of political conflicts (Ramon, 2008), and a special supplement of *International Social Work* on further research in this area (Ramon and Zaviršek, 2012, see Selected Publications). I certainly would like to continue this type of work, and see how it will take shape.

Another thing that relates to that is my mental health work in EMILIA, a European Union framework for six projects. It is about social inclusion, empowerment and recovery in mental health, which again I see as related to social work. I do not think it is accidental that the coordinator is a professor of mental health social work, Peter Ryan, University of Middlesex, and the whole ethos is very much a social work ethos. The project now ends after four-and-a-half years. I am involved in the publication from the project (Ryan, Ramon and Greachen, 2012, see Selected Publications). A group of three people is editing the book.

Personally, I am quite critical of mental health social work. It is too much bogged down by legal and not concerned enough with social aspects. It does not pay attention to individual psychological issues and social issues beyond enabling people to get benefits, which is a shame. How this might be taken further I am not sure, but I certainly would like to.

In which field do you think you made the biggest contribution?

Probably in the areas of user involvement and political conflict. I am sorry that my work in mental health has not had the same impact on social work because I think it is important. I would also mention my commitment to international social work.

At LSE, international social work was encouraged, but only if you chose carefully where you were going to do it. It has to be research and not development work. They did not like my involvement in setting up social work education in Armenia, Ukraine or Russia. Whether this was a particular LSE position I do not know, but today, with a lot more focus on the government university funding body's assessment of research achievement in university departments, this happens in other universities as well. I was able to show enough publications in peer-reviewed journals, so nobody could ever say I was neglecting these requirements, but they could not define all the funding that I received as research, and that did bother them.

What has social work education meant to you personally and professionally? Why did you choose it?

I am not sure how to answer this question. My first degree was in social work, due to personal autobiographical reasons. I wanted to be a social worker since I was about 14. I never thought I would be a social work academic, as I wanted to be a practitioner. I came into academia by accident, but do not regret it at all. I am probably more suited to it than to be a practitioner. I am actually grateful for what I got in the school of social work at the Hebrew University, which is where I did my first degree. We got a lot of input and attention to our personal developmental needs, input from different countries and different perspectives.

I was recruited to become an academic. I saw an interview by a researcher who was doing research on successful and less successful school graduates. This would not be possible today, but he offered me a job at the end of the interview. It gave me a very good basis, but the rest of my training was not as straightforward as my undergraduate degree in social work.

My PhD was in social work in a social administration department in the UK. In between, I did a degree in psychology and sociology and a masters in clinical psychology in Israel. I continued with the same topic for my PhD, and the supervision I got for the masters clinical psychology dissertation was enough to sustain me.

For me social work education is very important because it is the basis for preparing practitioners, but not just practitioners, also leaders of services and researchers. I would like it to be more research-oriented. To an extent, I see with some envy how nursing has developed. Nursing used not to have any research, and it is now much more research-oriented than undergraduate social work education. Nursing departments in the different health settings respect research more than social services departments do.

I am sorry that this is the case. I supervise PhD students from social work, nursing and sometimes other disciplines, and I can see the difference in their starting points. Even with a masters degree, social workers actually know a bit less. There are individual differences as some people from social work are very good and some from nursing are not necessarily so, but the research training in the social work qualification degree is not good enough.

What are the main challenges for social work and its education?

One of the challenges is to create a good evidence base for social work practice. I do not mean only the traditional evidence-based and not necessarily randomized control trial research, but research that takes the user perspective and the carer perspectives into account, and values both scientific and experiential knowledge. This is still a challenge.

However, I would also like social work education to support the profession and develop a more independent perspective, especially from health, than it has. Health is so influential in the UK as a model of how you should think and work when you are in any helping profession. My sense is that social work is retreating in terms of its unique message rather than expanding. Some of it, paradoxically, is because nursing is doing a lot more of what used to be social work. You could say that such influence is a success for social work, but what nursing brings is a mixture of a model from traditional medicine, with elements of a social model.

I would like social work to be more robust in its theory, in its research and practice. Many practitioners ignore research, even if they are force-fed with it in study days and similar initiatives, as there is no model of how you actually apply it in your everyday practice. This is a pity, and it is one of the major challenges for social work education, but social work education cannot meet this on its own.

How has social work and social work education changed during your career?

It has partly changed from a much more individualistic psychodynamic approach to understanding that many clients' problems come from social structures, but not necessarily from a Marxist position as some argued in the 1960s and '70s. It is accepting the social structure as given, affecting the life of individuals. However, it has not developed in a sense that it sees social work as mediating between the client and the impact of the social structure – what society does allow people who use social services to have. It is not enabling social workers and social work clients to get what they can, and to enhance their own problem-solving strategies. The increasing impact of the neoliberal approach to the economy and to society in many countries, including the UK, is highlighting the treatment of social work clients as undeserving citizens, thus retreating to Victorian attitudes.

Nevertheless, social work continues to an extent to be bogged down by the idea that because people come to us when they have problems, and serious ones, they are seen as being weak. Their resilience and strengths are not emphasized enough. I would like social work to develop beyond lip service on this issue, on how to use the strengths that people bring with them and build on this.

What would you like to see happening in social work, its education and IASSW in the future?

I would like social work education to focus more on involving users and creating models for involvement in practice. It has to be done, first, respecting the unique contribution of their experience, and second, taking into account their strengths and capacity for resilience. I mentioned earlier the importance of developing research and a robust theoretical perspective for social work.

International organizations like IASSW could play quite a major role. However, to do that it will have to move to the perspective of seeing clients as partners and not as recipients. I am not seeing that internationally, only in some pockets, and I do not see it emphasized.

There is a role for the international associations to look seriously at those aspects, thinking of their place within social work theory, research and practice, and encourage local member schools of social work in different countries to also consider those issues.

Selected publications

Ramon, S. (ed) (2008) *Social work in the context of political conflict*, Birmingham: Venture Press.

Ramon, S. and Zaviršek, D. (eds) (2009) *Critical edge issues in social work and social policy*, Ljubljana: Faculty of Social Work.

Ryan, P., Ramon, S. and Greachen, T. (2012) *Empowerment, lifelong learning and recovery in mental health: Towards a new paradigm*, Basingstoke: Palgrave Macmillan.

Ramon, S. and Zaviršek, D. (eds) (2012) 'Social work in the context of armed conflict', *International Social Work*, Special issue 55(5).

Duffy, J., Ramon, S., Guru, S., Lindsay, J., Cemlyn, S. and Nuttman-Shwartz, O. (2013) 'Developing a social work curriculum on political conflict: findings from an IASSW-funded project', *European Journal of Social Work*. 16(5): pp 689-707.

Notes

[1] At the time of the interview.

FOURTEEN

Silvia M. Staub-Bernasconi, 2010

Interviewed by Darja Zaviršek

Biography

 Silvia Staub-Bernasconi's (b. 1936) career in social work education was defined by her role as professor at Zurich School of Social Work from 1967-97. After she qualified in social work at this school, she studied social work (1963-67) on a United Nations Fellowship at the University of Minnesota, Minneapolis, and at Columbia University, New York. In Zurich, she became the first street social worker and worked with migrants. In the US, she worked with a group of black women and in community work on the Lower East Side. Coming back to Zurich, she studied sociology, social ethics and educational psychology at the University of Zurich, where she received her PhD (1979), followed by her *habilitation*[1] in 1996 at the Technical University of Berlin. After 30 years of professorship at the Zurich School, teaching and supervising social work with groups and with communities, she became a professor at the Technical University Berlin from 1997 until 2003. Her main topics were theories of social problems, social work as discipline and profession and social work as human rights profession. She has been on the academic board and teaching staff of the International Doctoral Studies in Social Work (INDOSOW), which involved several European universities.

When did you receive the award and what has it meant to you?

I received it in 2010 at the World Conference in Hong Kong. The first memory, which came to my mind when I learned I was elected, was a dinner with Katherine Kendall, Lynne Healy and some other colleagues at the IASSW Conference in 2001 in Montpellier, France. We talked about many things, but I was especially impressed with Katherine Kendall's historical and current knowledge about the profession and its development. It was the first time I had been invited to one of the many small, informal meetings taking place alongside conferences. Until then, I was just imagining how conference members, especially men, were being effective in networking and making plans. However, this was a most pleasant meeting of women without other goals than sharing experiences and a good dinner.

For me, the award honours my lifelong endeavours to develop a sound theory of social problems as the domain of social work and of social work as a discipline and profession. In recent decades, I integrated human rights into this frame, using a broad philosophical, ethical and action-theoretical framework, which could integrate many fragmented theoretical approaches and methods on different social levels, starting with work with individuals, families and communities and engagement with global issues in world society.

I was sure the award would also support my engagement in educational and curriculum policy in the German-speaking part of Europe, which I see as not well linked to the international community. Since the strong German faction in IASSW, founded in 1928 in Paris, left the Association when their request to dismiss Alice Salomon as secretary-general was not accepted by the board, Germany – now with about 80 schools of social work and several universities with departments of social pedagogy – has not manifested a strong interest in the international association. An exception is the Alice Salomon University of Applied Sciences.

What activities were of major importance for your professional career and its impact on social work and its education?

I would highlight three important points. First, the supervision given to me by a teacher, Lotty Brunschweiler, at the Zurich School of Social Work when, parallel to my studies and fieldwork in social work from 1958 to 1960, I started with street work with a gang in an industrial area of Zurich. This gang had destroyed parts of a leisure centre, beaten up former educators and were in a good deal of trouble with the police. The content of my thesis in 1960 comprised analyses of gang processes and my interventions. I showed how knowledge about group structures and processes, combined with democratic methodological principles in working with a street gang, were successful in gaining the respect, confidence and gradually the cooperation of its members in developing their own activities which would not bring them straightaway to the police station. Only many years later I realized, why this 'account' published in three editions, was especially successful in Germany. After years of 'black pedagogy'[2] in state agencies and, especially, in children's and young people's homes managed mostly by Christian denominations, this 'democratic counter-example' of social work practice with rebellious youngsters apparently convinced social workers and their teachers during the years of the 'Democratic Education Programs'. These were initiated in West Germany by the Allies, especially the US, after World War II. I am almost sure that without this starting point I would have ended up within the narrow borders of Switzerland.

Second, was my decision to study sociology as a major after returning from the US. I decided to write my PhD thesis to answer the question: what could be the special domain and transdisciplinary scientific base of social work? It took me a dozen years, alongside having a family and a job, and no financial support. Professor Heintz, a sociologist of world society and my major supervisor, appreciated especially the development of a theory of constructive and destructive power structures and social action. In contrast, many colleagues who had not studied social work were, to say the least, irritated by my writings. For them, social work was just a practice with more or less sound methods. Yet, the students got more and more enthusiastic about it, because it gave them a professional identity and orientation.

Parallel to my lectures, seminars and projects in Zurich, I was invited to many conferences, seminars, workshops, lectures and universities as guest professor in different European countries, confirming the proverb that nobody is a prophet in one's own country. The greatest attacks came from the universities in Germany, the educational sciences and social pedagogy. They spoke of a putsch against them. Yet, this was never my intention. I only wanted to promote the idea of a social work profession, which deals in a comprehensive way with social problems without the problematic heritage of dualisms between body and mind, individual and society, natural sciences and *Geisteswissenschaften* [human sciences]. Even more important, I wanted to oppose the theoretical top-down approach, starting with the social macro level of socio-economic, socio-political or legal conditions for social work, which ended mostly with a simple, reductionist image of the individual, defined as the socially deviant client.[3] It was in this phase that I realized what I had learned implicitly in my studies in the US. Namely, if we start with individuals, their needs, suffering, discrimination, powerlessness, but also with their resources and entitlements, we must follow a theoretical bottom-up approach of transforming privatized issues into professional help, as well as public, socio-political debates, claims and social rights issues, including a sophisticated analysis of power structures and sources of power. I think my book, *Social work as action science* (Staub-Bernasconi, 2007, see Selected Publications[4]), was and is a central frame of reference for this development.

During this wild 'high noon debate', the German Society of Social Work was founded. I, as its vice president, headed the theory development section until 2015. This created a platform for all these heated discussions. A subgroup developed a core curriculum for bachelors and masters studies in social work, which in its second, enlarged and precise version was ratified at the annual conference of the German society of social work in 2016. For a couple of years, we have had constructive collaborative networks between universities and universities of applied sciences, even in doctoral programmes of social work. This is why I am so grateful to Darja Zaviršek for setting up the INDOSOW project, for which we are looking for a new financial basis for the participation of doctoral students.

Third is surely the audacity of setting up a masters programme called 'Social Work as a Human Rights Profession', which started in 2002 in Berlin. It has survived all prognoses of opponents who were sure that there is no market for such a crazy, abstract, luxurious idea. It looked to them as if it were a naive fantasy of 'displacing clouds in the sky', which does not fit at all into the neo-liberal zeitgeist and the actual fiscal poverty of the state. But, interestingly enough, the notion of human rights seems to find its way, although slowly and not without resistance, into seminars, lectures, conferences, curricula, practice projects and the masters theses of more and more departments of social work in the German part of Europe. In 2014, we could start an international masters in Social Work as a Human Rights Profession at the Alice Salomon University of Applied Sciences in Berlin. It has students from all over the world, and especially from many crisis, conflict and war regions.

In which field do you think you made the biggest contribution?

You would have to ask my colleagues, supporters, as well as my opponents about this! If I have to give a personal statement, I would mention the following:

- The explication of the contribution of the philosophical and theoretical work of Mario Bunge in developing a disciplinary framework for social work as a profession. His theoretical framework offers the possibility of a transdisciplinary integration of atomized, particular knowledge under the general idea of 'integrated pluralism'. I was pleased to find a reference to Bunge in a newer discussion about 'Shaping the science of social work' in *Research on social work practice* (Brekke, 2012).
- The insight that social work does not have only a double mandate of 'help and control', often criticized as 'help *as* control', but a triple mandate. The first mandate comes from the client, the second from agencies and society, and the third from the profession itself. The last legitimates relative professional autonomy of judgement based on its obligation to science and human rights, and, if necessary, a self-formulated mandate, if organizational, social and political power structures impede it, for example, in failed states or pre- or post-war conflicts.
- The development of a relatively comprehensive theory of power processes, destructive and constructive power structures, power sources and empowerment.
- A contribution to the competence linking theory and practice, called the 'three-stage transformation step'.
- The development of a local masters, in German-speaking countries, and an international masters in social work and human rights. In both, all students have to develop a project of human rights implementation, either individually or in groups, either in their workplace, in the community or in relation to the UN or the European Council of Human Rights.

All this was always accompanied by personal counselling, social practice and research projects.

What did social work education mean to you personally and professionally? Why did you choose it?

For me personally, social work opened a completely new vision of the world after my four years of commercial school. I found a voice and explanation for a question I had had since my childhood: why is there so much misery, poverty, hate, war, terror and millions of refugees in the world, if God loves us? Why has Switzerland, surrounded by two wars in the middle of Europe, been protected from all their horror? Not even clerics could give me a satisfactory answer, so I decided to find out by myself. The disciplines I could have studied – law, medicine, economics or psychology – did not interest me. There was no sociology at that time at the University of Zurich, so I chose the School of Social Work as the only interesting alternative and hoped to find answers to some of my questions. Some answers came from my social work education, others during my studies in sociology, philosophy and the intense endeavours to grasp what had happened in Nazi Germany and the Holocaust, which is a never-ending process.

In the US, I was introduced to a combination of methods of social group work, community work and international social work. Arnold Rose, professor of social psychology and sociology, opened my eyes to the 'American dilemma', racism, its causes and consequences. The black students taught me, in practice, what racism, poverty and living in slums means.

My studies in sociology in Zurich happened at the same time as the student revolt of 1968. I was then confronted with the strong critique of social work as sustaining a worldwide capitalist system of discrimination and oppression of clients, which calls for revolution. The fantasy to change or even revolutionize the worldwide capitalist system with the support of social work or, even stranger, with the help of social work clients, seemed to me quite illusory. Yet, this criticism was the starting point to develop a theory of legitimate power and practice. This was based on having a legitimate goal formulated together with the clients, family, community members and on acting, if necessary, using alternative sources of power against the will of the power holders. Thus, I showed students and practitioners in countless seminars, projects and supervisions how, together with the clients, to get what they are entitled to. Alinsky's (1971: p 126) dictum, 'We will either find a way or make one!', became a leading principle when people faced obstacles. The main goal was to change oppressive, discriminating structures where social workers have access to these, namely families, communities, organizations, working places.

What was the importance of international work in your career?

My orientation to international social work has three roots. First, it was influenced by the experience of ethnic, religious and class diversity in my family. Second, especially, the UN Fellowship 1963-67 was of great importance. The UN building, the people visiting it and its personnel represented for me breathtaking internationality and multiculturalism and an agenda of worldwide, although conflictive, integration. Third, as professor at the Zurich School of Social Work I was responsible for what was then called *Ausländerproblem* [the foreigner or 'outsider' problem]. In order to learn more about international social work contexts, I planned my sabbaticals in various parts of the world: Rio, Brazil; Birmingham, UK; California, US; and Moscow, Russia.

However, the most decisive eye opener and engagement was the admission policy for political refugees of the Zurich School. The students came from different countries: Turkey after the Devjol process of 1980, then from former Yugoslavia, Chile, Eritrea and Iraq and so on. I realized that I could not teach social work without integrating their biography and sociocultural context. Many had experienced persecution, repression and jail in the most terrible prisons of their countries. When, in 1989, the death of communism and socialism and the victory of capitalism and liberalism were declared, many of them had serious personal crises. Had they been fighting in vain for a better world? What could give them new orientation and hope, and a place in society? What could the education contribute to this? Therefore, I had the idea to organize a seminar on human rights. It reattached them to a world community united by the idea of the dignity of human beings and the liberty and social rights of the individual as complementary to work for social change. This was the start of the institutionalization of seminars in human rights at the Zurich School. But finally, it was the request from Ellen Mourajev-Apostol, the IFSW and IASSW representative at the UN in Geneva, to be an expert reviewer of the first *UN manual of social work and human rights* (1992), which consolidated the idea that international human rights have to be a decisive part in all aspects of a social work curriculum.

Gradually, I also realized that it is not necessary to go to a foreign country to practice international social work. With immigrants representing 25 per cent of the Swiss population, one can practice it on one's own doorstep. Following this path I initiated, and have supervised for over 20 years, a taskforce for intercultural conflicts, racism and violence operating in the German part of Switzerland. It keeps me in close contact with all the problems and conflicts of intercultural living.

What were the major obstacles that you faced in your career?

Being born between the first and second feminist movements, the first obstacle was that my father decided that the school of commerce was enough for a daughter who would marry anyway. He supported my brother in his natural science studies and was proud to have a son who was the youngest full professor at the University of California. I was not happy with my first administrative job as secretary. This was my starting point to look for educational opportunities. Until the *habilitation* at the University of Berlin in 1997, my career was a typical feminine zigzag one, almost exclusively supported by women.

The second obstacle was my teaching and practising of empowerment according to my theory of power and power sources. Students of the University of Zurich asked me to apply for a professorship. According to a committee member whistleblower, they were afraid about social unrest! At that time, I was also a member of the Women's Council on Foreign Affairs and a founding member of the journal, *Olympe*, the name of the woman who wrote the Declaration of the Rights of Women of 1791 in revolutionary France, who was killed on the guillotine! Berlin was the much better alternative.

Apart from this, I cannot say I faced big obstacles. The biggest problem, which is still not solved for women today, is having to choose between children and a career. To feel that I could not give my daughter the care and attention she needed and wanted was hurtful. Nevertheless, after many painful reflections and dialogues about this, we now have a good, supporting relationship.

Another aspect is that I had to learn to do 'my thing' without support and at the beginning always with much criticism and the advice to forget it. This began with my street work, where I was discouraged because 'this is not for a woman'. Then I saw shaking heads when I dared to say that I was working on a general theory of social work: 'Forget it, social work is a field of practice'. Starting the project on racism, power and intercultural conflicts, I heard: 'This is dangerous, because it will stigmatize Swiss people as well as migrants'. When trying to get the Swiss Parliament to sign the European Social Charter, the reaction was: 'You have not the faintest chance with the actual power constellation in the parliament'. Yet, after skilful work and lobbying by four alumni of the Berlin masters on human rights, the *Bundesrat*, the government, has to present parliament with a 'message' requiring a vote, hopefully by the end of 2017 or in 2018.

When I published *Social work as a human rights profession*, the reactions were: 'Are you a victim of nostalgia about the student revolt of 1968?' Or: 'This is a job for lawyers. It is irresponsible to compete with lawyers in this field.' Those criticizing had not even realized that social rights, for which social work should be responsible according to its professional ethics, were not justiciable at that time. No lawyer would engage him or herself in any procedure to claim social rights. It is only since 2009 that the UN Assembly has accepted the right to individual claims for social rights. A theologian teaching social work was upset, that IASSW and IFSW had the audacity to define social justice and to claim human rights in their international documents. According to him, social workers have to accept the mandate defined by society, without consideration of the actual political constellation. A very disturbing position looking back into recent German history! Looking back, I never let myself be discouraged by such 'obstacles'. On the contrary, it mobilized all my creativity, energy and patience to work continually at what I think is worthwhile to fight for.

How has social work and its education changed?

A most significant change in many curricula and social practice is the introduction of neo-liberal concepts and efficiency management techniques. This means the dismissal of a serious diagnosis about the sufferings of clients, vulnerable individuals and groups, which have no opportunity to satisfy their needs. Systematic work has been replaced by more efficient solution-based methods. This dispossesses clients of their primary concerns and social workers of their domain, social problems. It thus hinders any thinking about power structures, which are in most cases important causes of clients' situations and often also those of social workers. It means 'fast-food' instruments and techniques like checklists instead of science-based assessments and action guidelines, or tailored, time-based activities. These blatantly counteract and destroy empathy and reflective dialogue as human and professional interactions. I know that many faculties, teachers, supervisors and practitioners resist this inhuman colonization. But until now they seem to have been marginalized and made themselves vulnerable, to the detriment of their clients.

This all shows the great necessity to have international associations of social work education and social work like IASSW, CSWE and IFSW, which can give orientation and guidelines to their members in difficult times. Their task is to reassure members that they are not alone if they fight for crucial convictions about a social work that brings the clients, their distresses, concerns and rights back into focus.

What would you like to see happening in social work, its education and IASSW in the future?

We have now had over 30 years of neo-liberal colonization and dozens, if not hundreds of critical analyses of it. I joined this choir, too. Yet, the ten years of developing and implementing a masters of social work, which sets human rights and corresponding projects and social practice at its core, have shown what can still be achieved, even under very unfavourable societal conditions. I think that now the time has come for social work to free itself from the neo-liberal code system and face the multitude of worldwide economic, political, ethnic, religious, gender-based, war, ecological and many other conflicts and disasters – and the millions of refugees within and between countries. It is a world constellation in which the rich countries cannot ignore any more that the refugees are 'here' because 'we' were 'there', and still are there. This requires a social work education that transcends national borders, for example to work on transnational social care and social cause chains (Staub-Bernasconi, 2014, see Selected Publications). The Global Agenda by IASSW, ICSW and IFSW (2012) is a good guideline for future curriculum development and social action. So let us be 'academic activists', as Briskman (2009) suggests. In many respects, we still benefit from academic freedom. Why do we not use this freedom to implement the content of our own international documents? However, most important, let us end the endless debate about whether social work has a political *or* professional mandate. With its triple mandate, referring to science-based action guidelines and methods as well as human rights and social justice as its ethical guidelines, there cannot be an either–or, but only a skilful combination of both.

Selected publications

Staub-Bernasconi, S. (1991) 'Social action, empowerment and social work: an integrative theoretical framework for social work and social work with groups', in A.Vinik and M. Levin (eds) *Social action in group work*, New York: Haworth.

Staub-Bernasconi, S. (2006) 'Social work: theory and methods', in G. Ritzer (ed) *The Blackwell encyclopedia of sociology*, New York: Blackwell: pp 41-46.

Staub-Bernasconi, S. (2007) *Soziale Arbeit als Handlungswissenschaft* [*Social work as action science*], Bern: Haupt.

Staub-Bernasconi, S, (2012) 'Human rights and their relevance for social work as theory and practice', in L. M. Healy and R. J. Link (eds) *Handbook of international social work*, New York: Oxford University Press: pp 30-36.

Staub-Bernasconi, S. (2014) 'Transcending disciplinary, professional and national borders in social work education', in C. Noble, H. Strauss and B. Littlechild (eds) *Crossing borders and blurring boundaries*, Sydney: Sydney University Press: pp 27-41.

Staub-Bernasconi, S. (2016) 'Social work and human rights: linking two traditions of human rights and social work', *Journal of Social Work and Human Rights*, 1(1): p 31.

Notes

[1] A recognition of post-doctoral academic standing awarded in central European universities.

[2] (SMS-B) '*Schwarze Pädagogik'* is a cluster of educational 'methods' working with menaces, degrading, dehumanizing, chastising, violent practices, even torture, which were then on the whole legitimated by Bible texts.

[3] (SMS-B) I stick to the concept of 'client', which was historically seen as an emancipatory one, instead of the functionalist concept 'user'.

[4] (GAA&MP) Although this book is only available in German, an earlier article in English is available (Staub-Bernasconi, 2003, see Bibliography) presenting some of Staub-Bernasconi's ideas.

FIFTEEN

Lena Dominelli, 2012

Interviewed by Helle Strauss

Biography

 Lena Dominelli's academic career included appointments in social work at Warwick University and professorships at Sheffield, Southampton and Durham universities in the UK. Her education led to a first degree from Simon Fraser University, British Columbia, MA (Sussex, 1969), and PhD (Sussex, 1979). Practice roles included work for the Batley Community Development Project. Leadership roles include the presidency of IASSW (1996-2004). Her publications include pioneering work on feminism, anti-racism, community work and green social work. (Some information here drawn from Callahan, 2008.)

What does the award mean to you?

It recognizes the work that I have done over many years with great joy and commitment because I wanted to change the world and make it a better place for everyone. To me, it is a real honour to be linked with someone like Katherine because she meant so much to me and I worked with her for many years. We had several values in common and developed a good relationship as we shared the profession's joys and tribulations. She had a great sense of humour. She used to say to me whenever I was late from my meetings: 'I will be in my purple pyjamas', because we shared the same hotel suite. When I was president of IASSW, she would take me to meet all the people that she knew to make sure I did not miss a thing, especially at CSWE meetings. She was a fantastic friend, funny and caring. In later years her physical health declined, but her mind was as sharp as a button. I said in a poem for her ninetieth birthday: 'Nobody could ever be like you; you're one of a kind' and I gave her the title 'Queen of Social Work'.

In 2008, two years before she died, she was speaking at a UN conference on the Social Work Day. I came on the train with her from her home outside Baltimore. She spoke for ten minutes without notes; I was just amazed at how wonderful she was, still mentally alert. On her hundredth birthday, she was very ill and frail, but again she still talked for ten minutes without notes. I gave her a bowl of recognition from IASSW and told her I was going to dedicate *Green social work* (Dominelli, 2012, see Selected Publications) to her. Her quick mind asked: 'How does green social work differ from good social work, Lena?'. This wonderful relationship I had with Katherine is what this award means to me, not the personal recognition, although that is important, because you do not get much of that in our profession.

What activities were of major importance for your professional development and career and its impact on social work education?

I started in social work as a community worker, and I was determined to make sure that social workers focused on community interventions as well as individuals and groups. I was fortunate to have Peter Leonard[1] as a colleague and my boss in my first social work job at Warwick University. He insisted that everyone did community work as part of their social work placement. My first writings were about community development, and I took a particular interest in women. That was important because it raised gender issues for community development, when no one was interested in it. I had, as a community worker, taken my local authority to the Employment Tribunal to get women's rights and equal pay in my employment. This is before equalities legislation in the UK had been implemented. The Sex Equality Act for women's equality in employment came into effect in 1975. Everybody treated it as a joke that I wanted the same pay: 'I am doing the team leader's job, but I am not getting paid for it like the guys are'. I had degrees that they did not have. Yet I was being paid less. Nevertheless, I did not get that recognition. They made me sit outside the tribunal door. I could hear them laughing and saying: 'She's gonna get married, what does she need the extra salary for?'. That motivated me to write *Women and community action* (Dominelli, 2006, see Selected Publications), although I did not write about my personal experiences. The book is now going into its third edition.

The second thing that was extremely important was class in relation to gender. I did much work on gender, and included class in all of my writings. Differentiated living experiences are important to acknowledge. With students, I organized the first feminist social work conference in the UK. Eventually, I wrote *Feminist social work*, initially with a colleague (Dominellli and McLeod, 1989). I probably would not have written this book without her. A later book on feminist social work, I wrote myself (Dominelli, 2002, see Selected Publications).

The third thing was writing *Anti-racist social work* (Dominelli, 2008, see Selected Publications). As a result of my experiences of racism as an immigrant who is different from the Anglo-Saxon norm, I became more aware about social justice in its broader sense. The passion that keeps me going is trying to eradicate social injustice, wherever and however I see it. Therefore, I decided to move into the latest and fourth thing, which I hope will have a big impact. That is *Green social work* (Dominelli, 2012, see Selected Publications), which links social and environmental justice in non-exploitative forms of social development; non-exploitative, that is, both of people and of Planet Earth. In all four areas, I linked theory with practice, running groups to change behaviour among violent men and to provide resources for abused women.

For me those are the four key things. Other people will tell you that critical theory is another important contribution, but I have always been constructively critical and reflective. I do insist on maintaining standards, principles, ethics and research. Along with colleagues, I have been pushing social work to be a research-led discipline. In the UK, I was the first one to start the demand that our ESRC (Economic and Social Research Council) recognize social work as a research-led discipline. I started that ball rolling in 1996, and then got colleagues in the Joint University Council Social Work Education Committee[2] involved. We struggled collectively for a decade before being granted this status. Thus, I started many things that were not on anyone else's agenda, and brought other people in.

In which field do you think you made the biggest contribution to social work and its education?

The areas are critical theory, anti-racist social work, feminist social work, working with violent offenders, and getting gender on the agenda for both social workers and probation officers to ensure that women's different experiences are taken on board. I hope for the future it will be about environmental justice and issues, and we need to develop new models and paradigms for disaster interventions and sustainable development. On that score, I am grateful to IASSW for electing me head of the Disaster Intervention Climate Change and Sustainability Committee. That has been a major milestone in my life.

What does social work education and social work mean to you professionally?

For me, social work is a broad, wide-ranging profession, and we are privileged to be part of that. The contribution that social work makes to enhancing people's well-being is one of the major ways of contributing through our practice to making the world a better place.

Social workers as professionals tend to be quite critical and reflective. We see and work with the injustices in the world, trying to make the world a little bit better, even if it is only at the individual level. It places great responsibility on social workers, but is one of the things that make it a worthwhile profession. The environment is the social, political, economic context as well as the physical geosphere. We are the only profession, as far as I am aware of, that claims such a broad remit. That is what is attractive about social work.

What does social work education mean to you personally and why did you choose it?

I fell into social work education rather than choosing it. As a community worker in a development project in northern England, I was shocked at the levels of poverty compared to the south. That was important, because it got me on a social work professional path that I had no idea about at the time. As a sociology PhD-trained student, I wanted to do something on poverty, economic decline. I had been taught by top professors including Kathleen Gough Aberle, Anthony Giddens and Tom Bottomore.[3] Therefore, I had ideas buzzing round in my head and got the opportunity to put them into practice. Because of my knowledge of Islam, and I could read and speak Arabic at the time, I was appointed team leader of a part of the Batley Community Development Project (CDP) in Dewsbury that dealt with the Gujarati Muslim community, which was challenging. This was in the mid-1970s when people were not really concerned about race and gender, let alone making it part of a local authority and Home Office-funded project.

In the CDPs, we discovered that the decline, which has continued in Britain, was economic rather than person-centred. We soon debunked the myth that the government had about lazy people who have bad housing and no jobs because they do not want to work. We were an activist group and, in Batley CDP, we used to talk about empowering local communities, having borrowed the terms from the American civil rights movements and people like Barbara Solomon, saying what poor people need are good jobs and decent housing (Solomon, 1976). Together, community workers took the local authorities to court for putting people into poor housing. I wanted to put some of our leaders in some of the appalling houses where ordinary people on benefits had to live. Therefore, we took them to court. We won the battle and lost the war because what did the state do? Not what we thought, which was to create new housing and improve old housing to make it habitable. They offered the housing to private landlords and put people in bed and breakfast accommodation. Poor families had nowhere to go but the streets during the day. I learned a bitter political lesson about how you try to initiate social change, which made me more successful in some of my subsequent attempts. As a result of our activism, the Batley CDP was closed down. We were seen as too radical, although ironically I was offered reappointment afterwards. I declined and took this local authority to the Employment Tribunal, again because they had violated our terms of contract, with the right to organize and empower communities. I argued that I had been constructively dismissed because the work was still there to be done, but the local authority was not allowing us to do it. That made nonsense of community development and what people wanted to do, so I won that battle as well, but refused to be reinstated.

Then I started looking for other jobs. I applied for one as a community work lecturer at Warwick University, and so did many of the other CDP workers. Peter Leonard thought students should be involved in selecting who was going to teach them. We had a wonderful time at the interview, which is all I can remember of it. Unexpectedly, I got the job, and accepted it because I wanted to make sure that all social workers did community work.

During Prime Minister Margaret Thatcher's administration in the UK,[4] social work became more separated from community work. I then retrained as a social worker, a probation officer and a residential worker. I did work in all those three areas so that I would know what I was talking about, however, always from a community dimension, linking community activities with statutory activities. I have never given that up, even in my work in the Gilesgate community, Durham, with renewable energy projects.[5] This work began with local residents asking me to do something about fuel poverty on the estate. In the 1970s, we addressed fuel poverty by helping people manage their minimal budgets or begging the utilities companies for concessions. If the fuel deprivation still existed 30 years later, we had to do something else.

Addressing this issue through the creation of energy-self-sufficient communities through renewable energies was doing something at the local level that could benefit the world more widely for climate change purposes. This light went on in my head while talking about electrical energy with colleagues who were engineers. The missing link between renewable and self-sufficient energy offered the community a new answer. From that point of view, I have always been very lucky, either been at the right point at the right time or met people who triggered my brain to think: 'Social workers can do this, should do this'.

Personally, social work has been an arena for change where you can do things that will make people's lives better.

What are the challenges of social work and its education?

There are some old and some new problems. Among the old problems is to get good professional training for social workers. Too many people call themselves social workers without training or experience. It goes back to the beginning of the profession, when people thought of it as a vocational calling, and misunderstood enthusiasm for professionalism. Getting social work recognized as having high status is an old problem. We are different from other professions because we engage with people to include them in solving the problems they face. We should be proud of that, not embarrassed by it.

Another old challenge is managerialism or 'new public management', which has increasingly bureaucratized our relationships with people. We are in danger of losing relational social work.

An additional old one is being a research-led profession. Many of our founding mothers were determined that social work should be a PhD-level profession. We still have not got that across the world, although some countries have done more than others.

Yet, another old problem is poverty; again some countries are better than others at dealing with it. Eighty per cent of our service users are poor and yet we hardly study poverty in UK social work anymore. When I trained, it was part of our social policy component. You cannot understand where the people we work with are coming from, if you do not understand poverty and its structural causes.

My current challenge is to make sure that social workers are properly trained for disaster interventions. This consideration is missing from the curriculum in the UK. This is also the case in social work education in many other countries, so green social work argues for the inclusion of disaster and environmental interventions in mainstream training.

The new problems of social work are getting human rights, social justice and environmental justice embedded in social work theory and practice. We still have to fight for an equal place for women. Again, some countries have done better than others, but on the whole women throughout the world are not equal.

Ethnicity and racism come from the same issue. We find unacceptable expressions of it wherever we go. Increasingly many governments, including those in the West, are denying people their basic democratic human rights, because they are concerned about terrorism. The right to speak as you wish with whom you wish is important. We should not see people as a threat to national security simply because they espouse unpopular views. Social workers have yet to learn how to deal appropriately with people who impose violence on others in pursuit of political power and with those who deprive others of their rights through judicial processes. These are new issues for social workers.

Climate change and the environment are crucially significant. The world's population is increasing; we are now over seven billion. If we cannot think of how to sustain people in their daily lives, in ways that do not ruin the Earth, none of us will be here. Collective action is essential, and social workers have a critical role to play in progressing the environmental and climate change agenda.

A new area, but also an old one, is working with people suffering from armed conflict. Domestic and communal violence have always been at the centre of social work practice in the community, in statutory and voluntary services, but we are seeing new dimensions to it as whole nations engage in civil wars for lengthy periods of time. Social and relief workers are being killed because they support and defend people's rights. Women and children are also the ones suffering inordinately in such conflicts.

Indigenous social work, with its links to environmental justice, may provide us with challenges that we must address. Indigenous people can remind us of how to treat the environment with respect. As I argued many years ago, we have the internationalization of social problems. Trafficking and sexual exploitation of children, although they were there before, have come up as big industries.

Another big challenge is the fiscal crisis. Actually, I want to redefine this as a crisis of capitalism. Capitalism is looking for new arenas to make profit by bringing down the welfare state and privatizing it to make money out of people's needs. It is immoral for those of us who believe in a social democratic ethos to society. That requires us to think about alternative economic relations that can help us promote people's well-being without costing the earth and by pooling risks to show solidarity and commitment to each other and planet Earth.

What is the importance of international work in your career?

It is an interesting and complicated question, because I am an internationalist. I have Italian, Canadian, British heritages so I feel my own biography is international. I have been involved in what other people call 'international social work' all my life. However, I wrote in 2000, that I do not think we have international social work yet. I would still argue we have to develop the theory and the practice of it. People going to other countries, crossing borders, call what they do international social work, just because they leave country X and go to country Y. Others say it is international if you exchange curricula and learn things from each other. These are all important activities, but I do not think they are international social work. The internationalist does not have to cross a national border because the international is wherever we are: people have migrated across the world ever since the beginning of humanity. Borders are bureaucratic conveniences and, at times, a way of managing people in an inhumane way.

I have been a player in the international arena in different guises supporting people through disasters, inventing new models for interventions, like the virtual helpline for people after the Christchurch earthquake, then passing it on to our Japanese colleagues after Fukushima and to Nepal after the earthquake in 2015. I have been involved in discussions at the UN, in different subjects: women, poverty, ethnicity and racism, climate change, unemployment, and older people. Whenever I felt I had something useful to say, I would become involved.

We need to learn how to theorize about people moving across borders and treating the local and the global as permeable. I have tried to come up with a new word; I had lots of laughs in Dubrovnik when I called it 'glogalisation', to indicate that the local and global are interactive. They thought I meant some kind of global brand. I have not used the term since. Sadly, I have not come up with a better one. I am involved in activities across national borders, engaging with internationalized social problems ranging from poverties to disasters, articulating an agenda for social work in the UN and in other places where we should have our voices heard. It is a huge area for us to continue to work on; as a profession, we are only scratching the surface.

What major obstacles have you faced in your career?

The professional challenges are to do a huge job. Social workers and social work educators have an enormous task ahead of us, with limited resources, usually in small departments with few students. What we achieve is amazing because we spread our resources so far and yet manage to achieve depth and change. I have had to struggle with lack of resourcing and recognition for the profession, and the devaluing of social work, like every one of my colleagues.

Some of my personal challenges have included being seen as an outsider, as a sociologist with community work credentials and radical roots in trade unionism. Some people found my commitment to my social justice principles hard to take. Practical responses have to be ethically justifiable by the principles that I use to guide my life. That gave me many problems, and I had to become a nomad academically. I could have taken various universities to the Equal Opportunities Commission[6] for not recognizing and promoting me, simply because I stood for social justice, human rights, and ending oppression whether it was for women, disabled, black or working-class people. Those involved know who they are, and will have to live with their conscience, but at least I know mine is clear.

How has social work changed?

It has changed for the better and for the worse. For the worse in becoming more bureaucratic and managerialist. Social services are managing people instead of responding to needs, as resources get tighter and public expenditure cuts deeper. We will have to do more with less. I was practising in social work when it had a local authority budget in the UK, and you exercised professional judgment to do what you thought was right for people. I would like to see those days come back. I realize we live in the world with state-created scarcities because politicians take decisions about where they are going to put our resources and where not to. I do have a PowerPoint presentation showing slides of homeless people and of corporate welfare, which shows the state giving tax-handouts to the bankers while poor people go hungry over a 100 year period, and that says it all.

What has changed in good ways? The profession is gaining more status despite the setbacks in places. In 1997, when I discussed abuse of the Canadian First Nations[7] in the residential schools in my book, *Sociology for social work* (Dominelli, 1997, see Selected Publications), nobody else in mainstream social work was talking about them. Now we have indigenous social work books all over the world.

Another positive change, at least in some countries, is that the voice of service users is being increasingly listened to. However, social workers could do more to form alliances with service users and be guided more by their agendas than the state's agendas. However, we then will have to be prepared to be faced with a demand to behave within professional boundaries. These boundaries in democratic societies should come from the people not from the politicians, who are promoting their own interests, of which we are often unaware. We should do more political analysis in social work education and research. I was fortunate because in my undergraduate degree, I did everything from natural science to social science disciplines. I think we need to move more into that direction and become more transdisciplinary.

I started as a social work educator in the late 1970s. At that time, practice was psychodynamic casework, some group work and the integrated methods based on systems theory. Although community work was included as a method in social work, it saw itself as quite distinct in its practice because it did not have the statutory remit that social workers did. As service users would stay on the caseload for a long time, there was a lively critique of psychodynamic casework in the UK, initially from practitioners through *Case Con*.[8] However, some change in approach was driven by corporatist agendas arguing that social case workers needed to make better use of their resources. Reid and Epstein (1972) were important in bringing that change about by promoting task-centred social work. While their agenda was quite conservative, there was another important agenda following on from the Settlement Movement's history and that was recent radical social work. At that point, Peter Leonard was bringing Marxism into social work. I knew Marxist theory from Tom Bottomore, and I knew about postmodernist inclinations as I had studied with Pierre Bourdieu[9] in France. For me the difference now is that there is a commitment to postmodernism's rejection of a search for one model that answers everything. Radical social work has become more sophisticated, including gender, disability, race and ethnicity, sexual orientation, and mental ill health, and has developed anti-oppressive and empowering forms of practice. It has also begun to address environmental justice, social justice, human rights, issues of citizenship, and the active citizen. These issues were not in social work when I started.

What would you like to see happen in social work, its education and IASSW in the future?

We need to be more aware of NGOs in our teaching and practice. I want the curriculum to reflect practice using indigenous knowledge, particularly the way in which it sees the holism between the person and their environment, including spirituality. One of the problems that we have today is crass materialism. I am not saying we do not want to have the latest labour-saving devices, but I do not want to guide my life around consuming, which capitalism encourages people to do. We need to include more about social – and environmental – justice and see the world as interdependent, and acknowledge that if some people are privileged, it usually happens at somebody else's expense. We need to figure out how we are all going to share everything in this world equitably and fairly. Social workers need to observe and challenge the lack of human rights, including in our own countries. I will keep asking: why does the Universal Declaration of Human Rights say that every person is entitled to food, clothing, shelter, healthcare, education and social services, yet, whenever you cross a border, you have to prove you have insurance before you can get help? This challenges us as social workers to say: 'If people are in need, we should respond to them'.

It leads me to my next argument: that I would like to see social work become a universal service like health and education and a curriculum that backs that up. I believe in universal services because targeted services lead to residual, means-test services, which decline in the way they are delivered and in quality. The best way of ensuring quality is having articulate active citizens who can hold practitioners to account and say: 'You have not given me what I am entitled to'.

What can IASSW do? We need to develop a much stronger voice in the international arena, linking the international and the national on local levels. It needs to form alliances with others, not just with IFSW and ICSW, which we are doing. I like to think I played no small role in authenticating that, and also with other agencies including the environmental movement and equal rights' movements. We need to develop more our roles in helping people to defend their human rights, and in having a critical voice rooted in empirical data so as to not come across as just being good-hearted. IASSW needs to become more inclusive of many parts of the world where we are still not well represented. We have to find more resources to maintain and expand the organization, not just in membership but also sponsoring funds for core activities that would allow it to live up to its ideals and mission.

Selected publications

Dominelli, L. (1997) *Sociology for social work*, Basingstoke: Palgrave.

Dominelli, L. (2002) *Feminist social work theory and practice*, Basingstoke: Palgrave Macmillan.

Dominelli, L. (2006) *Women and community action* (2nd edn), Bristol: Policy Press.

Dominelli, L. (2008) *Anti-racist social work* (3rd edn), Basingstoke: Palgrave Macmillan.

Dominelli, L. (2012) *Green social work: From environmental crises to environmental justice*, Cambridge: Polity.

Notes

[1] Peter Leonard (d. 2013), first professor in the Department of Applied Social Studies, University of Warwick, later Director of the School of Social Work, McGill University; co-author of *Social work practice under capitalism* (Corrigan and Leonard, 1978).

[2] The UK representative body for social work education programmes.

[3] Kathleen Gough Aberle (1925-90), British anthropologist and feminist, author of *Rural change in Southeast India, 1950s–1980s* (1989) and *Political economy in Vietnam* (1990); Anthony Giddens (b. 1938) British sociologist, author of *The consequences of modernity* (1991) and *The third way: The renewal of social democracy* (2013); Thomas Burton Bottomore (1920-92), British Marxist sociologist, Professor of Sociology, University of Sussex, 1968-85, author of *Classes in modern society* (1965).

[4] 1979-90.

[5] Information about the Gilesgate Energy Initiative is available at: https://www.dur. ac.uk/ihrr/vulnerabilityresearch/transcendingrisk/gilesgateproject/

[6] The UK body at the time of the interview for enforcing equal treatment of women and men; now replaced by the Equality and Human Rights Commission.

[7] Indigenous peoples of the Americas, that is ethnic groups present before settlement by peoples from colonial powers. In Canada, the term is accepted not to include Inuit and Méti peoples.

[8] *Case Con*, a British federation of radical social workers, active in the 1970s, deriving from a radical magazine of the same name whose title was an ironic comment on *Case Conference*, a professional journal title of the 1950s and '60s.

[9] Pierre Bourdieu (1930-2002) French intellectual, from 1968 director of the *Centre de Sociologie Européenne*, Paris.

SIXTEEN

Lynne Healy, 2014

Interviewed by Gurid Aga Askeland

Biography

Lynne Healy's (b. 1947) career-defining role was as faculty member in the University of Connecticut, School of Social Work from 1978-2015. She was promoted to professor in 1992 and granted the university's highest title, Board of Trustees Distinguished Professor, in 2012. Her education led to a BA, Asian Studies, Brown University; MSW, community organization, University of Connecticut; PhD, Rutgers University. Practice roles included work as a family casework assistant, a social caseworker in child welfare services, and director of a community information and referral service. Leadership roles include: board of directors, secretary, vice president and human rights roles in IASSW; poverty and social development advocacy as IASSW representative with the UN; and international and national roles with NASW and CSWE. Publications include books on human rights, international social work, social service management, and shorter works on ethical and practice issues in social work.

When did you receive the award and on what basis? What has it meant to you?

I only received it two days ago! However, I had been informed several months before. It is an extremely meaningful award for several reasons, but obviously because it bears Katherine Kendall's name. Also, because it is an honour that IASSW gives for contributions to international social work education, it is an important career recognition.

While it is personally rewarding that your colleagues think you deserve this, I am at a stage in my career where things to put on my CV do not matter. My university and school of social work were impressed and pleased about the award. The greatest honour is to be recognized by your colleagues in your field and in the association.

Then it is important because of the personal connection I had with Katherine Kendall. In the future, there will be Kendall awardees who will be removed from that. We have a connectedness that future professional scholars will only have by reading about it. I remember a conversation with Katherine. She was reflecting that she had personally known every president of the IASSW except Alice Salomon. She connected back to 1949 or 1950, and so these periods of history are passing away.

What activities were of major importance for your professional career and its impact on social work and its education?

My biggest contribution has probably been my writings on international social work, especially the textbook (Healy, 2008b, see Selected Publications), and I am hoping to do a new edition. Originally, I sent Katherine an outline of what I wanted to do. She thought it was impossible. It was too broad, too comprehensive; she did not see that it would be feasible. Nevertheless, she was happy with the result. At that time, most writing about international social work was very general. They were, 'It is nice to have a world view, we should be more international', but that was where all the writings stopped, even by people I greatly respect.

My primary teaching is at the masters level, which in the US is a practical degree, the main degree for people who do social work. Therefore, that vague notion about international social work did not have meaning for most students and schools. Students do not have to travel outside the borders to practise, but they have to be more competent and knowledgeable about the ways that globalization affects where they live. That is why the subtitle of the book is *Professional action in an interdependent world*. I emphasize students' responsibilities as active citizens in the social policy area. Almost no policy issue is domestic. You and I are sitting here in Australia, where one of the biggest news items is about how Australia's policy about asylum seekers is damaging. We could look at the same in my own country. It is irresponsible for social workers to be silent about these issues. My biggest intellectual contribution is probably to get more specific about international social work, its dimensions, how can it be meaningful to a practice profession?

I am focusing more on human rights. I teach in a university that has made a major interdisciplinary commitment to human rights. Human rights are a framework that can link the local and the global. It is a set of global standards that are highly relevant and consistent with social work values. It can help students see how knowledge of global processes and standards can improve their local practice. Therefore, I have recently done some writing about human rights, especially the clash between culture and universal rights. Many social workers struggle with areas where cultural practices violate international human rights standards.

What has social work and its education meant to you professionally?

Social work was an accidental career. My undergraduate university did not teach social work, and I had no thought about being a social worker. Growing up, I did not know much about social work, and I knew no social workers. I came from a rural area and had summer jobs working for the YMCA in day camps; I thought that was interesting. I knew it was a career to work for the YMCA, so I talked with the head of office in Providence, Rhode Island, where my undergraduate university was. He accidentally handed me an internal study saying that people choosing social work instead of a career in the YMCA were more intelligent. It made me think about social work. I also had an interesting summer position working in a neighbourhood antipoverty programme.

I went from undergraduate school to work as a social caseworker in a state-run child welfare agency, completely untrained, no social work education. That was a way of hiring people back then. After three years, I went on to get a masters in social work, majoring in community organizing. After three years of casework in social welfare, mostly with people living in poverty, I felt frustrated with the idea of casework relationship. With no training, I was not doing intensive casework. What I was doing did not change the lives of the people I was working with, so I thought it would be better to work on a more macro level. After my MSW, I held several positions before I decided to go for a PhD and move into teaching.

I did my thesis on international dimensions in social work education. My advisor, Werner Boehm, initially worried that it would not be quantitative enough. But he was supportive and recommended that I contact Katherine Kendall for assistance, an advice that changed my career in many ways. Then (1982) I did not know who she was, and started to read about her. The more I read, the more intimidated I felt, so I wrote her a letter. She immediately called me. I went to New York, told her what my interest was, and we chatted for several hours. By the end of the afternoon, she asked if I wanted to spend the night. She was helpful in the dissertation study, especially when I wanted to do in-depth interviews with people well-known in international education. If Katherine told them they needed to speak with me, they spoke with me. She became an important person in my life and our friendship lasted until her death in 2010.

In some ways, I did launch my career with the doctoral dissertation, because it formed the basis of some articles, and through doing the dissertation, I met many people involved in international aspects of social work.

I had gotten involved in professional organizations early in my career. Nevertheless, I expected that, after my masters, I would return to the child welfare field, perhaps in staff training, staff development work. I never did that, because different paths were created. I hoped that my first-year field placement would be in the macro side of child welfare or emphasizing women. This was 1972, and I was very interested in women's issues. Instead, I was assigned disappointingly to the National Association of Social Workers to work with the president of the State Chapter. Nevertheless, it was meaningful for the rest of my career, because I got involved in the work of the professional association. They nominated me in my second year to be student member on the National Board of Directors, NASW. There I was, at 26, meeting leaders in our field. From then on, once you are in the door, you are in the door. I was then nominated for many other committees.

In the 1980s, I got appointed to the International Committee of CSWE. Beginning in IASSW, I became a regular conference-goer, the first one in 1980 in Hong Kong. Then I went to England in 1982 while I was working on my doctoral dissertation and, in 1984, to Montreal.

In 1986, I was asked to be on the programme committee for the Tokyo Conference for the IASSW. I am unsure how the chair of the programme committee, Yoko Kojima,[1] knew of me. She was Japanese, lived and taught in Japan, but her American husband lived in Connecticut, so she made several visits to the US during the planning process. That may have been why she invited me on the programme committee, to have somebody to talk to, while visiting her husband.

What is the importance of international work in your career?

Our school celebrates an international social work day every year. This year (2015),[2] my colleagues asked me to be the speaker, and I spoke about social work at the UN. Graduate students do their internships at the UN and I am their field instructor. They do a great job, extending the work of the IASSW volunteers, because they are there for 20 hours a week, for the academic year. I insisted that they include the two UN interns to talk about their work after I presented. We also invited back a former UN intern, a young man who graduated a couple of years ago and is now a policy associate in Washington DC, in the office of one of our US senators. Inspiring students to become involved more globally has been central to my career.

I got involved with the UN seven years ago, as a member of a team of five people representing IASSW in activities with the UN in New York. I have been serving on the NGO committee for social development, and I have done a variety of things. We have the ability to write position statements for some of the official meetings. These are translated into the UN languages, and posted on the official websites as IASSW statements. I have spoken at and organized workshops, what the UN calls 'side events'. This year I was invited by Sergei Zelenev,[3] to speak on a panel organized by UNESCO on inequality within and between nations, which is one of IASSWs priorities.

In January 2015, I took over as the main representative, which is one of the reasons I am retiring from full-time teaching. Because I need time to do my voluntary work, I have to give up my pay to do a successful job on behalf of IASSW. It is interesting, and an opportunity to raise the profile of social work at the UN, and among other NGOs, and more importantly, to contribute to some of the big issues relevant to social work that the UN is dealing with. One of my goals as the main representative is to get members around the world without access to the UN headquarters, in Geneva or New York, to be active in the processes online.

I have recently been following the Post-2015 Agenda[4] and signed IASSW on to some advocacy statements around inequality. We were able to get inequality in the Post-2015 Agenda. We have written something promoting human rights, but that has not been successful. The sustainable development goals are disappointing; they do not have human rights language at all.

Ever since I was a new social worker, our professional organizations have been important to me. That is how we make a difference, by having a collective voice at the national and international levels. There is only a handful of opportunities for involvement. I was lucky! When I was a new faculty member, I asked our dean: 'How do I get more involved in international social work?' His advice was to forget it. It was a closed club. Fortunately, I did not listen to him. For many of us, careers are accidental or a path we had not considered opens up.

One of the most meaningful exchange relationships that our school of social work established was with the University of the West Indies, specially its Jamaica campus, an active partnership in the years since 1992. It has been mutually beneficial, with student exchange for field internships, but probably the majority of the connections has been faculty exchange and joint work. Several members of our teaching faculty have jointly written with colleagues from their faculty. It has given me an opportunity to become familiar with another educational system and to work in depth on some of the challenges around development and migration. To meet great colleagues there has been inspiring; many are now friends and we have visited and stayed in each other's homes.

There has been a variety of other activities. I did a faculty development workshop for the Copenhagen School of Social Work at their summer retreat. I have done consultations and an external evaluation for the University of Mauritius. As part of an IASSW team, I was on an evaluation visit to the United Arab Emirates and Abu Dhabi. Then there are a lot of things from afar, as external examiner on doctoral dissertations for South Africa, Ethiopia and India. I was in Israel recently as the main consultant speaker at an international social work institute held at a college.

What challenges have you experienced during your career?

Let me start with an area of disappointment. The lack of support for IASSW within the United States makes me sad. It is shameful that such a small proportion of our schools currently belong to the association. There is less commitment to professionalism now, including our professional associations. We have about 200 MSW and doctoral programmes in the US. Probably less than a third of them are members. When Katherine was alive, even in her nineties, she was a constant advocate with the deans, and would go to their meetings and push IASSW.

My own roles have been mixed. About a decade ago, I wanted to become less involved in the business side of the professional association and more in the substantive work, like the UN work on human rights. Then I took over part of a term as vice president representing NACASSW. Running for secretary was not what I had intended to do. Anyway, I did it. Being an officer is a challenge; we are all volunteers, so there is always this nagging feeling that you are not doing enough.

My university was delighted that I was secretary. However, they did not give me any workload release.

Another change for social work is that teaching and mentoring students and professional activities are less valued than publishing. It is only going to worsen, with less commitment by the faculty to being active professionally or in the community.

In the realm of scholarship and publications, the view of what is acceptable is increasingly narrow. Some educators in Israel said to me that one school has told the faculty members that only five journals are valued for publications, and they have to publish in those journals. None of them are Israeli or based in the Middle East. Similarly, South African scholars informed me that they were told the only concern is journal impact factors. This means that people are encouraged to publish only in a narrow set of professional journals; all based pretty much in the UK and the US. Thus, scholars in Africa and Asia are told: 'Do not write for your local body. Write something that will be accepted by American or British edited journals.' It is a new kind of imperialism. Even within the US, it is having a chilling effect on creativity. Scholars are encouraged to write about mainstream topics. I have been lucky; I got academic tenure before these pressures were as intense as they are now. I have been free to write what I wanted to, in the journals I wanted to, and to assist colleagues in the Caribbean to launch and sustain their *Caribbean Journal of Social Work*, which would not be valued based on journal impact factors. My scholarship in international social work gets cited by people who are writing about international social work. The main body of work in the United States is about clinical and mental health social work. If you want many citations, you need to be writing about those topics.

This pressure obviously is also having a terrible impact on language, which is a huge challenge today. I am concerned about that as well.

For social work there are always new problems. Certain things that social workers are dealing with now, were not an issue in the beginning of my career, like AIDS. I was just exchanging emails with Gidraph Wairire[5] in Kenya, and he expressed sorrow, concerns and fear of terrorism. Norway has also suffered from one of these terrible homegrown attacks, as we have in Connecticut. How do you balance concern over the dangers with encouraging people to live their lives and not be afraid?

All these new problems, but you can also look back and say, there have been victories too. One of my projects is research at the IASSW archives[6] on what happened during the apartheid era in social work education in South Africa. In the United States, we have seen the most rapid shift in public opinion ever around the topic of rights of gays and lesbians, in which campaign social work was early involved. It is exciting that people and cultures can change, and this feeds into issues and arguments on human rights in the profession. Cultures are not static. The United States used to be where Uganda is today on homosexuality, a huge shift in one generation.

How has social work and its education changed?

We are a contextual profession. Therefore, both new social trends and problems affect social work education, how we would teach, and think about social issues. Within IASSW, we have certainly seen the growth of social work education, because of the social structural changes, not all positive, in countries where 30 years ago there was none: in Russia, China, and Vietnam. Thus, there has been opening up of the profession. People within IASSW are worried about Asian instead of American dominance, which is quite interesting.

The status of social work in the US is stronger than, say, in the UK, from my scholarship reading. The profession seems more attacked in the UK than in the US. Certainly, salary conditions have generally improved in the US, and we now have legal regulation. Every state has some formal licensing of social work, which has increased the status of the profession. Social work tends, with a lot of advocacy from our national bodies, to be written into federal legislation for mental health care. In the US, masters–level social workers are on the par with PhD-level psychologists in provision of mental health care, and social workers provide the majority of it. That is not typical around the world. Thus, the status is high, but the services that social workers provide are still subject to budget cuts. Social workers in the US operate under constrains of our poor welfare system. We are still far from having universal healthcare. We have complex insurance regulations, so it is frustrating to get people the services they need, which makes practice on the ground difficult.

In addition to focusing on international social work, I teach the administration concentration. Students are now less likely to select administration or policy because they are worried that they will not qualify for a license since most of the licensing is on clinical practice. It has shifted students' priorities toward the mental health direct service role. I am not happy about that. A fear of not qualifying for a credential has become a major factor in students' choice of study.

In the 1970s in the US, the focus was on women´s liberation and advocating for equality for women. At that time in the US, although women were the majority of social workers, almost all deans of schools of social work and administrators at major agencies were men. Therefore, there was a lot of activism around gender in the profession. With a colleague, I did some early writings on women. Even now, much of my concern around human rights is with gender. One of my articles on gender has gotten lots of comments on universalism and cultural relativism in social work ethics. Issues around gender, sexuality and roles within families generate the most heated conversations about culture and human rights, so I am still interested in gender. I get frustrated with younger social workers who do not recognize gender issues that they are facing.

I wrote my major text on international social work alone. Working alone, you miss the opportunity to talk over issues where you might be stuck or need some help. Recently, I have done some joint writing to bring along junior colleagues. Four of us co-edited a book recently on human rights and social work education (Libal et al, 2014). We had a great partnership and a good time. I was asked to write an article for a special Africa issue of a journal. I wanted to co-author with an African colleague, so I reached out to someone I knew (Healy and Kamya, 2014, see Selected Publications). It is always a rewarding challenge to cooperate with someone you have never written with before.

What major obstacles have you faced in your career?

Initially there were obstacles in being a woman and being taken seriously. My first job after my masters programme as a director of our state chapter of NASW meant that I was the paid staff person in our professional association at 26. At times, that was a challenge.

The profession in the US is preoccupied with micro. One major challenge initially that has changed somewhat, is that people in the US are inward looking. It was strange, therefore, when I developed an interest in international social work, then to be seen as on the margins of professional concerns. People were not interested in the international, and not concerned about learning more. When we first tried to get a course in our school on working with immigrants and refugees, some senior faculty members said: 'We are not interested in that; we are interested in working with people here'. They are here, that is why we want the course. There was resistance to the idea of international conferences. It was difficult to get articles on the topic accepted in major journals in the US, because it was assumed that no one was interested. There is still a massive American ignorance of the world, people not knowing even basic facts about what is going on in the world. There is definitely now a much larger group of educators and students across the US, who are interested in having a more global view on a range of topics. My major interest is not training people to be social workers in Bangladesh, but to be better social workers in the US by understanding what is going on in the world, how these issues intersect with our practice, and how professionals have a responsibility to be knowledgeable and influence our own policy. People in other countries often say to me, that they wished American social workers would do more advocacy at home for better foreign policy.

What would you like to see happening in social work, its education and in IASSW in the future?

I would love to see a strong IASSW with educational programmes around the world supporting the association. I would like for us be able to mobilize our members to participate more effectively, including feeding in their expertise to the UN processes. Obviously, if we have more members, we will have a stronger financial base and be able to have professional staff again. I would like our professional associations to collaborate meaningfully. On the international scene, we are not very powerful and need to cooperate, not fight. However, unfortunately human beings do not always work that way. Working on the Global Agenda (IASSW/ICSW/IFSW, 2012) has not prevented other conflicts, which impeded progress at the global level.

I would like social work education to reclaim the balance among the three functions of educators: to prepare and excite social workers; to contribute to the growth of knowledge; to contribute to policy making, community-based projects and professional activities.

What I found exciting about being an academic was to have this balance among these three functions, and not solely be directed toward research. With a narrow definition of what research should be, social work education will weaken.

Social work has made a lot of progress in the last 30 or 40 years. When I read about what went on in the 1910s and 1920s and read some of the work of our wonderful foremothers in the early twentieth century, for example on migration, I am not sure we have done much better than to rediscover what we knew back then. We really had some amazing predecessors in this field. Social workers were using human rights language and arguments about the rights of immigrants back in the 1920s. It is very powerful, all there in our history. It is exciting, but it is also like what are we doing? Have we really made progress? At least we can rediscover.

What has social work education meant to you personally?

As I approach retirement, I am worrying about finding a way to continue interacting with creative, bright young people who have commitment to the profession. It is exciting to interact and keep up with some of our graduates. Those kinds of things have kept us in social work education so long.

I cannot think what my life would have been like without social work. My son was raised in the IASSW. My husband and I took him with us to so many conferences that when he was seven, he asked me, 'Mom, are we invited to any good meetings this summer?' That suggests how intertwined the personal and the professional have been. The international piece of it, I never have regretted. I am glad that I graduated from the university when there was discrimination against women in a number of careers. If I had graduated 20 years later, I might have become a lawyer instead. I am glad I am a social worker.

The reward for being involved internationally has been the connection to people from all over the world. I have a picture in my bedroom taken at Narda Razack's[7] house during one of the board meetings. In her recreation room, seated on the couch was a group of people from all six continents. I love that picture, because I have gained so much from interacting with wonderful social work educators from every corner of the inhabited world. Some of them have become such dear friends. It was one of the best weeks of our lives in Norway with international friends when you [the interviewer] hosted us.

I grew up in a small village with 500 people, in the state of Vermont, one of our most rural ones, where my father and his father had grown up. We never travelled, and I lived there until I went off to university. However, my father travelled all over the world with the army air force during World War II. My goal as a child was that someday I hoped to be able to see Arizona. I never thought I would have the opportunities that social work has given me.

Selected publications

Healy, L. M. (2007) 'Universalism and cultural relativism in social work ethics', *International Social Work*, 50:1, pp 11–26.

Healy, L. M. (2008a) 'Exploring the history of social work as a human rights profession', *International Social Work*, 51:6, pp 735–48.

Healy, L. M. (2008b) *International social work: Professional action in an interdependent world* (2nd edn), New York: Oxford University Press.

Healy, L. M. and Link, R. J. (eds) (2012) *Handbook on international social work: Human rights, development and the global profession*, New York: Oxford University Press.

Healy, L. and Kamya, H. (2014) 'Ethics and international discourse in social work: The case of Uganda's anti-homosexuality legislation', *Ethics and Social Welfare*, 8(2): pp 151-69.

Notes

[1] Professor of Rehabilitation, Japan Women's University in the 1980s, co-editor of *Peace and social work education* (Kojima and Hosaka, 1987).

[2] (GAA&MP) While the first part of the interview took place at the conference in 2014 where Lynne Healy received the award, the second part was completed in 2015.

[3] Executive Director, ICSW, formerly working in various UN social development leadership roles.

[4] The Post-2015 Development Agenda, a UN process to develop a future global social development framework: https://sustainabledevelopment.un.org/post2015.

[5] Dr Gidraph G. Wairire, Senior Lecturer, Department of Sociology and Social Work, University of Nairobi, Vice President, IASSW.

[6] The IASSW archives for 1928-98 are held at the Social Work History Archives, University of Minnesota: http://archives.lib.umn.edu/repositories/11/resources/755.

[7] Narda Razack, Professor, School of Social Work, York University, Toronto, Canada.

SEVENTEEN

Abye Tasse, 2016

Interviewed by Gurid Aga Askeland

Biography

Abye Tasse was a refugee from Ethiopia, becoming a French citizen in 2000. After posts as a sociocultural *animateur* and journalist and following social science and social work studies in Toulouse, Montpellier, Rouen, Le Havre and Paris, he gained a PhD at L'Ecole des Hautes Etudes en Sciences Sociales in Paris. After a variety of senior posts in social work education in France, he took up professorships and advisory posts in Ethiopia, Mauritania and Comoros leading the development of new social work education programmes. He was president of IASSW, 2004-08.

What do you think the award will mean to you?

I will know when I receive it what it will imply emotionally. Professionally, it is about recognition by peers of my contribution to social work around the world. I will be the first from the African region to receive this award, so it acknowledges the contribution of international social work education from Africa. The most important aspect of this recognition for me is that maybe it will open up doors for others, showing that international social work contributions come from different parts of the world. Armaity Desai from India received the award in 1992, but since then the awardees have been concentrated in Europe and the US.

It is an acknowledgement for past political support I was granted in developing schools of social work in different parts of the world, in Ethiopia, Mauritania. People who helped me are also recognized by it.

What activities have been of major importance for your professional career and its impact on social work and its education?

Besides working as social work educator, I worked for over six years as an *animateur sociaux culturelle* [social worker] in France, in a very marginalized area when I was young. While teaching in France, my school became a member of a big three-year programme supporting child protection in Romania. We supported eight Romanian universities in different parts of the country for several years, developing practice education; previously it was more theoretical. I also supported schools of social work in Cameroon when I was in France.

Then came the development of schools of social work in Ethiopia and Mauritania. In Mauritania, there was no previous school of social work and I supported the creation of a social work programme. Ethiopia had a vibrant social work education 30 years ago. However, this was closed during the military regime. With the help of many others, I restarted it. These are the most practical contributions.

The contribution to the IASSW board during my presidency (2004–08) was chiefly in two areas. First, developing the Global Agenda (IASSW/ICSW/IFSW, 2012) will have, I hope, the most lasting impact on social work education and social work. The second area was to go, as president, beyond frontiers. Membership among the Chinese schools started to grew during the time I was president. Social work in China is well developed now and, since Angie Yuen-Tsang[1] became president in 2008, more schools from China have joined IASSW. When I was elected as president of IASSW, Asia-Pacific Region had been having a really difficult time, restarting thanks to people like Tatsuru Akimoto[2] and others.

What did you do in Ethiopia?

The social work programme in Ethiopia was closed down in 1976. Before I came back, people had tried to reopen it but, for different reasons, had not succeeded. Eight months before I arrived in 2004, I started preparing, working with colleagues, among them Professor Seyoum G. Selassie.[3] He had worked hard for the re-establishment of the school of social work for a long time. When he asked me to do something about social work education, I found that there were no teachers because he and two others, who had been engaged in the programme 30 years previously, had retired. Some other very active individuals were for different reasons not able to make it happen.

Without human resources, how could we develop social work programmes?

Because I was engaged in IASSW, I thought it was possible to mobilize colleagues from different parts of the world for this endeavour. I had listened to a discourse on solidarity and social work in conferences and meetings around the world, so I thought that there were people who could be engaged and really believed that it was possible to take solidarity seriously. Before I left France, I wrote an open letter – sending it everywhere – reminding colleagues that they often affirm their solidarity with people who do not have resources to achieve social work education. I informed them that I was going back to Ethiopia to re-establish a school of social work and that we needed their support. Over 60 people responded positively to my request. It was a fantastic solidarity move, even though some colleagues could not believe that this venture was possible.

Strategically, it was difficult to start with a BA programme, because this would have required more teachers and it could not be done in a simple way. We decided to start with a masters programme, as that would be more flexible. The idea was to create, with a masters, a human resource who would be able to teach and develop their own programmes. After discussion among those engaged in the development, we opted to admit 40 students in the first cohort.

We had immense support from Alice Butterfield and Nathan Links,[4] who had been engaged preparing for re-establishing a social work programme before my arrival in Ethiopia. The first cohort of students knew from the beginning that it would require hard work and a different kind of engagement from being a student at a university programme with permanent professors. The students on the first course were active because they were waiting for it. In the history of social work in Ethiopia, there had been no masters programme.

A huge number of people applied, many with a degree in social sciences. Those who entered the first course had already social work experience, which they were able to articulate easily. Colleagues coming to teach described the students they met as brilliant, engaged, hardworking. For most of our colleagues from abroad this was not just a class, it was something besides that, which was very important.

After the first group of students graduated in July, we started the first ever PhD programme in August, because our plan was to develop a human resource able to teach. We knew that having colleagues coming from abroad to support the venture was important to start with, but not sustainable in the long term.

Eight students from the first masters course started the PhD programme. To secure the quality of the programme, we mixed US and European models, basing it on both research and teaching. They followed compulsory modules for two years; among these was a teaching module. Students, once they finalized the course work, started co-teaching with colleagues from abroad. In the ten years since this programme started, there have been over 30 PhD holders in social work trained in that university. From the start of the social work programme in 2004, Ethiopia is now endowed with bachelors programmes of social work and two or three masters programmes in different universities, where masters and PhD holders in social work are employed.

That was a fantastic experience, because it was not only social work education but higher education in general that dared to do things. It opened other programmes to developing PhDs. The social work programme was unique, and colleagues from psychiatry and computer science started programmes using the same model. From 1950 to 2008, Addis Ababa University produced only 60 PhD holders. Since we started the PhD programmes, hundreds have graduated.

Three or four people with a PhD in social work are now vice presidents of universities. Others are deans, or deans of colleges, and some are heads of department. The programme did not only have high quality, but it gave people strong motivation and dedication. So, recognition should go not only to me or to the teachers, but also to the students who embraced the programme.

I knew when I arrived that I was going to leave the country after five or six years. When the first students started the second year of the PhD courses, I decided to take two students each year to be assistant deans while they pursued their PhDs. This had never been experienced before, at least in Ethiopia. Every year we changed assistant deans, and by the time I left, six of the students had already had that position. They had not only been trained as social workers and educators, but also as social work education leaders. I remember Emebet Mulugeta, one of the students and assistant dean in 2008, saying at a conference to 800 people that our education is not only about our own social work training, it is also about leadership. Now when I see these students in various positions in different universities, I feel that the objective has been achieved.

It is a unique example of how a poor university can create human resources by attracting talented professors from different parts of the world that it could not afford. You could have the best people in social work internationally coming to teach. People were wanting to come because it was an interesting experience. None was paid, but they were really engaged. What makes it unique is that based on social work values it is possible to transform something through solidarity, and then to accept that the time arrives for leadership to be given away. It shows that social work can empower people to do what they want to happen. The PhD holders and colleagues since are more structured and organized in a very clear fashion. They do not need people like me now, except as a colleague who can give some feedback from time to time. My role has shifted, as they are able to do the job themselves. This approach to practice, value and engagement encapsulates social work education and social work.

What about Mauritania and Comoros?

What I did in Mauritania was different. There were no social work educators, and none who wanted to be engaged in social work and had practice experience. The first thing was to train some people to get social work experience. We then started with a BA degree and, since I had not been a dean at the university in Mauritania, I was supporting and advising colleagues in the process of creating the social work programme. We collectively developed a new institute called the Institute of Professional Education where the school of social work is located.

Again, this became a very impressive programme because we asked the students to be involved, practically and financially. For example, the first year we asked the students to contribute financially to the development of the school. Other resources we found from the 'French cooperation' informally, a French development agency, to match the student contribution to equip students with personal computers. This had never been seen in Mauritanian universities, and again the level of engagement and involvement of students in social work was totally different from that of other students.

Now I am here in Comoros. I arrived just four months ago, as we speak, and we are discussing with colleges how to develop similar programmes as in Mauritania or Ethiopia, attempting to see what model will work. It may be a bachelors or a masters programme; this has not yet been decided.

What has social work and its education meant to you professionally and personally?

Social work has impressed me as an area for professional development. I became engaged in social work during my youth in France in a highly marginalized migrant area. Social work in France was very open then, very articulate and militant. Engagement was possible. I worked in a difficult district, and we used to go and discuss with young people who were saying that 'we're going to prison'. We were not only social workers but also older brothers. They came to realize that someone cared about them, not only giving them norms, but also engaging them in activities. I found it possible to contribute, although modestly, in the process of transformation and integration of youth and young adults into the society. Those people influenced my life in general as well as my work. After that experience, I wanted to take part in social work.

We are now reconstructing what happened many years ago, so it is difficult to say why I chose social work. It was a combination of many things, but emotionally this was it. I did my bachelors, masters and PhD in France, and I got French citizenship in 2000. I was interested in international relations, which I studied at university. This deepened during my PhD research, a comparative study of migration in France and in the US.

For me, the professional and personal are related. I was not in my country of origin at the start of my professional life. I arrived in France as a political refugee in 1979, and was not supposed to be involved in political activities. Social work engagement is not political in the sense of political party but, because you combine it with doing things, you could see there are other models of engagement, both professionally and socially. I think that is what social work and its education mean for me professionally, real engagement and the possibility of doing something. As you see, social work has been an entire life engagement. You could link the professional to the personal and the personal to the social. That is how it worked for me.

What challenges have you experienced during your career?

There have been two areas of concern for me in social work education. One was to incorporate social justice and social development and identify contributions to that. The other was the attempt to give academic credibility to the profession. These two concerns are in tension. In the late 1970s and early '80s, social work education in Europe and especially in France was radically politically oriented.

One of the challenges in the early 2000s and even today is that it has become too technical. In recent years, it has sought to become like other disciplines in academic areas. For me, the challenge in social work education has been how to deal with being just another academic area of education. You have to consider the history, remembering why we need social work education. I have also been a sociology student. People like Bourdieu wrote about sociology as an army of combat for social justice. How could social work lead to articulating the struggle for social justice? That is probably the higher-level challenge that I can see.

It is important to champion other values: the value of brotherhood. People often talk about equity, but not about fraternity. The French people have this *fraternité* or brotherhood concept that is really important to me. While concepts of equality and liberty are well developed and analyzed in social work, fraternity remains largely untouched. Equality and democratic rights do not work without the fraternity component. The equality of rights comes to life if we include brotherhood. Social work has to be very careful about what we are engaging in, because if you get into a pure academic area these values may not be major components.

Liberty is not only for individuals. It is also for the collective, how to bond with others without disrespect, but acknowledging and being with others. My equality only becomes real in relation to others. People are now talking more about equity than equality because equality is a difficult issue. We have to be careful because the subjectivity of equity means that it cannot replace equality. We will have to rethink how to teach this, and how it works in reality. There are many elements related to it, like users' rights. Users may be part of the problem or the solution. This has to be considered from not only a theoretical perspective, but also how to deal with it in practice.

When I was elected the president of IASSW, I announced at the first board meeting that I would not run for another period. Many people asked why and I said because I wanted people to know that I would like to feel free from the beginning to do something, rather than to work for re-election. Four years was enough, because when I was elected, I became the tenth president in 80 years. When you have 193 countries in the world, for every country to have one member as president, it would take many hundreds of years. Although having four years to achieve something as president was important, I knew that I would have more than four years' involvement in IASSW, so that was not a problem for me. Nevertheless, it was also one way of saying to people: can we bring our discourse closer into practice?

I have been privileged because everywhere I found people who supported me in my career beyond their duty. I have met very few direct obstacles. Maybe my career was not extraordinary in itself, only what I really wanted to do with it. In France, I worked with people who supported me, including support to become the director general of the Institute for Social Work and Social Development. I was probably the first person from the immigrant population to get this kind of position. As people have been very supportive, challenges were in myself rather than coming from outside.

What would you highlight as most important in your international work?

Migration has really been important to me and I hope I have contributed to new perspectives on it. This is related to my own history. International migration has not been well articulated in social work, and there are difficulties in researching and teaching it.

The second area of enormous importance to me is higher education in social work. We have a discourse where we talk about African and Asian perspectives, and respecting them, but I am not sure if we have been able to develop strong perspectives that put meat on the bones on this. Social work education continues to be dominated by Western perspectives. The development of indigenous perspectives remains very fragile. We have achieved the political acceptance of integration of indigenous social work into the corpus of international social work; however, we need to work from the other end to make it real. We need to focus on the contribution of indigenous social work, not only for Africa and Asia, but also as a contribution to make international social work stronger. What it means in theory and practice continues to be an undiscovered or unchallenged area. I do not know what we mean when we say that there is an African perspective. People like Vishantie Sewpaul[5] have attempted to use Ubuntu, the South African indigenous conceptualization of humanity, for a different kind of social work. It is interesting to explore the relationship between brotherhood and Ubuntu, and what kind of practices might emerge from that. There are programmes within different disciplines, such as psychology and sociology that attempt to include African perspectives. How these are taken into account in African social work education programmes is a real question.

We have to test the slogans. Let me take the example of solidarity. Many people say that Europeans are very individualistic compared to Africans, and that Africans are very communitarian. My observation today is that this is a misunderstanding. It is true that Europeans achieve less organic solidarity. For me, however, they are collectivists in a different way, as they organize society under 'administrative solidarity'. Aid for older people, free social care, universal healthcare systems and other support systems are a form of collectivism. In many areas of Africa, people are losing the traditional, organic forms of solidarity, without developing public systems that replace it. We are losing force as communitarians. One could question if the current African way of organizing society is not equally individualistic as the one observed in Europe and even more so. We have to re-discuss seriously the discourse on how far solidarity reaches, and see if we have to invent new and better forms. Today, inequality is growing much faster than development, and inequality is a basis for future problems. If we do not work on this, solidarity will belong to the past rather than to the practice of today.

What would you like to see happening in social work in the future?

The Global Agenda (IASSW/ICSW/IFSW, 2012) is really one of the structuring tools for the future of social work for developing a collective voice. It is already happening, but we are still at the beginning. What I want to change is that the collective voice should begin to articulate more social issues and new perspectives for social work education, and also to project itself across boundaries working with other disciplines. Maybe social work in rural areas should be working with people in agriculture, in development and in education. There are so many fields that social work education should be engaged in, because the Western social work model is not going to fit on other continents. Even European countries will probably in the future not have the same state provision as today. That means that family responsibilities will have to be reorganized, not only the state provision. Today the unemployment rate in France is over 10 per cent. What does that mean for social work education? If social provision is not just about giving out money, but trying to organize people to invent areas of engagement for development and new processes, social work education needs to change. New forms of economy are emerging, and new experiences gained. How is social work going to embrace and support communities using new technology? All these areas remain almost untouched. We still do our interviews, using interview techniques. We really have to rethink the entire system because the world now is different.

Going back to the Global Agenda, I proposed it originally for the three parties, IASSW, IFSW and ICSW, in London 2006 when I was president, but it is difficult to say it was my idea. We collectively developed the leadership. We launched two important things. One was the Global Agenda itself and the other was to link our conferences to the Global Agenda and to our political engagement in social work education, social work and social development, and how to be visible. Since the conference in Adelaide, I have been the chair. I encouraged Antoinette Lombard from South Africa to take over, as she is very interested and knowledgeable. She is now giving very impressive leadership on the Global Agenda, and most probably, another directions will emerge. We should continue to be militant, or to advocate, but we do not need a position to do that. There is enough space for people who want to act and invent something new. When you have reached a goal, you should move on; there are so many things to do that a whole life is not enough.

Anything you would highlight from your period as a president?

IASSW is a big organization. Lena Dominelli started before me to open it up, and since I became the president, I have been concerned about bringing us together and becoming more international. Now we have had presidents from China and India. There are people in other parts of the world who can do things.

The criteria for the award recognized that I got the chance to be 'international' in one way. It is very difficult, not for me personally, but for colleagues from Africa to attend conferences and cooperate on joint publications due to lack of resources. They cannot go or publish everywhere because their areas may not be of interest for major publications. It has been argued that people who were funded in the past by the solidarity fund for conferences should not be eligible subsequently because we have to support new applicants first. However, colleagues coming from Western countries, including myself, can go to conferences regularly supported by their universities. People using solidarity funds cannot. Sometimes, even people from the Global South are thinking in this mechanistic way, because the dominant system has been collectively accepted.

We seek to value people on the same level but raise awareness that there are invisible criteria. English is not the language of many people. Most conferences, most publications, are in English and we accept that. Academic recognitions are still based on that. Let us have other criteria, other selection processes. We do not need to change everything, but to acknowledge that the difficulties persist and we must deal with them. Many people who have international recognition are invited to different places, including myself. I am not sure that we deserve it more than others who are invisible because they do not have access to resources, and not because they do not have something interesting to offer. It feels good to be acknowledged but at the same time, as I said earlier, it was motivating as the president of IASSW to contribute to opening up the leadership position for people coming from elsewhere.

How did you get into the French secondment programme?

This happened by accident when I arrived in Ethiopia. The university approached the ambassador and asked France to support my position at Addis Ababa University. That is how the secondment programme started.

Here I am working as an advisor for the Minister of Education and Research of the United Comoros. I was working as advisor to the Minister of Higher Education and Research in Mauritania earlier for over five years.

What would you like to see happening in IASSW in the future?

More opening, more diversity, more engagement. IASSW should become a platform for involvement, not only for board discussion. Now with the Global Agenda, with regional seminars, including the board seminars, things are happening. We should be able to mobilize more people, not only every other year, when there is an international conference, but in an ongoing fashion. Sending statements, which we are doing, is good, but not sufficient. We have to *do* something and develop other forms of engagement. Maybe many new fields would emerge, and that is fine.

My Katherine Kendall Award speech at the conference will be about 'Voices against Walls'. All these walls that are being built around the world to limit access for people; walls people climb to try to survive. This is my history. I cannot imagine what would have happened to me without the opportunity to go to France. Maybe I would have died. By being able to come to France, I have contributed in my modest fashion in places where I have been. I do not think that we should consider migrants as a burden, but also as people. Sometimes these people have left their country because they are victims of wars that they did not start. They are not responsible, and developed countries have to be more responsible. Such issues should really be visible and IASSW should argue for them. The Global Agenda topic this year is about 'Dignity and worth of people'. With an increasing number of asylum seekers and refugees in the world, we should be able to recast the issue of migration. We should be involved in this, not only criticizing states but coming up with innovative solutions.

It is obvious that my background has influenced all my life, the way I think and behave. I was born in Addis Ababa. When I was 14 or 15, Ethiopia was in political turmoil, and most of us at that age were engaged politically. Sometimes now, it is funny to see young people being awake all night, going out in the early morning to buy a new version of games. When I was 15, we could pass a night waiting for a new political book to come. That is how I became politically engaged. I remember the books I read. I am not sure that nowadays I still understand them correctly, but at that time, I thought I did. They are very complex.

I left my country at a very young age as political refugee to escape the military dictatorship. Thousands of young women and men were killed or detained and tortured. I had to go to Eritrea, then walk many miles across the interior to Sudan at the age of 16. Then I went to Egypt and eventually to France. All this creates a person. This was not exceptional; thousands of young people did the same. We thought that the future looked bright; everything was possible. The circumstances I lived under for a long time in Sudan were economically and socially very difficult. We used to go to the library and read books while we did not have enough to eat.

It is possible to go against the odds. Taking risks is something my own history is full of; to experiment, to fail, would mean starting again, but what is there to lose? When you have nothing, you have nothing to lose. We opened a school of social work, and many people said it is impossible, there is no quality. Maybe we have not reached the Harvard level of social work, but if you focus on what others have and you do not have, then you cannot work. It is all about taking risks, but not unconsidered risks. We joined forces on a collective journey, risk-taking to create a better life for all. The risk was for everybody but we took it collectively; that is probably why we achieved some good results. It has been a journey, not alone but with others. My journey to Sudan was not a lonely one; we were many. My journey back to Ethiopia and the school of social work, I was not alone. There are many people, who came to assist. However, I was not just doing it for others; for me it was also coming back to my country of origin, and contributing gave me a sense of doing something important. It was also for my kids, to live in the country of their parents for some time, and to feel comfortable.

Selected publications

Tasse, A. (2004) *Parcours d'Ethiopiens en France et aux Etats-Unis: Les nouvelles formes de migration*, [Comparative studies of Ethiopian Migrants in France and the USA: New type of Migration], Paris: l'Harmattan.

Tasse, A. and Butterfield, A. K. (2012) (eds) *Social work and social development: Lessons from Africa*, London: Routledge.

Tasse, A. (ed) (2014) 'Global agenda promoting social and economic equalities, *International Social Work*, (Special edn) 57(4).

Tasse, A. (2015) 'Trajectoire d'un militant. Abdul, de l'Institut d'Etat du pétrole de Moscou à la guérilla éthiopienne', [Abdul, trajectory of a Militant. From the National Institute of Petrol of Moscow to the Ethiopian Guerrilla] in M. de Saint Martin, G. S. Ghellab and K. Mellakh (eds) *Etudier à l'Est: Expériences de diplômés africains*, [*Studying in the East: Experiences of African Graduates*] Paris: Karthala-FMSH: pp 129-143.

Tasse, A. (2015) 'Child soldiers as victims and actors: lessons from Ethiopia', in J. D. Wright (ed) *International encyclopedia of the social & behavioral sciences*, Vol 3 (2nd ed) Oxford: Elsevier: pp 439-44.

Notes

[1] Yuen Tsang Woon-ki, Angelina; Professor, Vice President, Student and Global Affairs, Hong Kong Polytechnic University.

[2] Tatsuru Akimoto, Professor and Director, Social Work Research Institute, Asian Centre for Welfare in Society, Japan College of Social Work, Professor Emeritus, Japan Women's University.

[3] Professor Seyoum Gebre-Selassie (1936–2007), sociologist and social development writer and practitioner.

[4] Both from Jane Addams College of Social Work, University of Illinois, Chicago, USA.

[5] Vishantie Sewpaul, Senior Professor of Social Work, University of Kwazulu-Natal.

Bibliography

Abo-el-Nasr, M. M. (1997) 'Egypt', in N. Mayadas, T. D. Watts and D. Elliott (eds) *International handbook on social work theory and practice*, Westport, CT: Greenwood, pp 205-22.

Aguilar, M. A. (1995) 'Mexico and Central America', in T. D. Watts, D. Elliott and N. S. Mayadas (eds) (1995) *International handbook on social work education*, Westport, CT: Greenwood, pp 43-64.

Akimoto, T. (2008) 'What is international social work? Its contribution to social work in a global society', Paper given at the Symposium of the 100th Anniversary of the Alice Salomon Hochschule, Berlin 'Soziale Arbeit und Gesundheit – Facetten ihrer Politisierung', https://www.ash-berlin.eu/100-Jahre-ASH/symposium/akimoto.htm.

Akimoto, T. (2013) 'What can Buddhism contribute to the professional social work? An essential element it has somewhere lost', in E. Sakamoto, (ed) *The roles of Buddhism in social work: Vietnam and Japan*, Hanoi: University of Social Sciences and Humanities, Vietnam National University/Chiba: Shukutoku University/Tokyo: Social Work Research Institute Asian Center for Welfare in Society ACWelS), Japan College Of Social Work, pp 1-3.

Alinsky, S. D. (1971) *Rules for radicals*, New York: Random House.

Almanzor, A. (1974) 'Introduction', in IASSW (ed) *A developmental outlook for social work education*, New York: International Association of Schools of Social Work, pp 7-10.

Ashencaen Crabtree, S., Husain, F. and Spalek, B. (2008) *Islam and social work: Debating values, transforming practice*, Bristol: Policy Press.

Askeland, G. A. (2007) 'Globalisation and a flood of travellers. Flooded travellers and social justice', in L. Dominelli (ed) *Revitalising communities in a globalising world*, Aldershot: Ashgate, pp 271-80.

Askeland, G. A. and Payne, M. (2001) 'What is valid knowledge for social workers?', *Social Work in Europe*, 8(3): 13-23.

Askeland, G. A. and Døhlie, E. (2006) 'Internasjonalt sosialt arbeid: når sosialarbeidaren kryssar grenser', in E. Døhlie and G. A. Askeland (eds) *Intenasjonalt sosialt arbeid: innsats på andres arena*, Oslo: Universitetsforlaget.

Askeland, G. A., Mulugeta, E., Ero, D., Negeri, D., Mengsteab, M., Bekele, S. and Alemu, T. (2010) 'Contextual social work in Ethiopia', Paper given to the Conference of the International Association of Schools of Social Work/International Federation of Social Workers/International Council on Social Work, Hong Kong, 10-14 June.

Askeland, G. A., Døhlie, E. and Grosvold, K. (2016) 'International field placement in social work: Relevant for working in the home country', *International Social Work*, http://journals.sagepub.com/doi/abs/10.1177/0020872816655200.

Association of Social Work Education in Africa (1973) *Case studies of social development in Africa*, vol 1, Addis Ababa: ASWEA.

Association of Social Work Education in Africa (1974) *Case studies of social development in Africa*, vol 2, Addis Ababa: ASWEA.

Association of Social Work Education in Africa (1982a) '1981 minutes of the General Assembly of Social Work Education in Africa, June 5, 1981', in *ASWEA seminar on guidelines for the development of training in family welfare*, Doc. 15, Addis Ababa: ASWEA.

Association of Social Work Education in Africa (1982b) *Seminar on the organization and delivery of social services to rural Africa*, Doc. 19, Addis Ababa: ASWEA.

ASWEA (1982c) *3rd Seminar on the organization and delivery of social services to rural areas in Africa*, Book 6: 10, Addis Ababa: ASWEA.

Bagdonas, A. (2001) 'Practical and academic aspects of social work development in Lithuania', in P. Helppikangas (ed) *Social work and civil society from an international perspective*, Rovaniemi: Lapin Yliopisto, pp 37–83.

Barclay, P. (2001) 'Robin Huws Jones. Innovative spirit behind social work reforms', *Guardian*, 9 July 2001. https://www.theguardian.com/news/2001/jul/09/guardianobituaries.socialsciences

Barretta-Herman, A., Leung, P., Littlechild, B., Parada, H. and Wairire, G. D. (2016) 'The changing status and growth of social work education worldwide: Process, findings and implications of the IASSW 2010 census', *International Social Work*, 59(4): 459–78.

Bauman, Z. (2000) *Liquid modernity*, Cambridge: Polity.

Beecher, B., Reeves, J., Eggertsen, L. and Furuto, S. (2010) 'International students' views about transferability in social work education and practice', *International Social Work* 53(2): 203–16.

Beless, D. (2004) 'A profile in excellence: Katherine A. Kendall', in *New Global Development*, 1&2: 5–7.

Bettmann, J. E., Jacques, G. and Frost, C. J. (eds) (2013) *International social work practice: Case studies from a global context*, London: Routledge.

Beveridge Report (1942) *Social Insurance and Allied Services* (Cmd 6404) London: HMSO.

Billups, J. O. (ed) (2002a) *Faithful angels: Portraits of international social work notables*, Washington, DC: NASW Press.

Billups, J. O. (ed) (2002b) 'Herman D. Stein', in J. O. Billups (ed) *Faithful angels: Portraits of international social work notables*, Washington DC: NASW Press, pp 255-72.

Billups, J. O. (ed) (2002c) 'Katherine A. Kendall', in *Faithful angels: Portraits of international social work notables*, Washington, DC: NASW Press, pp 145-63

Billups, J. O. (ed) (2002d) 'Robin Huws Jones', in J. O. Billups (ed) *Faithful angels: Portraits of international social work notables*, Washington, DC: NASW Press, pp 133-44.

Blavo, E. Q. and Apt, N. A. (1997) 'Ghana', in N. Mayadas, T. D. Watts and D. Elliott (eds) *International handbook on social work theory and practice*, Westport, CT: Greenwood, pp 320-43.

Boehm, W. W. (1959) *Objectives of the social work curriculum for the future*, (vol 1: Social Work Curriculum Study), New York, NY: Council on Social Work Education.

Bottomore, T. B. (1965) *Classes in modern society*, London: Allen and Unwin.

Brandwein, R. A. (2005) 'Katherine Kendall: a social work institution', *Affilia*, 20(1): 103-10.

Brauns, H.-J. and Kramer, D. (1991) 'Social work education and professional development', in M. Hill (ed) *Social work and the European Community: The social policy and practice contexts*, London: Jessica Kingsley, pp 80-99.

Brekke, J. (2012) 'Shaping the science of social work', *Research on Social Work Practice*, 22(5): 455-64.

Briskman, L. (2009) 'Academic activism for political change: opposing mandatory detention of asylum seekers', in D. Bennett, J. Earnest and M. Tanji (eds) *People, place and power: Australia and the Asia Pacific*, Perth: Curtin University of Technology, pp 190-207.

Briskman, L. (2009) 'Recasting social work: Human rights and political activism', Eileen Younghusband Lecture, IASSW conference, Durban 2008, Typescript.

Bronfenbrenner, U. (1979) *The ecology of human development: Experimental by nature and design*, Cambridge, MA: Harvard University Press.

Bunge, M. (1974-1989) *Treatise on basic philosophy* (8 vols), Dordrecht: Dreidel.

Butterfield, A. and Tasse, A. (2013) *Social development and social work: Learning from Africa*, London: Routledge.

Callahan, M. (2008) 'Lena Dominelli (United Kingdom), President 1996-2004', *Social Work and Society*, 16(1), http://www.socwork.net/sws/article/view/107/396.

Chan, C. L. W. and Chow, N. W. S. (1992) *More welfare after economic reform? Welfare development in the People's Republic of China*, Hong Kong: Centre for Urban Planning and Environmental Development, University of Hong Kong.

Chow, N. (1997) 'China', in N. Mayadas, T. D. Watts and D. Elliott (eds) *International handbook on social work theory and practice*, Westport, CT: Greenwood, pp 282-300.

Cohen, B.-Z. and Guttmann, D. (1998) 'Social work education in Israel', in F. M. Loewenberg (ed) *Meeting the challenges of a changing society: Fifty years of social work in Israel*, Jerusalem: Magnes Press, The Hebrew University, pp 300-20.

Corrigan, P. and Leonard, P. (1978) *Social work practice under capitalism: A Marxist approach*, Basingstoke: Macmillan.

Cox, D. (1995) 'Asia and the Pacific', in T. D. Watts, D. Elliott and N. S. Mayadas (eds) *International handbook on social work education*, Westport, CT: Greenwood, pp 321-38.

Cox, D. and Pawar, M. (2013) *International social work: Issues, strategies, and programs*, Thousand Oaks, CA: Sage.

CWRU (1998) August (in-house magazine of Case Western Reserve University) [no longer publicly available online].

Desai, A. S. (1972) 'Curriculum development', in IASSW *New themes in social work education*, New York, NY: International Association of School of Social Work, pp 89-108.

Desai, A. S. (1985-86) 'The foundations of social work education in India', *Indian Journal of Social Work*, 46(1).

Desai, A. S. (2003) 'Value orientation of higher education', in M. M. Luther (ed) *Building a vibrant India: Democracy, development and ethics*, New Delhi: Tata McGraw Hill, pp 271-88.

Desai, A. S. (2007) 'Disaster and social work responses', in L. Dominelli (ed) *Revitalising communities in a globalising world*, Aldershot: Ashgate, pp 297-314.

Desai, A. S. (2009) 'Catalyzing higher education and school education linkages', in M. Mukhopadhyay (ed) *Quality school education for all*, New Delhi: Educational Technology and Management Academy, pp 47-65.

Desai, A. S. (2012) 'Transforming higher education for gender equality', in A. S. Kolaskar and M. Dash (eds) *Women and society: The road to change*, Oxford: Oxford University Press, pp 60-85.

Devine, E. T. (1906) *Efficiency and relief: A programme for social work*, New York, NY: Columbia University Press.

Dominelli. L. (1997) *Sociology for social work*, Basingstoke: Palgrave.

Dominelli, L. (1998) 'Foreword', in K. A. Kendall, *IASSW The first fifty years 1928-1978: A tribute to the founders*, Alexandra, VA: International Association of Social Work.

Dominelli, L. (2002) *Feminist social work theory and practice*, Basingstoke: Palgrave Macmillan.

Dominelli, L. (2006) *Women and community action* (2nd edn), Bristol: Policy Press.

Dominelli, L. (ed) (2007) *Revitalising communities in a globalising world*, Aldershot: Ashgate.

Dominelli, L. (2008) *Anti-racist social work* (3rd edn), Basingstoke: Palgrave Macmillan.

Dominelli, L. (2010) *Social work in a globalising world*, Cambridge: Polity.

Dominelli, L. (2012) *Green social work: From environmental crises to environmental justice*, Cambridge: Polity.

Dominelli, L. (ed) (2013) *Decolonizing social work*, Aldershot: Ashgate.

Dominelli, L. and E. McCleod (1989) *Feminist social work*, Basingstoke: Macmillan.

Duffy, J., Ramon, S., Guru, S., Lindsay, J., Cemlyn, S. and Nuttman-Shwartz, O. (2013) 'Developing a social work curriculum on political conflict: findings from an IASSW-funded project', *European Journal of Social Work*, 16(5): 689-707.

Ealy, S. D. and Lloyd, D. (eds) (2004) 'The Eric Voegelin-Willmoore Kendall correspondence', *Political Science Reviewer*, 33(1): 357-412.

Estes, R. (2010) 'United States-based conceptualization of international social work education', https://www.researchgate.net/publication/270589444_US-Based_Conceptualization_of_Education_for_International_Social_Work.

Farman Farmaien, S. (1992) *Daughter of Persia: A woman's journey from her father's harem through the Islamic revolution*, London: Bantam.

Fish, J. and Karban, K. (eds) (2015) *Lesbian, gay, bisexual and trans health inequalities: International perspectives in social work*, Bristol: Policy Press.

Foxwell, E. (2014a) *American contributions to global social work: CSWE recipients of the IASSW Katherine Kendall Memorial Award*, Alexandria, VA: Council on Social Work Education.

Foxwell, E. (2014b) 'Katherine A. Kendall and the Kendall Memorial Award', in E. Foxwell, *American contributions to global social work: CSWE recipients of the IASSW Katherine Kendall Memorial Award*, Alexandria, VA: Council on Social Work Education, pp 3-5.

Freire, P. (1972) *Pedagogy of the oppressed*, Harmondsworth: Penguin.

Furuto, S. B. C. L. (2014) 'Social welfare contrasted in East Asia and the Pacific', in S. B. C. L. Furuto (ed) *Social welfare in East Asia and the Pacific*, New York, NY: Columbia University Press, pp 249-78.

Garber, R. (1992) *Katherine A. Kendall Distinguished Service Award*, Alexandria, VA: Council on Social Work Education.

Garber, R. (2000) 'World census of social work and social development education', *Canadian Social Work*, 2(1): 198-215.

Giddens, A. (1991) *The consequences of modernity*, Cambridge: Polity.

Giddens, A. (2013) *The third way: The renewal of social democracy*, Cambridge: Polity.

Ginet, M. L. (1963) 'Comments on specialization in social work education', *International Social Work*, 6(2): 26-7.

Goodman, R. (1998) 'The Japanese-style welfare state and the delivery of personal social services', in R. Goodman, G. White and H.-J. Kwon (eds) *The East Asian welfare model: Welfare orientalism and the state*, London: Routledge, pp 139-58.

Gough, K. (1989) *Rural change in Southeast India, 1950s–1980s*, New Delhi: Oxford University Press.

Gough, K. (1990) *Political economy in Vietnam*, Berkeley, CA: Folklore Institute.

Graham, M. (2002) *Social work and African-centred world views*, Birmingham: Venture.

Gray, M. and Fook, J. (2004) 'The quest for a universal social work: some issues and implications', *Social Work Education*, 23 (5): 625-44.

Gray, M., Coates, J. and Yellow Bird, M. (eds) (2008) *Indigenous social work around the world*, Farnham: Ashgate.

Gray, M., Coates, J., Yellow Bird, M. and Hetherington, T. (eds) (2013) *Decolonizing social work*, Farnham: Ashgate.

Green, E. C. (1999) 'National trends, regional differences, local circumstances: social welfare in New Orleans, 1870s-1920s', in E. C. Green (ed) *Before the New Deal: Social welfare in the South, 1830-1930*, Athens, GA: University of Georgia Press, pp 81-99.

Guzzetta, C. (1995) 'Central and Eastern Europe', in T. D. Watts, D. Elliott and N. S. Mayadas (eds) *International handbook on social work education*, Westport, CT: Greenwood, pp 191-209.

Harris, J., Borodkina, O., Brodtkorb, E., Evans, T., Kessl, F., Schnurr, S. and Slettebø, T. (2015) 'International travelling knowledge in social work: an analytical framework', *European Journal of Social Work*, 18(4): 481-94.

Hart, M. A. (2008) 'Critical reflection on an aboriginal approach to helping', in M. Gray, J. Coates and M. Yellow Bird (eds) *Indigenous social work around the world*, Aldershot: Ashgate.

Healy, L.M. (2007) 'Universalism and cultural relativism in social work ethics', *International Social Work*, 50(1): 11-26.

Healy, L. M. (2008a) 'Exploring the history of social work as a human rights profession', *International Social Work*, 51(6): 735–48.

Healy, L. M. (2008b) *International social work: Professional action in an interdependent world* (2nd edn), New York, NY: Oxford University Press.

Healy, L. (2008c) 'Introduction: a brief journey through the 80 year history of the International Association of Schools of Social Work', *Social Work and Society* (6)1: www.socwork.net/sws/article/view/98/387.

Healy, L M. (2008d) 'Katherine A. Kendall (USA), Honorary President since 1978', *Social Work and Society*, 6(1): http://www.socwork.net/sws/article/view/109/398.

Healy, L. (2012) 'Defining international social work', in L. Healy and R. Link (eds) *Handbook of international social work: Human rights, development, and the global profession*, New York, NY: Oxford University Press.

Healy, L. M. and Kamya, H. (2014) 'Ethics and international discourse in social work: the case of Uganda's anti-homosexuality legislation', *Ethics and Social Welfare*, 8(2): 151–69.

Healy, L. M. and Link, R. J. (eds) (2011) *Handbook of international social work: Human rights, development, and the global profession*, New York, NY: Oxford University Press.

Healy, L. M. and Thomas, R. L. (2007) '*International social work*: A retrospective in the 50th year', *International Social Work*, 50(5): 581–96.

Helfgot, J. H. (1981) *Professional reforming: Mobilization for youth and the failure of social science*, New York, NY: D. C. Heath.

Hermansen, O. (1991) 'Historisk beskrivelse af socialrådgiverutdannelsen i Danmark', *Nordisk Socialt Arbete*, 11: 41–8.

Hessle, S. (ed) (2001) *International standard setting of higher social work education* (Stockholm Studies of Social Work 17), Stockholm: Stockholm University, Department of Social Work.

Hessle, S. (2013) 'Child welfare development in Sweden', in P. Welbourne and J. Dixon (eds) *Child protection and child welfare: A global appraisal of cultures, policy and practice*, London: Jessica Kingsley Publishers.

Hessle, S. (ed) (2014) *Social work – social development* (vols I-III), Farnham: Ashgate.

Hessle, S. (2015) 'Child, family and the external world: Establishing policies in a dialogue with increased migration' (Plenary speech at the Finnish Congress of Social Work, February 2015), *Tutkiva Sosiaalityo 2015*, 5–9: http://www.talentia.isinteksas.com/mag/tutkivasosiaalityo2015.php.

Hessle, S. and Zaviršek, D. (eds) (2005) *Sustainable development in social work: The case of a regional network in the Balkans*, Stockholm: Stockholm University, Department of Social Work.

Hochschild, J. L. (2009) 'Conducting intensive interviews and elite interviews', Workshop on Interdisciplinary Standards for Systematic Qualitative Research [internet]: http://scholar.harvard.edu/jlhochschild/publications/conducting-intensive-interviews-and-elite-interviews.

Hodge, P. (1980) 'Social work education', in P. Hodge (ed) *Community problems and social work in Southeast Asia*, Hong Kong: Hong Kong University Press, pp 67-9.

Hokenstad, M. C. and Kendall, K. A. (eds) (1988) *Gerontological social work: International perspectives*, New York, NY: Routledge.

Hokenstad, M. C., Khinduka, S. K. and Midgley, J. (eds) (1992) *Profiles in international social work*, Washington, DC: NASW Press.

Hokenstad, M. C. and Midgley, J. (eds) (1997) *Issues in international social work: Global challenges for a new century*, Washington, DC: NASW Press.

Hokenstad, M. C. and Midgley, J. (eds) (2004) *Lessons from abroad: Adapting international social welfare innovations*, Washington, DC: NASW Press.

Hokenstad, M. C. and Rigby, B. D. (ed) (1977) *Participation in teaching and learning for social work educators*, New York: International Association of Schools of Social Work.

Hort, S. E. O. and McMuphy, S. C. (1997) 'Sweden', in N. S. Mayadas, T. D. Watts and D. Elliott (eds) *International handbook on social work theory and practice*, Westport, CT: Greenwood, pp 144-60.

Huegler, N., Lyons, K. and Pawar, M. (2012) 'Setting the scene', in K. Lyons, T. Hokenstad, M. Pawar, N. Huegler and N. Hall (eds) *The Sage handbook of international social work*, London: Sage: pp 1-33.

Hugman, R. (2010) *Understanding international social work: A critical analysis*, Basingstoke: Palgrave Macmillan.

Huws Jones, R. (1970) 'Social values and social work education', in K. A. Kendall (ed) *Social work values in an age of discontent*, New York, NY: Council on Social Work Education, pp 35-45.

Huws Jones, R. (1971) *The doctor and the social services*, London: Athlone.

Iacovetta, F. (1998) 'Parents, daughters, and family court intrusions into working-class life', in F. Iacovetta and W. Mitchinson (eds) *On the Case: Explorations in social history*, Toronto: University of Toronto Press, 312-37.

IASSW (2016a) 'IASSW Structure & List of Committees', www.iassw-aiets.org/about-iassw/iassw-structure-list-of-committees/.

IASSW (2016b) 'Mission statement', www.iassw-aiets.org/about-iassw/mission-statement.

IASSW/IFSW (2014) 'Global definition of social work', www.iassw-aiets.org/global-definition-of-social-work-review-of-the-global-definition/.

IASSW/ICSW/IFSW (2012) 'Global agenda for social work and social development: Commitment to action', Berne: International Federation of Social Workers, http://ifsw.org/get-involved/agenda-for-social-work/.

Ife, J. (2001) 'Local and global practice: relocating social work as a human rights profession in the new global order', *European Journal of Social Work*, 4(1): 5-15.

IFSW/IASSW (2004) 'Ethics in social work, statement of principles', Bern: International Federation of Social Workers and International Association of Schools of Social Work: www.iassw-aiets.org/wp-content/uploads/2015/10/Ethics-in-Social-Work-Statement-IFSW-IASSW-2004.pdf.

Imru, H. (1972) *The important role of supervision in social welfare organization*, Addis Ababa: ASWEA/AESA Information Centre.

Indian Journal of Social Work (1999) 'Career profile of Prof. Armaity S. Desai' *Indian Journal of Social Work*, 61(2): 300-15.

Infoplease (2016) 'Languages spoken in each country of the world', www.infoplease.com/ipa/A0855611.html.

International Committee of Schools of Social Work (1929) Protocol adopted 12 June, www.alice-salomon-archiv.de/online.htm.

Jennison, T. and Lundy, C. (2011) *One hundred years of social work: A history of the profession in English Canada 1900-2000*, Waterloo: Wilfred Laurier University Press.

Jones, C. (1976) 'The foundations of social work education' (Working Papers in Sociology 11), Durham: University of Durham Department of Sociology and Social Administration.

Jónsdóttir, S. (1991) 'Socionomutbildningen på Island', *Nordisk Socialt Arbete*, 11: 57-63.

Jordan, B. (2000) *Social work and the third way: Tough love as social policy*, London: Sage.

Jordan, B. (2008) *Why the third way failed: Economics, morality and the origins of the 'big society'*, Bristol: Policy Press.

Jordan, B. (2014) *Welfare and well-being: Social value in public policy*, Bristol: Policy Press.

Josefsson, C. (2001) 'Porträtt Harriet Jakobsson' ['Portrait of Harriet Jakobsson'], *Socionomen*, 2: 55-8.

Jovelin, E. (2010) 'The evolution of social work as a profession in France', in P. Erath and B. Littlechild (eds) *Social work across Europe: Accounts from sixteen countries*, Ostrava: University of Ostrava/European Research Institute for Social Work/Albert, pp 55-66.

Katherine A. Kendall Institute (2016) *Katherine A. Kendall (1910-2010)*, Retrieved 30 January 2016 from: http://www.cswe.org/CentersInitiatives/KAKI/AboutKAKI/KatherineKendall.aspx.

Katz, M. B. (1996) *In the shadow of the poor house: A social history of welfare in America* (rev. edn), New York: Basic.

Kearney, N. (1999) 'Preface', in C. Skehill, *The nature of social work in Ireland: A historical perspective*, Lewiston, NY: Edward Mellen, pp xi-xiii.

Kendall, K. A. (1977) *Final Report: International development of qualified social work manpower for population and family planning activities*, New York, NY: IASSW.

Kendall, K. A. (1978) *Reflections on social work education 1950-1978*, New York/Vienna: International Association of Schools of Social Work.

Kendall, K. A. (1979) Toward reciprocity in technical assistance through collegial relationships, *International Social Work*, 22(1): 2-8.

Kendall, K. A. (ed) (1986) *Eileen Blackey: Pathfinder for the profession*, Silver Spring, MD: National Association of Social Workers.

Kendall, K. A. (1989) 'IASSW and social work education in the fifties, sixties and seventies', in *60 Jahre IASSW: International Association of Schools of Social Work*, Berlin: Fachhochschule für Sozialarbeit und Sozialpedagogik, pp 15-25.

Kendall, K. A. (1994) *The challenges of internationalism in social work: past, present and future*, (Paper 2, Inaugural Conference) Connecticut, CT: University of Connecticut Center for International Social Work. Retrieved 3 February 2016 from: http://digitalcommons.uconn.edu/sw_intlconf/2.

Kendall, K. A. (1998) *IASSW The first fifty years 1928-1978: A tribute to the founders*, Alexandra, VA: International Association of Schools of Social Work.

Kendall, K. A. (2000) *Social work education: Its origins in Europe*, Alexandria, VA: Council of Social Work Education.

Kendall, K. A. (2002) *Council on Social Work Education: Its antecedents and the first twenty years*, Alexandria, VA: Council on Social Work Education.

Kendall, K. A. (2003) *Herman D. Stein, challenge and change in social work education: Toward a world view*, Alexandria, VA: Council on Social Work Education.

Kendall, K. A. (2005) *Council on Social Work Education: Its antecendents and first twenty years*, Alexandria, VA: Council on Social Work Education.

Kendall, W. (1941) *John Locke and the Doctrine of Majority Rule* (Illinois Studies in the Social Sciences, 26:2), Urbana, IL: University of Illinois Press.

Kezar, A. (2003) 'Transformational elite interviews: principles and problems', *Qualitative Inquiry*, 9(3): 395-415.

Klaassen, D. (2016a) 'Condolence letters on death of mother, 1980 (Box 4, folder 4)', *Katherine A. Kendall papers: Series 2. Family Correspondence, 1940-1995*, Minneapolis, MN: Social Work History Archives. Retrieved 13 February2016 from: http://special.lib.umn.edu/findaid/xml/sw0097.xml#series2.

Klaassen, D. (2016b) *Katherine A. Kendall papers: Series 3. Correspondence with Professional Colleagues and Friends, 1940-2006 (Boxes 6-14)*, Retrieved 27 March 2016 from: http://special.lib.umn.edu/findaid/xml/sw0097.xml#series3.

Klaassen, D. (2016c) *Katherine A. Kendall papers: Series 5. Publications and Writings, 1939-2006. (Boxes 19-24)*, Retrieved 27 March 2016 from: http://special.lib.umn.edu/findaid/xml/sw0097.xml#series5.

Kniephoff-Knebel, A. and Seibel, F. W. (2008) 'Establishing international cooperation in social work education: the first decade of the International Committee of Schools for Social Work (ICSSW)', *International Social Work*, 51(6): 790–812.

Kojima, Y. and Hosaka, T. (eds) (1987) *Peace and social work education: Proceedings of the 23rd International Congress of Schools of Social Work*, Vienna: International Association of Schools of Social Work.

Kramer, D. and Brauns, H.-J. (1995a) 'Europe', in T. D. Watts, D. Elliott and N. S. Mayadas (eds) *International handbook on social work education*, Westport, CT: Greenwood, pp 103-22.

Kramer, D. and Brauns, H.-J. (1995b) 'Germany', in T. D. Watts, D. Elliott and N. S. Mayadas (eds) (1995) *International handbook on social work education*, Westport, CT: Greenwood, pp 177-89.

Kreitzer, L. (2012) *Social work in Africa: Exploring culturally relevant education and practice in Ghana*, Calgary: University of Calgary Press.

Kreitzer, L. (2005)'Queen mothers and social workers: a potential collaboration between traditional authority and social work in Ghana', http://dspace.ucalgary.ca/bitstream/1880/42980/7/Queen_Mothers_need_social_workers.pdf.

Lavalette, M. and Ferguson, I. (eds) (2007) *International social work and the radical tradition*, Birmingham: Venture Press.

Les, E. (1997) 'Poland', in N. Mayadas, T. D. Watts and D. Elliott (eds) *International handbook on social work theory and practice*, Westport, CT: Greenwood, pp 184-202.

Libal, K. R., Berthold, S. M., Thomas, R. L. and Healy, L. M. (eds) (2014) *Advancing human rights in social work education*, Alexandria, VA: Council on Social Work Education.

Lin, K. and Chan, R. K. H. (2015) 'Repositioning three models of social policy with reference to East Asian welfare systems', *International Social Work*, November, 58(6): 831-9.

Lindsay, J. (2007) 'The impact of the 2nd Intifada: an exploration of the experiences of Palestinian psychosocial counselors and social workers', *Illness, Crisis, and Loss*, 15(2): 137-53.

Lindsay, J., Baidoun, M. and Jones, D. N. (2011) 'Case study: working with sexual abuse in East Jerusalem', *Ethics and Social Welfare*, 5(3): 298-305.

Loney, M. (1983) *Community against government*, London: Heinemann.

Lorenz, W. (1994) *Social work in a changing Europe*, London: Routledge.

Lorenz, W. (2001) *Facing up to history: Social work between timeless universalism and contingent particularism*, Houten/Diagem: Bohn Stafleu Van Loghum.

Lyons, K., Hokenstad, T., Pawar, M., Huegler, N. and Hall, N. (eds) (2012) *The Sage handbook of international social work*, London: Sage.

Macadam, E. (1925) *The equipment of the social worker*, London: Unwin.

Maeda, K. K. (1995) 'Japan', in T. D. Watts, D. Elliott and N. S. Mayadas (eds) *International handbook on social work education*, Westport, CT: Greenwood, pp 389-402.

Majumdar, R. (1968) 'Social work in ancient and medieval India', in A. R. Wadia (ed) *History and philosophy of social work in India*, (2nd edn), Bombay: Allied, pp 16-24.

Mandal, K. S. (1995) 'India', in T. D. Watts, D. Elliott and N. S. Mayadas (eds) *International handbook on social work education*, Westport, CT: Greenwood, pp 355-65.

Mandel School of Social Sciences (2016) 'M. C. 'Terry' Hokenstad: biographical sketch', Cleveland, OH: Case Western Reserve University, http://msass.case.edu/faculty/thokenstad/.

Martínes-Román, M. A. (2007) 'Social work education in Europe: the Bologna process and the challenges for the future of social work', in E. Frost, M. J. Freitas and A. Campanini (eds) *Social work education in Europe*, Rome: Carocci, pp 23-37.

Martino, F. S. (1960) 'Social welfare in Italy', *International Social Work*, 3(3): 1-5.

Mayadas, N., Watts, T. D. and Elliott, D. (eds) (1997) *International handbook on social work theory and practice*, Westport, CT: Greenwood.

Mwansa, L.-K. J. (2010) 'Challenges facing social work in Africa', *International Social Work*, 59(1): 129-36.

Nagpaul, H. (1972) 'The diffusion of American social work education in India: problems and issues', *International Social Work*, 15(1): 3-17.

Nash, G. H. (1975) 'Willmoore Kendall: conservative iconoclast (1)', *Modern Age*, Spring 1975: 127-35.

Nimmagadda, J. and Martell, D. R. (2008) 'Home-made social work: the two-way transfer of social work knowledge between India and the USA', in M. Gray, J. Coates and M. Yellow Bird (eds) (2008) *Indigenous social work around the world*, Aldershot: Ashgate: pp 141-52.

Noble, C., Strauss, H. and Littlechild, B. (eds) (2014) *Global social work: Crossing borders, blurring boundaries*, Sydney: Sydney University Press.

Ntusi, T. M. (1997) 'South Africa', in N. Mayadas, T. D. Watts, and D. Elliott (eds) *International handbook on social work theory and practice*, Westport, CT: Greenwood, pp 344-65.

Oettinger, K. B. and Stansbury, J. D. (1972) *Population and family planning: Analytical abstracts for social work educators and related disciplines*, New York, NY: International Association of Schools of Social Work.

Okafor, D. I. (2004) *Social work in Nigeria: A historical perspective*, Onitsha: Mid-Field.

Olcott, A. (2009) '"Peeling facts off the face of the unknown": revisiting the legacy: Sherman Kent, Willmoore Kendall, and George Pettee—strategic intelligence in the digital age', *Studies in Intelligence*, 53(2). Retrieved 3 February 2016 from: https://www.cia.gov/library/center-for-the-study-of-intelligence/csi-publications/csi-studies/studies/vol53no2/peeling-facts-off-the-face-of-the-unknown.html

One Nation (2016) 'Country codes list', http://www.nationsonline.org/oneworld/country_code_list.htm.

Osei-Hwedie, K. (1993) 'The challenge of social work in Africa: starting the indigenisation process', *Journal of Social Development in Africa*, 8(1): 19-30.

Osei-Hwedie, K. and Rankopo, M. J. (2008) 'Developing culturally relevant social work education in Africa: the case of Botswana', in M. Gray, J. Coates and M. Yellow Bird (eds) *Indigenous social work around the world: Towards culturally relevant education and practice*, Aldershot: Ashgate.

Otte, C. and Olsson, K.-G. (2007) 'Professionalism in social work and the education of social workers: a cross-cultural perspective', in E. Frost, M. J. Freitas and A. Campanini (eds) *Social work education in Europe*, Rome: Carocci, pp 89-101.

Pathak, S. H. (1968) 'Medical social work', in A. R. Wadia (ed) *History and philosophy of social work in India*, Bombay: Allied, pp 347-56.

Payne, M. (2005) *The origins of social work: Continuity and change*, Basingstoke: Palgrave Macmillan.

Payne, M. and Askeland, G. A. (2008) *Globalization and international social work: Postmodern change and challenge*, Aldershot: Ashgate.

Pernell, R. B. (1972) 'New trends in curriculum development as seen in graduate schools of social work in the United States', in IASSW, *New themes in social work education*, New York, NY: International Association of Schools of Social Work, pp 109-17.

Pollitt, C. (1993) *Managerialism and the public services: Cuts or cultural change in the 1990s*, Oxford: Blackwell.

Queiro-Tajalli, I. (1995) 'Argentina' in T. D. Watts, D. Elliott and N. S. Mayadas (eds) *International handbook on social work education*, Westport, CT: Greenwood, pp 65-85.

Ragab, I. A. (1995) 'Middle East and Egypt', in T. D. Watts, D. Elliott, and N. S. Mayadas (eds) *International handbook on social work education*, Westport, CT: Greenwood, pp 281-304.

Ragab, I. A. (2016) 'The Islamic perspective on social work: a conceptual framework', *International Social Work*, (59)3: 325-42.

Ramon, S. (1985) *Psychiatry in Britain: Meaning and policy*, London: Croom Helm.

Ramon, S. (1991) *Beyond community care: Normalisation and integration work*, Basingstoke: Macmillan.

Ramon, S. (ed) (2008) *Social work in the context of political conflict*, Birmingham: Venture Press.

Ramon, S. and Giannichedda, M. G. (eds) (1988) *Psychiatry in transition: The British and Italian experiences*, London: Pluto.

Ramos, H., Costa e Silva, S., Ramos Pontes, F. A., Fernandez, A. and Furtado, N. K. C. (2014) 'Collective teacher efficacy beliefs: a critical review of the literature', *International Journal of Humanities and Social Science*, 4(7): 178-88.

Rankopo, M. J. and Osei-Hwedie, K. (2011) 'Globalization and culturally relevant social work: African perspectives on indigenization', *International Social Work*, 54(1): 137-147.

Rao, V. (1984) *World Guide to Social Work Education*, (2nd ed) (ed. K. A. Kendall) Vienna: International Association of Schools of Social Work.

Rater-Garcette, C. (1996) *La Professionnalisation du Travail Social: action sociale, syndicalisme, formation: 1880-1920*, Paris: L'Harmattan.

Reid, W. J. and Epstein, L. (1972) *Task-Centered Practice*, New York, NY: Columbia University Press.

Resnick, R.P. (1995) 'South America', in T. D. Watts, D. Elliott and N. S, Mayadas (eds) *International handbook on social work education*, Westport, CT: Greenwood, pp 87-102.

Robertson, J. M. (1980) 'Two decades of social work education in Singapore and Malaysia', in P. Hodge (ed) *Community problems and social work in Southeast Asia*, Hong Kong: Hong Kong University Press, pp 70-78.

Ross, E, L. (ed) (1978) *Black heritage in social welfare 1860-1930*, Metuchen, NJ: Scarecrow Press.

Sabater, J. (2001) 'Social work education and training: the Spanish experience', in A. Adams, P. Erath and S. M. Shardlow (eds) *Key themes in European social work: Theory, practice, perspectives*, Lyme Regis: Russell House, pp 85-94.

Salomon, A. (1937*) Education for social work: A sociological interpretation based on an international survey* (edited by ICSSW), Zurich: Verlag für Recht und Gesellschaft.

Salomon, A. (1958) 'Die Wohlfarthrtsschule in der sozialen Entwicklung unsere Zeit', in H. Muthesius (ed) *Alice Salomon, die Begründerindes sozialen Frauenberufs in Deutschland*, Köln: Carl Heymanns Verlag, pp 234-5.

Salomon, A. (2004) *Character is destiny: The autobiography of Alice Salomon*, (Lees, A., ed.) Ann Arbor, MI: University of Michigan Press.

Satka, M. (1995) *Making social citizenship: Conceptual practices from the Finnish Poor Law to professional social work*, Jyväskylä: SoPhi.

Seebohm Committee (1968) *Report of the Committee on Local Authority and Allied Personal Social Services* (Cmnd 3703) London: HMSO.

Seibel, F. W. (2003) 'Social work in central and eastern Europe', in C. Labonté-Roset, E. Marynowicz-Hetka and J. Szmagalski (eds) *Social work education and practice in today's Europe: Challenges and diversity of responses*, Katowice: Śląsk, pp 263-76.

Selassie, S. G. (ed) (1989) *Social development agents in rural transformation in Africa*, Addis Ababa: ASWEA.

Semigina, T. (2014) 'About IASSW: IASSW Membership Committee', *Social Dialogue*, 9: 53.

Sewpaul, V. and Jones, D. N. (2004) 'Global standards for the education and training of the social work profession', Adelaide: General Assemblies of the IASSW and IFSW. Retrieved from: http://cdn.ifsw.org/assets/ifsw_65044-3.pdf.

Shawky, A. (1972) 'Social work education in Africa', *International Social Work*, 15(3): 3-16.

Singh, K. (1999) *Rural development: Principles, policy and management*, New Delhi: Sage.

Sinha, D. and Kao, H. S. R. (1988) *Social values and development: Asian perspectives*, New Delhi: Sage.

Smith, M. J. (1965) *Professional education of social work in Britain: An historical account*, London: Allen and Unwin.

Social Welfare History Project (2016a) 'Biographical highlights of Mrs Katherine A. Kendall, PhD, ACSW', in *Katherine A. Kendall (1910 – 2010): Social work pioneer, educator and first educational secretary of the Council of Social Work Education*, The Social Welfare History Project. Retrieved 9 February 2016 from: http://www.socialwelfarehistory. com/people/kendall-katherine/.

Social Welfare History Project (2016b) *Ernest Witte (1904-1986) – Social Worker, Educator and Administrator*, The Social Welfare History Project. Retrieved 10 February 2016 from: http://www.socialwelfarehistory. com/people/witte-ernest/.

Social Welfare History Project (2016c) *Council on Social Work Education: Dr. Kendall's Appointment*, The Social Welfare History Project. Retrieved 21 February 2016 from: http://www.socialwelfarehistory. com/organizations/council-on-social-work-education-dr-kendalls-appointment/.

Solomon, B. B. (1976) *Black empowerment: Social work in oppressed communities*, New York, NY: Columbia University Press.

Specht, H. and Courtney, M. (1994) *Unfaithful Angels: How social work abandoned its mission*, New York, NY: Free Press.

Staub-Berlusconi, S. (2003) 'Social work as transdisciplinary science of social problems and social action – program and educational practice', in C. Labonté-Roset, E. Marynowicz-Hetka and J. Szmagalski (eds) *Social work education and practice in today's Europe: Challenges and diversity of responses*, Katowice: Śląsk.

Staub-Berlusconi, S. (2007) *Soziale Arbeit als Handlungswissenschaft: systemtheoretische Grundlagen und professionelle Praxis - ein Lehrbuch*, Bern: Haupt.

Stein, H. D. (ed) (1966) *Social perspectives on behavior: A reader in social science for social work and related professions*, New York, NY: The Free Press.

Stein, H. D. (ed) (1968) *Social theory and social invention*, Cleveland, OH: Press of Case Western Reserve University.

Stein, H. D. (ed) (1969) *The crisis in welfare in Cleveland. Report of the Mayor's Commission* (Mayor's Commission on the Crisis in Welfare), Cleveland, OH: Case Western Reserve University.

Stein, H. D. (ed) (1981) *Organization and the human services: Cross-disciplinary reflections*, Philadelphia, PA: Temple University Press.

Stein, H. D. (2003) *Challenge and change in social work education: Towards a world view, Selected papers*, (Aronoff, N. D., ed) Alexandria, VA: Council on Social Work Education.

Stein, H. D. and Cloward, R. A. (1967) *Social perspective on behavior*, New York, NY: Free Press.

Stiglitz, J. (2002) *Globalization and its discontents*, New York, NY: Norton.

Stoškova, R. and Chytil, O. (1998) 'The progress of social policy and social work in the Czech Republic', in S. Ylinen (ed) *Social work in public health symposium*, Kuopio: Koupion Yliopistollinen Opetussosiaalikeskus, pp 81–103.

Sundt Rasmussen, S. (1991) 'Sosionomutdanningen i Norge 1920–1990. Et historisk tilbakeblikk', *Nordisk Socialt Arbete*, 11: 21–30.

Takahashi, M. (1997) *The emergence of welfare society in Japan*, Aldershot: Avebury.

Tice, C. J. and Long, D. D. (2009) *International social work policy and practice: Practical insights and perspectives*, Hoboken, NJ: Wiley.

Tulva, T. (1997) (ed) 'Developing social work in Estonia', in T. Tulva (ed) *Some aspects of Estonian social work and social policy*, Tallinn: Tallinn University of Educational Sciences, pp 5–14.

Ugiagbe, E. O. (2015) 'Social work is context-bound: The need for indigenization of social work practice in Nigeria', *International Social Work*, 58(6): 790–801.

United Nations (1948) 'Universal declaration of human rights' (UN General Assembly Resolution 217A), http://www.un.org/en/universal-declaration-human-rights/.

United Nations (1950) *Training for Social Work: An international survey*, Lake Success, NY: United Nations.

United Nations (1958) *Training for social work: Third international survey*, New York, NY: United Nations.

United Nations (2016) 'About MDGs: what they are', http://www.unmillenniumproject.org/goals/.

United Nations Economic and Social Council (2016) 'Millennium Development Goals and post-2015 Development Agenda', http://www.un.org/en/ecosoc/about/mdg.shtml.

Vladinska, N. (1994) 'Tendencies in the development of social work/social pedagogy education in Bulgaria', In IASSW, *Paper from the 1994 Congress: Papers giving a review of the situation in a particular country*, Manchester: Department of Applied Community Studies, Manchester Metropolitan University, Paper 6.

Walton, R. and Elliott, D. (1995) 'United Kingdom', in T. D. Watts, D. Elliott, D. and N. S. Mayadas (eds) *International handbook on social work education*, Westport, CT: Greenwood, pp 123-45.

Walton, R. G. (1975) *Women in social work*, London: Routledge.

Watkins, J. (2010) 'Katherine A. Kendall: the founder of international social work', in A. Lieberman, (ed) *Women in Social Work who have Changed the World*, Chicago, IL: Lyceum, pp 167-81.

Watts, T. D., Elliott, D. and Mayadas, N. S. (eds) (1995) *International handbook on social work education*, Westport, CT: Greenwood.

Wieler, J. (1989) 'The impact of Alice Salomon on social work education', in *60 Jahre IASSW: International Association of Schools of Social Work*, Berlin: Fachhochschule für Sozialarbeit und Sozialpädagogik, pp 15-25.

Williams, C. (2016) (ed) *Social work and the city: Urban themes in 21st-Century social work*, Basingstoke: Palgrave Macmillan.

Worldometers (2016) 'World population rankings 2014', http://www.worldometers.info/world-population/population-by-country/.

Xu, Qingwen (2006) 'Defining international social work: a social service agency perspective', *International Social Work*, 49(6): 679-82.

Yelaja, S. A. (1970) 'Towards a reconceptualization of the social work profession in India', *Applied Social Studies*, 2(1): 21-6.

Yimam, A. (1990) *Social development in Africa 1950-1985: Methodological perspectives and future prospects*, Aldershot: Avebury.

Younghusband Report (1959) *Report of the Working Party on Social Workers in the Local Authority Health and Welfare Services*, London: HMSO.

Younghusband, E. (1978) *Social work in Britain: 1950-1975*, London: Allen and Unwin.

Zierer, B. (2010) 'Social work in Austria', in P. Erath and B. Littlechild (eds) *Social work across Europe: Accounts from sixteen countries*, Ostrava: University of Ostrava/European Research Institute for Social Work/Albert, pp 8-18.

Index